Gender Warriors

Teaching Gender

Series Editor

Patricia Leavy (*USA*)

International Editorial Board

Tony E. Adams (*Northeastern Illinois University, USA*)
Paula Banerjee (*University of Calcutta, India*)
Nitza Berkovitch (*Ben Gurion University, Israel*)
Robin Boylorn (*University of Alabama, USA*)
Máiréad Dunne (*University of Sussex, UK*)
Mary Holmes (*University of Edinburgh, UK*)
Laurel Richardson (*Ohio State University (Emerita), USA*)
Sophie Tamas (*Carleton University, Ottawa, Canada*)

Scope

Teaching Gender publishes monographs, anthologies and reference books that deal centrally with gender and/or sexuality. The books are intended to be used in undergraduate and graduate classes across the disciplines. The series aims to promote social justice with an emphasis on feminist, multicultural and critical perspectives.

Please consult www.patricialeavy.com for submission requirements (click the book series tab).

VOLUME 10

The titles published in this series are listed at *brill.com/gend*

Gender Warriors

Reading Contemporary Urban Fantasy

Edited by

U. Melissa Anyiwo and Amanda Jo Hobson

BRILL

SENSE

LEIDEN | BOSTON

Cover illustration: Image by Steve Anyiwo

All chapters in this book have undergone peer review.

The Library of Congress Cataloging-in-Publication Data is available online at
http://catalog.loc.gov

ISSN 2542-9205
ISBN 978-90-04-39408-7 (paperback)
ISBN 978-90-04-39409-4 (hardback)
ISBN 978-90-04-39410-0 (e-book)

ADVANCED PRAISE FOR
GENDER WARRIORS

"The theme that most resonates with me in U. Melissa Anyiwo and Amanda Jo Hobson's *Gender Warriors: Reading Contemporary Urban Fantasy* is the importance of perception. As a CJ scholar, it can be challenging to impress upon my students (many whom are active criminal justice practitioners) why perception is so vitally important. The chapters in Anyiwo and Hobson's edited text all examine perception in some way no matter the specific lens (queer lens of Buffy and the current political climate by Guitar's chapter or a postfeminist response to Harry Potter in fan fiction in Coker's chapter for example). By identifying and examining the manifest and latent content that is found in all forms of communication, students can learn to deconstruct how messages are perceived and understand how perceptions shape trust and relationships. In current times, this level of critical analysis is imperative to the work of cultivating and maintaining strong community and police relationships. Understanding and appreciating the various lenses through which information is filtered (race, class, gender, among many others) and how perception drives decision-making is paramount to fostering strong, healthy, crime resistant communities and sustainable and equitable justice."
– Rebecca Allen Paynich, Professor of Criminal Justice Curry College, and author of *Law Enforcement in the United States* (Jones & Bartlett Learning, 2011) and *Fundamentals of Crime Mapping* (Jones & Bartlett Learning, 2018)

"U. Melissa Anyiwo and Amanda Jo Hobson's *Gender Warriors: Reading Contemporary Urban Fantasy* offers provocative assessments of a wide range of popular culture texts and icons. Focusing particularly on representations of gender, sexuality, class, and race, this collection offers nuanced interpretations of the often contradictory messages and ideologies embedded within the urban fantasy genre. Anyiwo's analysis of the Showtime series *Penny Dreadful*, for example, contends that the series simultaneously contests and reinforces dominant cultural representations of Otherness, and persuasively reveals how the show's attempt to reposition canonical literary monsters as sympathetic protagonists implicitly reinscribes white male privilege and traditional axes of difference along gendered and racial lines. Thoughtfully curated and theoretically cohesive, *Gender Warriors* will undoubtedly serve as an invaluable resource for anyone interested in popular culture studies, intersectional feminism, and film/television studies."

– Katherine Lee, Associate Professor of English and Gender Studies, Indiana State University, and contributor to the *Encyclopedia of Racism in American Film* (Rowman & Littlefield, 2018).

"When I teach critical theory to undergraduate students I'm often looking for ways to help them connect with material that can often be dense and abstract. Gender Warriors is a collection useful for not only teaching feminist theory, but other schools and traditions working well with everything from Virginia Woolf's A Room of One's Own (using Sarah Smith's 'Empowering or Fetishizing: Wonder Woman Takes the Bechdel Test') to Roland Barthes's 'Death of the Author' (using Cait Coker's 'The Problematic Fan-Girl: Cassandra Glare's Gendered Revisions in the Mortal Instrument Series'). Most interesting is Ana G. Gal's 'Tough Women, Patriarchal Violence, and the Problem of Non-Intersectional Feminism in Les Wiseman's Underworld Series' which performs a deft deconstruction of the going analysis of the Underworld Series. Although often thought of as feminist, Gal shows how the series carries with it more than just a trace of the patriarchy. Many undergraduate students are familiar with one-sided social media-friendly essays on these topics and will benefit greatly from the depth and insight found in this collection. Gender Warriors forces us to question previous analyses of urban fantasy, making us reenvision what we thought we already saw clearly enough."

– Jennifer Schomburg Kanke, Florida State University and editor of *Pleiades Book Review*

CONTENTS

ACKNOWLEDGEMENTS

This book is dedicated to Rhonda Nicol, an amazing friend and scholar that passed away in November 2016. In many ways, this is Rho's project, as it was our conversations about gender in urban fantasy and her passion for the genre that led to this volume.

Special thanks go to Patricia Leavy for her support, patience, and scholarship. Her intellectual activism and commitment to giving back to the community of feminist scholars continues to inspire our work.

We would like to thank our reviewers, Rebecca Allen Paynich, Katherine Lee, and Jennifer Schomburg Kanke, for the uncompensated time they took to read our manuscript and offer valuable feedback.

Amanda would like to thank my wonderful and supportive parents, Jo and Donn Hobson, who always believe in me no matter what. To Chris Reghetti-Feyler, Andy Feyler, and Dr. Amy French, because whenever I falter you are there to support me. To my brilliant nephews and niece, Blaike, Noah, Jase, and Madison, you are the reason I fight to create change and justice in our world. You give me so much joy as I watch you grow every day. Finally, I dedicate this book to the memory of my baby brother, Donn Anderson Hobson III, you have left a legacy of four beautiful and amazing children that are the bright stars of our world.

Melissa would like to dedicate this work to the gender warriors in her life including Carrie Cokely, Julie King Davies, Sally Hepton, Shannon Johnson, Patricia Leavy, Victoria Moss, Rebecca Paynich, Sarah Smith, Talia Welsh, and many more, who prove that a true feminist doesn't need labels or rules or limits, they just do it, every day. The warriors who unknowingly paved this road-my mother Agatha, Aunty Glynn, Aunty Cecile and all my aunts-who taught me about sisterhood, and how none of us need do this alone. To my emerging warriors – Nkechi, Chidera, Maeve, Freya, Maya, Kali, and baby girl XX-be brave, be whomever *you* want to be; trust me, it's better that way. Finally, to the greatest gender warrior in my life, my brother Steve, our amazing cover artist. Through his ungendered support, he has created three girls (and counting), each independent, confident, and amazing in their own ways. The future truly is female, but it takes fathers to raise all their children to believe there are no limits to our dreams.

ACKNOWLEDGEMENTS

Our gratitude goes to our contributors who have stuck with us through this process. Their knowledge and insights into gender, ethnicity and the urban fantasy universe guided this work helping shape scholarship in this field.

Hope strengthens. Fear kills.
— *Mac Lane* (Karen Marie Moning, 2011)

AMANDA JO HOBSON AND U. MELISSA ANYIWO

1. INTRODUCTION

What Is Urban Fantasy?

If you have ever walked through a bookstore, you will likely recognize the urban fantasy genre from cover art alone: a singular person stands with the city in the background. If the individual is a woman, she stands with her back to you and holds a weapon in her hand, typically a sword but potentially a gun or knife. She looks over her shoulder at you, and her hip is cocked. If the cover has a man, he faces you, perhaps even making eye contact through the image. He, too, wields a weapon, a sword or knife, never a gun, but perhaps his hands are up as if he is casting magic at you. Under the covers and on screen, urban fantasy showcases flashy magic, including special effects in the visual texts, and features complicated narratives that usually follow an ensemble cast and multiple storylines.

According to the internet, urban fantasy (UF) is essentially any film, television show, or novel that features the fantastical or paranormal. The problem is that simply being a story about magic or the paranormal is not enough to make it urban fantasy. The ambiguity of UF as a genre grows from the blending of many genres into one. Urban fantasy complicates the idea that genres are stable with fixed borders and consistent iconography. Though the hallmark of genres is recognizable internal patterns, genre is inherently fluid with messy boundaries. The urban fantasy genre blends together romance, horror, science fiction, fantasy, mystery, detective fiction, and sometimes adds comedy or young or new adult elements, all set with the urban landscape as a backdrop. More importantly, the city and (sub)urban spaces play an essential role within the narrative to the point in which the location itself is a character in the plot. The city is alive, not simply as a location but creating both obstacles and aids for the protagonists.

One of the difficulties of categorization is that some series may have individual novels that either do or do not engage the urban as a vivid and complete character, meaning that a series that is predominantly urban fantasy may have novels that are hybrid genres but not "urban" and other series have singular novels that fully embrace the urban landscape. For instance,

© KONINKLIJKE BRILL NV, LEIDEN, 2019 | DOI:10.1163/9789004394100_001

Charlaine Harris's *Sookie Stackhouse Series,* otherwise known as the *Southern Vampire Mysteries*, is primarily set in an alternate-universe in the dangerous but ultimately bucolic small town of Bon Temps, Louisiana, but there are novels in the series intensely focused on the urban space, such as *Living Dead in Dallas* (2002). In the novel, Dallas nearly destroys Sookie, making the city itself one of the villains of the novel along with the enemy vampires. The opposite is true of *Penny Dreadful* (2014–2016), which is focused intensely on the rapidly changing and monstrous fin-de-siècle London from its dark sewers and seedy brothels to the lights and gore of the theatrical stage to grand glowing ballrooms. Yet, there are episodes that side-line the character of the city moving to the country side.

The use of the fantastical and the urban setting are core elements but not the only ones necessary to the genre. As with so many other more traditional fantasies, urban fantasy typically occurs in series and, in the literary form, often in long-running series, in which the action transpires over years and even decades. UF requires extensive world-building and interweaves character development with the creation of intricate details of a complex and fantastical world. Because of the scope of the worlds being created within the urban fantasy universe, a series that spans many books and across years is necessary in order for the creator to have the time and space to build these sophisticated magical spaces. Moreover, in these series, the elements of the urban fantasy universes change, developing over time as if it, too, is a character within the narrative. The universe character matures and deepens along with the other more traditional types of character.

The origins of UF are disputed in literary scholarship with scholars and bloggers arguing for as far back as ancient Greek beginnings and others arguing for a start in the 1990s,[1] but this is merely an anachronist tendency of literary criticism and applying contemporary terminology and ideology onto art of the past is problematic. Alexander C. Irvine states, that it "has also been retroactively extended to include virtually every work of the fantastic that takes place in a city or has a contemporary setting that occasionally incorporates a city, with the result that any particularity the term once had is now diffused in a fog of contradiction" (2012, p. 200). Framing urban fantasy means understanding the genre in its fluidity and also building constraints, allowing the genre to have meaning.

We set the foundation of contemporary urban fantasy with the publication of Laurell K. Hamilton's *Anita Blake, Vampire Hunter Series*, starting with *Guilty Pleasures* in 1993 and establishing its genre conventions. *Anita Blake* is an evolving blend of horror, detective fiction, crime fiction, romance, and fantasy. In addition to employing the unique blend of genre traits, Hamilton builds a deep connection to the urban landscape, specifically St. Louis, Missouri, with the features of the city being integral to the overall narrative of the series. From the Blood District to cemeteries and the many crime scenes Anita visits, the cityscape of St. Louis is a character that builds obstacles and opportunities for Anita. *Anita Blake* instigates the necessity for world-building over the course of a long-running series, allowing for the evolution of the characters and the series itself. Hamilton's engagement with urban fantasy grows to include elements of erotic fiction and melodrama. The world of *Anita Blake* continues to unfold, endlessly expanding in scope and issues, as well as companion characters and bigger and more dangerous villains. The series also initiates a trend in urban fantasy of a first-person, often female, narrator that has a strong personality, a compelling back-story, and a preternatural power that grows exponentially. It is the introduction of a kick-ass heroine that establishes both Blake as a character and the genre as whole. With twenty-five books and counting, *Anita Blake* is not just the point of origin but an on-going example of what works about the genre.

As UF grew in popularity in the early 2000s, the rise of the paranormal romance sub-genre created a unique generic problem: a difficult area of grey between definitions of urban fantasy and paranormal romance. The difference between these two categorizations is really an issue of nuance and emphasis. In paranormal romance, the core of the narrative is the romantic relationship between the two main protagonists, and each novel ends with a Happily Ever After (HEA) necessary for definition of the romance genre as a whole. Sarah Wendell and Candy Tan (2009) write, "It's extremely rare for romance novels to have true sequels; the Happily Ever After definitively marks the end of the story arc for the hero and heroine, since the focus of the romance novel is overwhelmingly the discovery and securing of romantic love" (p. 104).[2] The relationships in UF universes are frequently as intricately constructed as the worlds of which they are a part. As UF plays with conceptions of reality and gender, the authors also address and reimagine the normative constructions of relationships. These series often feature queer and polyamorous relationships in the ways that mainstream romance has only more recently begun to do. Because UF does not rely upon the HEA, the authors explore dating and sexual relationships outside of the paired monogamous couple of the traditional romance, meaning that the audience has the opportunity to watch the characters experiment with different romantic and sexual partners as they discover their own approach to love, sex, and family. Though urban fantasy includes and may even foreground the romantic relationship of the protagonists, the focus of urban fantasy is on the fantastical mystery or trials the protagonists must overcome, typically defeating mystical enemies and even saving the world.

3

Paranormal romance has clearly been influenced by urban fantasy, as it now includes long-running series, with each entry focusing on a different couple, connected somehow to the previous novel(s). UF also allows for shifting narrative perspectives, as many series focus on ensemble casts that all act as protagonists pushing the series forward and more importantly involved in overcoming whatever disaster has befallen the world. Some series sit in the grey area between paranormal romance and urban fantasy. For instance, J.R. Ward's *Black Dagger Brotherhood Series* foregrounds the romantic relationships of individual couples and early in the series appeared to give the couples traditional HEAs, but as the series has continued and the world has expanded in complicated new ways, their stories have continued to evolve and weave into later texts, including new books foregrounding couples that have already had "their" novel.

There is a trend in major popular franchises that are minimally connected to cities being listed as urban fantasy. One of the most obvious examples is the *Harry Potter Series*. Googling urban fantasy films finds *Harry Potter* showing up heavily in the top results, but the novel series does not show up in the top results for a similar fiction search. *Harry Potter*, however, is not urban fantasy; it is young adult fantasy. This is true for both the novel and the film series. Both are primarily set at Hogwarts School of Witchcraft and Wizardry, which is in the Highlands of Scotland. Indeed, Hogwarts is a living character within the series with its self-moving stairs and passageways, its hidden chambers, and its rooms that bend to the wishes of individuals in need, so perhaps *Harry Potter* is school fantasy. Occasionally, Harry and his friends spend time in London, but the bulk of the series, especially of the films, occurs in the castle and in other rural settings. When Harry, Hermione, and Ron are in London, the city plays no role within the narrative other than as a location for the events to occur, and the location most frequently featured in the city is Diagon Alley. While Diagon Alley is a magical location filled with hidden dangers and mystical tools, it plays a miniscule role in the overall narrative. Harry, Hermione and Ron embark on epic adventures both in fighting the forces of evil in the guise of Lord Voldemort but also in overcoming the obstacles of adolescence. It is this combination of their magic, the quest to overcome evil, and their growth and development as human beings as well as the lack of urban setting that makes *Harry Potter* a young adult, rather than an urban fantasy series.

Urban fantasy, as a genre, is as complex as the stories and world-building created within the texts. The promise of UF is that it is a genre in which radical transformation of norms can occur; genre destabilized, and identity categories unraveled and remade. When the world is built on fantasy and magic, there is such possibility for revolutionary creation of social norms and mores. While it does undermine concepts of fixed genre, more often than not urban fantasy reinforces pre-existing hierarchical structures of oppression based on both traditional identity markers—race, gender, sexuality, etc.—and creating new categories of oppression—wizard/muggle, Seelie/Unseelie, Fae/human, etc. The authors of the subsequent chapters discuss the liberating and the limiting potentials of urban fantasy, specifically as the genre engages with issues of identity. The complicated nature of the genre and the representations of gender created the necessity for *Gender Warriors: Reading Contemporary Urban Fantasy*, a volume of classroom ready original essays that allow readers to explore the place of urban fantasy within contemporary popular culture and demonstrate the importance of addressing gender within broader cultural questions.

As we mentioned earlier, the cover of a book creates expectations for the viewer about genre conventions and narrative structure. The cover of our text is no exception, and we invite the reader to return to the cover art here. The image itself sparked a debate between us because we all saw distinctive elements at play and that singular image told each of us a different narrative. Within the character, we saw either the pin-up girl or the warrior woman, the passive woman restrained or the powerful, sexy, and feminine African woman pushing at the stereotypes that constrain her. In the course of our conversations about the art, we began to come together to view her position as reflective of the tension between the pin-up girl and the warrior woman, the disempowered and the empowered. These conversations highlight long-standing debates about the male gaze, feminism, women's sexuality, and womanhood. Steven Anyiwo, graphic designer and cover artist, centered the image on addressing "the issue of gender being confined to stereotypes present in everyday life" (personal communication, July 17, 2018). The image, like many of the UF heroines at the heart of this book, unsettles expectations of womanhood and the image of the warrior woman, underscoring the conflicting messages women receive and embody about their gender. In her conversation about pin-ups, Maria Elena Buszek (2006) writes, "While many pin-ups are indeed silly caricatures of women that mean to construct their humiliation and passivity as turn-ons [for a perceived male audience], the genre has also represented the sexualized woman as self-aware, assertive, strong, and independent" (p. 8). The cover image articulates the arguments the chapters within this text make about the constructions of gender, sexuality, and race within UF: the women warriors in these universes are complicated characters that perform their gender in normative and contradictive ways both upholding and unraveling gendered conventions.

The volume opens with vampire scholar Candace Benefiel as she explores issues of upending gendered expectations in "Creating the Urban Fantasy Heroine: Gender Displacement in Laurell K. Hamilton's *Anita Blake, Vampire Hunter Series*." Benefiel argues that the heroine and narrator, Anita Blake, evolves from a young woman who is gifted with preternatural abilities and vampire slayer that longs for a traditional family into a necromancer and living vampire—succubus—who engages in polyamorous relationships, creating a sense of gender as a contentious category within Hamilton's world.

Sarah Smith's "Empowering or Fetishizing: *Wonder Woman* Takes the Bechdel Test" articulates the issue of gender representation in media. Smith explores "The Bechdel Test" as a tool for examining portrayals of women, specifically in film, applying the test to *Wonder Woman* (2017). She argues that it is necessary to build skills in media literacy and understanding the impact of media on issues of identity. Smith contends that "The Bechdel Test" does not in fact offer an in-depth approach to determining if the representation of women in a film truly makes it feminist or even some well-rounded examples of women. Despite this, Wonder Woman remains an empowering image that has united generations of women in the belief that gender is no barrier to heroism.

In "The Vampiric Nature of Transmedia Storytelling in the Buffyverse," Jenna Guitar takes us into the world of *Buffy the Vampire Slayer* (BtVS) and the ever expanding Buffyverse. Guitar demonstrates that *BtVS* has continued to be a source of academic and fan discourse beyond the show's seven-year television run and carries on to this day in comic book form with an additional five seasons and counting. She explores the continuation of the Buffyverse across those multiple platforms, which she argues points to new trends in the way that media is consumed and re-consumed, garnering new audiences and igniting old fandoms. This includes an in-depth look at the fan-run podcast, *Buffering the Vampire Slayer*, in which the creators—Jenny Owen Youngs and Kristin Russo—watch and commentate on each episode in chronological order, while also serving up an original song that recaps each episode and critiquing the show through a feminist and queer lens. Guitar contends that *Buffy* continues to matter today not only because of the high quality of the show, but ultimately through its ability to vampirically transcend time and remain accessible to new generations of viewers through the use of new transmedia.

Co-editor Amanda Hobson addresses the history of witchcraft in popular culture and its prevalence in the genre in "Bewitching Bodies: Sex, Violence, and Magic in Urban Fantasy." Arguing that history shows a specifically gendered image of the witch, Hobson articulates the ways in which urban fantasy relies on tropes of female hypersexuality and sexualized violence as methods for mystical power enhancement. She explores images of the witch or magic wielder character across literature and television with examples such as *Anita Blake* (1993–present), *The Magicians* (2015–present), *Charmed* (1998–2006), and more.

In "Fighting and Feminist Expression: The Argent Family and the Limits of Female Agency in *Teen Wolf*," Lauren Rocha explores the portrayals of the women on MTV's *Teen Wolf*, specifically that of Victoria Argent and her daughter Allison. Rocha highlights the mother-daughter pair, addressing the question of gender subversion in the familial power structure and the show's treatment of anxieties surrounding female empowerment and deviant femininity. She also examines the relationships between Chris Argent, Victoria's husband and Allison's father, and Gerard, the patriarch of the family, in order to explore anxieties regarding masculinity and to emphasize the series' theme of male dominance and reinstatement of male gender norms.

In "Tough Women, Patriarchal Violence, and the Problem of Non-Intersectional Feminism in Les Wiseman's *Underworld Series*," Ana G. Gal discusses Selene as a powerful and resourceful female warrior that "kicks ass" in her shiny black rubber costume, despite having to navigate a space dominated by the violent decisions and actions of a toxic masculinity. Gal examines the gender dynamics operating within the franchise, focusing primarily on how the series as a whole, despite its promise to challenge the values of patriarchy, ultimately serves to legitimize only one single strain of feminism—white and mainstream—and antagonizes alternate femininity. She argues that Selene's whiteness and vampire ancestry and the unilateral representation of female Lycans as bestial bodies project the failure of white feminism to treat intersectionality as essential to the understanding and construction of gender.

Cait Coker explores the intersections of urban fantasy and the world of fandom in "The Problematic Fan-Girl: Cassandra Clare's Gendered Revisions in *The Mortal Instrument Series*." She articulates the sense of déjà vu the audience might feel reading the series as a hormone-fueled derivative of the *Harry Potter* mega franchise. Coker details Clare's beginnings as a fanfic writer online, sharing numerous highly popular stories that were read by thousands, if not millions, of readers. This included the *Harry Potter* based series "The Draco Trilogy" that consisted of three novel-length stories focused on the characters as teenagers, though written and shared online before the release of Rowling's novels during that time period, which Clare uses as the backbone for *The Mortal Instruments Series*. Coker's chapter discusses *The Mortal Instruments*' origins within *Harry Potter* fandom and how Clare's revising of elements from her fanfic serve as a postfeminist response to Rowling's more traditional iterations of gender roles.

Co-editor U. Melissa Anyiwo unpacks the complex landscape of monstrous texts in "A Monstrous Narrative: Unraveling Gender and Ethnic Archetypes in Showtime's *Penny Dreadful*." By deconstructing the core archetypes that appear to create a beautifully complex and enlightened version of the Victorian Age, Anyiwo argues that the embedded assumptions of the creators actually reinforce ideas that have changed little over time. In this way she argues that the apparent enlightenment at the heart of urban fantasy itself remains informed by a Victorian sense of cultural imperialism.

The final two chapters offer practical guides to exploring the worlds of urban fantasy. "The Urban Fantasy Classroom" offers questions and activities for classroom use, offering a way to delve deeper into the material presented in the chapters as well as additional examples of genre texts. These exercises prod critical thinking around issues of genre, history, literary and film criticism, and identity. In many cases the questions were written by the authors, ensuring their direct relevance to the content. The final chapter looks more broadly at urban fantasy, suggesting other novels, television and literary series, and films for the reader to watch or read and/or incorporate into the classroom. We offer this list of narratives that demonstrate the variety and scope of urban fantasy as well as texts that explicitly illustrate the genre's engagement in explorations of identity and the genre's exponential capacity for world-building.

Urban fantasy stretches the imagination by contributing spectacular universes filled with magic and mystery, while keeping its audience grounded in the familiar setting of an urban landscape albeit a potentially alien one. The genre is known for the manner in which it pushes the boundaries of possibilities not just for magic and in its own internal worlds, but it also expands the borders of genre and identity. Urban fantasy is so ubiquitous that it is nearly unavoidable in our media, showing up in our novels and on all of our screens from tablets and televisions to iPhones and IMAX to e-readers and streaming online. Though this means that the genre is often misunderstood and left undefined, the role of urban fantasy in our contemporary popular culture is undeniable.

NOTES

[1] For scholarship that argues for earlier origins, see Alexander C. Irvine's "Urban Fantasy" in the *Cambridge Companion to Fantasy Literature* (2012), John Clute's "Urban Fantasy" in *The Greenwood Encyclopedia of Science Fiction and Fantasy* (2005), Farah Mendlesohn's *Rhetorics of Fantasy* (2008), Mendlesohn and Edward James's *A Short History of Fantasy* (2009), and Helen Young's *Race and Popular Fantasy Literature* (2016).

[2] For more on the romance genre, explore the Romance Writers of America webpage at http://my.rwa.org/romance. I also recommend *A Natural History of the Romance Novel* by Pamela Regis (2003) and *Happily Ever After: The Romance Story in Popular Culture* by Catherine Roach.

REFERENCES

Buszek, M. E. (2006). *Pin-up grrrls: Feminism, sexuality, popular culture*. Durham, NC: Duke University Press.

Irvine, A. C. (2012). Urban fantasy. In E. James & F. Mendlesohn (Eds.), *The Cambridge companion to fantasy literature* (pp. 200–213). New York, NY: Cambridge University Press.

Wendell, S., & Tan, C. (2009). *Beyond heaving bosoms: The smart bitches' guide to romance novels*. New York, NY: Fireside Books.

Amanda Jo Hobson
Women's Resource Center
Indiana State University

U. Melissa Anyiwo
Department of Politics and History
Curry College

CANDACE BENEFIEL

2. CREATING THE URBAN FANTASY HEROINE

Gender Displacement in Laurell K. Hamilton's Anita Blake,
Vampire Hunter Series

Note from the editors: In August 2017, Candace passed away after a difficult battle with cancer. She asked that the editors finish the edits for her chapter, and therefore, Amanda Jo Hobson and U. Melissa Anyiwo completed the text.

***

In Laurell K. Hamilton's *Anita Blake, Vampire Hunter Series*, audiences are introduced to a complex alternate world in which vampires and lycanthropes are real and out in the open. For the last twenty-five plus years and in twenty-five novels and counting, Anita Blake, the crime solving necromancer and protagonist, has thrilled and infuriated audiences with her gender- and genre-bending exploits. Alongside the supernatural crime solving is a tale of love, romance, and gender displacement. As the quintessential urban fantasy series, Hamilton's work illustrates its core genre-blending themes of hardboiled detective fiction, mystery, horror, gothic romance, and erotica, providing the core example of originality that defined an entirely new genre. Beyond its themes of the paranormal in an urban setting, Hamilton also creates the kick-ass heroine archetype, blurring the lines between genders and offering a very contemporary look at the modern woman. This chapter explores Anita's gender-defying journey towards a non-traditional sex life caused by her growing list of superhuman powers, becoming a study of the complexities of womanhood in the contemporary world.

Anita Blake, heroine and narrator, begins her journey as a young woman hoping for the conventions of normality exemplified by a little house in the suburbs with a white picket fence. Yet, from her first encounter with her reanimated dog, her preternatural talent sends her on a path from animator of zombies and vampire slayer to succubus, necromancer, and living vampire whose decidedly unconventional home life includes a bevy of shifter and vampire lovers. Through her, Hamilton creates what will become the central character traits of this new type of heroine described by Daniel Abraham as:

© KONINKLIJKE BRILL NV, LEIDEN, 2019 | DOI:10.1163/9789004394100_002

A kick-ass woman with a variety of possible lovers … She's been forced into power—either through accident of birth or by being transformed without her permission—and is therefore innocent of one of the central feminine cultural sins: ambition. She is in relationships primarily with men rather than in community with women. "Bad boys" want her, and they won't be bad to her. (2010)

Imbued with a condition known as the *ardeur*, Anita is eventually forced to abandon her conventional attitudes toward sex and the dream of a "normal" life and accept not just a need for multiple sexual partners but a hyper-female agency in sex as a means of survival for herself as well as her lovers and extended preternatural family. Her desire for the traditional home and family structure transforms over the course of the series, allowing her to embrace the unique blended family—polyamorous emotional and sexual partners with adopted siblings and adult children.

None of these changes are her fault, of course, and each addition of power towards a goddess-like heroine, who feeds on sex and anger, happens against her will ensuring her mystical augmentations are always freed from a direct challenge to patriarchy. Her struggles to create an identity, or accept an identity authentically hers, was perhaps an attempt by Hamilton to express her own attitudes towards the potential for a Disney version of reality,

Love conquers all: I knew that was a lie by the time I was ten. The adults around me had proven that. In fact, when I was young I was never getting married. I never dreamed of my wedding, or fantasized about the perfect man, because I didn't believe in a perfect anything. By the time I was a teenager I'd seen too much harsh reality, real violence, death. It's not the stuff to make you dream about Prince Charming. (2010, p. 41)

Anita's attempts to free herself from the gendered indoctrination, which limits our dreams, becomes the true central struggle over the series that began with *Guilty Pleasures* in 1993, and her evolution reflects both Hamilton's growth and the changing attitudes towards conceptions of gender. As has become the template for the urban warrior, Anita transforms from a celibate young woman that sees herself firmly on the human side of the monster/human divide, despite her unusual abilities to raise and control zombies and her side-line as a consultant to a police task force engaged in preternatural investigations. She becomes, over the course of the series, a polyamorous woman whose metaphysical powers have increased to the point that she is regarded as less, or possibly more, than human. This growth becomes the path of Charlaine Harris's Sookie Stackhouse, Patricia Briggs's Mercedes Thompson, Les

Wiseman's Selene of the *Underworld Series*, Cat Crawford of Jeaniene Frost's *Night Huntress Series*, and an endless series of other protagonists, creating a powerful genre expectation of dynamic and complicated female protagonists.

For Anita and the women of urban fantasy, the journey is always a complicated one. Hamilton's early novels focus not only on murder and mayhem arising from the uneasy coexistence of the vampires, werewolves, and other preternatural creatures with the humans of St. Louis but also on Anita's growing attraction to the master vampire of the city, Jean-Claude an element that begins to transform her understanding that the line between monster and human is far more complex.[1] At first, she insists that as a vampire executioner and living human, she cannot become romantically involved with the head monster. Add into the mix the handsome alpha werewolf Richard, and Anita finds her grasp on what she considers righteous morality slipping.

Yet Anita does not want to have it all; indeed she fights tooth and nail against the confining traditional image of womanhood. She clings to the veneer of "normal" far beyond when it becomes clear to the reader she is no longer simply a human with a bit of power. This reckless and obtuse behavior nearly kills Damien and severely harms Anita and Nathaniel. After Anita develops the *ardeur*, her power becomes so strong that she is a living master level vampire (succubus), and she becomes the master to a vampire and creates a new triumvirate of power with that vampire and a lycanthrope, in addition to the one she developed earlier in the series with Jean-Claude and Richard Zeeman. Because she resists recognizing that she cannot live as if she is fully human with human morality any longer, all three are severely drained, and the vampire almost dies, when Anita refuses to feed the *ardeur* by having sex, in *Cerulean Sins* (2003). This is not the only time that this occurs, showing the importance of accepting one's authentic self even if that contradicts what you belief it must be.

What is most fascinating with Anita is that she acknowledges the impact of her self-denial even before she almost accidentally causes harm to others. She confesses in *Narcissus in Chains*, "I'd fought so long and so hard not to be what I was. Not to be Jean-Claude's human servant, not to be Richard's lupa, not to be anything to anyone. Everyone seemed to be paying the price for that. I hated having other people pay the price for my problems" (Hamilton, 2002, p. 555), but, at this point in the series, she cannot yet give up her tight grasp on the idea of "normal," especially her position as a "regular" human with a conventional sexuality. During this time in the series, Anita begins to view herself as monstrous, and Hamilton continues to delve into the oppositions at the heart of so much of urban fantasy and popular culture, such as defining good and evil or human and monster. Hamilton writes,

Ever notice that you're a "good woman," but a "bad girl"? Because the moment you own your sexuality, society still tries to make you less. You're not a woman anymore, you're just a girl. The idea seems to be that you'll grow up and learn the error of your ways, and then you'll be a woman again, a good one. Well, I have grown up, and so has Anita, and we're both just fine the way we are, being not good women, but good people." (2010, p. 13)

This commentary clearly plays a role in the way Hamilton writes Anita, especially around issues of sex and gender dynamics. As she begins to accept herself, the reader sees Anita embrace the concept of being "fine just as she is."

For much of the series, Anita actually functions like the worst aspects of the normative stereotypes of both genders in a relationship, exhibiting aspects of male and female gender performance and creating a persona that is unique to her. She's emotionally withholding, making her men work endlessly to figure out her moods and unending emotional landmines. She's certainly a commitment-phobe, completely terrified of committing to anything except a code of honor that often does more harm than good, and is as slippery as a wet eel. Judith Butler has commented that "gender is in no way a stable identity or locus of agency from which various acts proceed; rather, it is an identity tenuously constituted in time—an identity instituted through a stylized repetition of acts" (1988, p. 519). Anita adapts gendered norms to fit her specific purposes in given situations. The identity she has constructed seems to be as stable as she can make it, although she stands on shifting sands of circumstance, and must continuously repeat the acts that make her both worthy of male respect as an equal, and that confirm her identity as a female sexual agent.

When it comes to sex, especially in the middle period of books, she's a complete hypocrite (and knows it) sleeping with a litany of men and having lots of random sexual encounters to satisfy her *ardeur*. Yet she cannot abide any man in her life even being interested in another person let alone having sex with them, including Jean-Claude who must also contend with his own *ardeur*. For instance, in *Narcissus in Chains*, Jean-Claude's former lover Asher, who on occasion also has sex with Anita, tells Anita that Jean-Claude is refusing to have sex with him even though they both desire it. Asher says, "He refuses my bed, because he fears that you would … what is the American word … dump him, if you knew he were sleeping with a man" (2002, p. 77). Anita's response is that she would breakup with Jean-Claude because she does not want him to have sex with anyone else,[2] though he is allowed to do some touching of others if Anita is having sex with them. The hypocrisy is evident when less than one hundred pages later Anita has sex with Micah, a wereleopard that she met mere hours earlier (2002, p. 156).

Hamilton emphasizes these traits and the characters bending of gendered norms even in choices and conversations about clothing with Jean-Claude and Anita. Jean-Claude's masculinity, from his appearance to his perceived overbearing wooing, plays a consistent role throughout the series, often as a counterpoint to Anita herself. In *Bloody Bones*, Anita describes her vampire boyfriend's attire in detail:

> [Jean-Claude] stood in the doorway leading to the bedroom. The shirt had long, full sleeves that had been gathered in three puffs down the length of the arm to end in a spill of cloth that framed his long, pale fingers. The collar was high and tied with a white cravat that spilled lace down the front of him, tucked into a vest. It was black and velvety with pinpricks of silver on it. Thigh-high black boots fit his legs like a second skin … His hair was nearly as black as the vest, making it hard to tell where the curls ended and the velvety cloth began. A silver and onyx stick pin that I'd seen before pierced the white lace at his chest. (Hamilton, 1996, pp. 137–138)

In a later novel, *The Killing Dance*, she clarifies as if to remind the reader that even in his frilly attire, Jean-Claude is truly an uber masculine master vampire. "He was one of those men who was beautiful rather than handsome, but the face was masculine; you wouldn't mistake him for female, even with the long hair. In fact, there was something terribly masculine about Jean-Claude, no matter how much lace he wore" (1997, p. 10). This emphasis on Jean-Claude's masculinity draws the attention to the binary Hamilton attempts to establish between him and Anita. Because if Jean-Claude is hypermasculine even in his velvet and lace, then Hamilton seems to want the reader to understand that Anita is still feminine even in her jeans, tennis shoes, and polo shirts. Anita, always a fan of practical clothing, describes one of her outfits, "I was wearing black jeans and a royal blue polo shirt" (1996b, p. 176), which is a fairly common description of her outfits. With a profession that requires her to spend a good deal of her working life wading through muddy cemeteries and bloody crime scenes not to mention sacrificing small animals to raise the dead, she has developed a clothing sense somewhat more pedestrian than that of the vampire who revels in velvet, lace, and leather. Still, if her clothing is not frilly, she is nevertheless portrayed as having a stereotypically feminine interest in making sure she is color-coordinated, and Hamilton is careful to make Anita (and the reader) cognizant of how her hair looks, and even, from time to time, her cosmetics.

Anita, when she is not actively involved in hunting down and dispatching rogue preternaturals, performs a straightforwardly heteronormative femininity with strong submissive overtones. Readers are often given details of how she tames her unruly hair, and carefully color coordinates her outfits, so that the swooshes on her Nikes matches the color of her shirt. Moreover, from the time she becomes involved personally and politically with Jean-Claude, the reader is given multiple instances when the vampire, whose own visual iconography of long hair, soft lacy shirts, and delicate pallor give him a sexually indeterminate aesthetic, choreographs the costuming of his minions, including Anita in his constructed tableaux. Her growing acceptance of his 'right' to do so is consistently presented as an example of her personal growth, and Anita grows to understand, though not enjoy, that clothing is a costume for vampire politics. She still complains—loudly and frequently—about the clothes Jean-Claude chooses for her, particularly because they are typically ultra-feminine and show a vast amount of skin. In *Cerulean Sins*, Anita's interior monologue gives the reader several pages of description of her attire as well as the rest of her group's as they prepare to meet the envoy from the Vampire Council. She describes in minute detail and shares her discontent, "I had, of course, complained about my clothes. The black velvet and blue silk seemed to be offering my breasts up like pale ripe fruits. The colors emphasized the near translucence of my skin with the undertone of blue highlights" (Hamilton, 2003, p. 285). Though Anita is willing to begrudgingly play dress-up, she is more inclined to comfortable attire. Anita is an embodiment of the idea that even the strongest and ardently feminist heroine must conform to femininity. As Lilith Saintcrow writes, "All strides in feminism aside, girls are still supposed to be soft, feminine, nurturing, passive recipients of male action" (2010, p. 31).

From the beginning, gender role reversal is a core theme in the novels, and it goes deeper than clothing. In *Guilty Pleasures*, Anita and the readers meet Phillip, a sexy stripper and play toy of multiple vampires, as evidenced by his many bite scars. In his introduction of Phillip's act, Jean-Claude tells the predominantly female audience that Phillip "shares your fantasy. He wanted to know how the sweetest of kisses would feel. He has gone before you" (Hamilton, 1993, p. 14). By identifying the stripper as having the same desires as the audience, he transforms Phillip into one of them, a woman. In Phillip's actual striptease, he presents himself, and his many bite scars, as an objectified, sexualized—and damaged—body. The women are not so much invited to lust after his body, but to want to be him, to experience what he has experienced under the fangs of the vampires. Indeed, later in the act, a vampire joins Phillip on stage, biting him in full view of the audience. Anita, however, sees the bite as less than enticing, and her description of it makes her disgust obvious: "They were both kneeling; the vampire had one of Phillip's arms pinned behind his back. One hand gripped Phillip's long hair, pulling his neck back at a painful angle. Phillip's eyes were wide and terrified" (Hamilton, 1993, p. 18). Phillip functions as the archetypal damsel in distress there only to be saved. As the plot progresses, Phillip becomes a go-between for the vampires and Anita and develops a tenuous friendship with him. In several instances, he is assumed by others to be her lover, and he delights in acting the part, touching her frequently, slipping an arm around her waist. There is always the implication that this physical closeness is for him to claim her for her protection. Anita truly believes she needs no protector—a belief that is frequently proven to be true, while Phillip, poor bite-addicted, scarred Phillip, constantly searches for the security he can never find. He flirts and poses constantly because his sexuality and attractiveness are the only power he has in the world further marking him as feminine, relying on the stereotype that femininity means a reliance on physical beauty for personal protection and financial gain.

In this way, Hamilton continuously unsteadies expected gender binaries creating a series that challenges traditional critiques of romance, and this functioning as one example of the move away from the limits of romance into an entirely new genre. For many romance readers of the late 1990s and early 2000s, the hallmark of a romance novel was a monogamous couple, who frequently even got married in the epilogue. Anita, however, has a myriad of lovers—at this point one cannot name or count all of them—is engaged to and lives with three of them and has regular date nights with several others. She also has recently begun having sex with women. This lack of a stable monogamous relationship left some readers at best perplexed and at worst angry. Hamilton writes,

> A lot of my female audience thought of [the novels] as romances. That was fine with me, until I wrote the unforgiveable. I had Anita choose the wrong man [Jean-Claude instead of werewolf Richard] … I am not romance. I've broken too many rules. I'm not mystery because I've broken their genre rules by having the relationships be important. I am neither fish nor fowl, for any genre. (2010, pp. 41–42)

It is precisely because she breaks the rules of genre that she can posit a hybridized vision of gender. Anita's gendered identity grows out of what she must do to survive and save those she cares about, as opposed to what is normative or what makes sense within the boundaries of a particular genre. Often Anita's experiences, thoughts, and behaviors are uncomfortable for the reader precisely because they do not easily sit within the lines of gender norms or genre tropes. Anita and her lovers demonstrate that by hybridizing gender, blending genres, and complicating sexuality more options exist for the writer and her readers.

Despite the emphasis on power through sex and romantic relationships in the series, Anita's journey is not limited to the expanding horizons of her sexual knowledge. She transforms female sexual agency and her career in law enforcement into a gender role blurring exercise in challenging and subverting male hegemony. The series was not accidentally subversive, Hamilton knew going in that it was time for a new type of female protagonist,

> I started reading a lot of hardboiled detective fiction … and I read a lot of strong female protagonists. But there was one problem … The men got to cuss, the women rarely; the men got to kill people and not feel bad about it, if the women killed someone they had to feel really, really bad about it afterward and it had to be an extreme situation; the men got to have sex, often and on stage and very casually, but if the women had sex it had to be offstage, very sanitized. I thought this was unfair. (Tiedemann, 2003)

Hamilton creates a character that has normatively male behaviour patterns, especially in work and dating, but is strongly coded as female and feminine. She is petite and pale, frequently referring to herself as a china doll. For instance, when Anita is trying on a bridesmaid's dress, she thinks, "I just stared at myself in the mirrors. My hair and eyes match, black hair, eyes so dark brown they look black. They are my mother's Latin darkness. But my skin is pale, my father's Germanic blood. Put some make-up on me and I look not unlike a china doll. Put me in a puffy pink dress and I look delicate, dainty, petite. Dammit" (Hamilton, 1994, p. 15). She is coded as attractive and exotic.

Anita's appearance negatively impacts her perceived ability to perform activities coded as stereotypically masculine, but her metaphysical powers are not so constricted. In particular, Hamilton often contrasts Anita's appearance as a petite, attractive woman with her ability to out-think, out-shoot, and generally out-do the police, frequently portrayed as large, aggressive males who resent the intrusion of any woman into their masculine preserve. In the earlier books, this is generally limited to verbal exchanges, and by the end of the most recent novels, Anita is often validated in the eyes of her male colleagues through her expertise and her unflinching focus on the investigation at hand. As the series progresses and her metaphysical power grows, she often finds herself the target of overt hostility, expressed in terms of sexual harassment and actions designed to undermine both her authority and her active participation in police investigations. Curiously, she is attacked both for expressions of her female sexuality, which have long since transcended the socially acceptable norm, and for her intrusive incursions into the masculine sphere of law enforcement.

Anita's begins a crusade to be accepted by her colleagues at the beginning of the series. *Guilty Pleasures* introduces us to her as a character who has been working both as an animator and a police consultant, for some time reflecting the early 1990s consideration of women struggling to find their voices in all male working environments. Anita is not on her first case with the police when we meet her, and, yet, they still tease her mercilessly at crime scenes, in ways verging on or actually becoming harassment. Even the team leader, Dolph, who is usually supportive, engages in the gendered harassment.

> [Dolph] closed his notebook and looked at me. He was almost grinning. "The secretary said you were at a bachelorette party." He wiggled his eyebrows. "Hoochie coochie."
>
> "Don't give me a hard time, Dolph."
>
> …
>
> The rest of the men waved at me and called in unison, "We love you."
>
> "Give me a break."
>
> One called, "If I'd known you liked to see naked men, we could have worked something out." (Hamilton, 1993, pp. 24–25)

Anita dislikes the catcalling, a typical mode of sexual harassment, but she puts up with it as real women are forced to, firing off comebacks in the hopes that the police officers will ultimately accept her as a valued colleague. The Regional Preternatural Investigation Team (RPIT), the police taskforce Anita consults with, regularly engages in this kind of sexualized banter, which seems to indicate in many ways that Anita is "just one of the guys." As the above quotation demonstrates though, there is always an edge to the teasing. It grows worse over the course of the novels, especially when the perception is that she is "sleeping with the enemy" after she begins having sexual relationships with Jean-Claude and the other "monsters." Dolph verbally attacks Anita at a crime scene about her sex life, he says "You're either one of us, or you're one of them, Anita." When Anita asks "One of what," he responds "Monster." An angry Anita asks, "Are you calling me a monster." To which Dolph replies, "I'm saying you're going to have to choose whether you're one of them, or one of us" (2003, p. 263). For Anita, this type of dichotomous approach to the monsters is problematic. Even though she has trouble accepting herself as not exactly human, she no longer sees the issue of monstrosity as completely dualistic. Anita has seen too many evil, monstrous humans to believe humans have the moral authority to judge vampires, werewolves, or other supernatural beings as monstrous by nature. Moreover, Dolph's and the other law enforcement officer's preoccupation with Anita's sex life is quite specifically gendered, as they seek to police her sexual partners and pleasures. In this way, Anita not only gender bends, but she blends the conceptions of women in law enforcement.

All this being said, it seems clear that Anita would have some difficulties and confusion in her life regarding gender appropriate behavior even without the preternatural influences at work. As a woman, given the male-dominated state of law enforcement, both in the early '90s when the series began, and continuing to the present day, she represents a fundamental threat to the patriarchal hegemony by being a woman uniquely qualified to perform a traditionally male function. Her relationships within the preternatural community, specifically her sexual relationships, only enhance her ability to do her job. She started with an affinity for the dead, an ability to animate corpses and a degree in preternatural biology. She developed, through her link with Jean Claude and her other men, strength, ability to heal, and an insight into the workings of the vampire subculture. When she contracted several strains of lycanthropy, instead of becoming a handicap, it gave her enhanced senses and an expertise in shapeshifters, which was basically unparalleled in law enforcement. Her career, especially her work with the police, demands that she suppress traditional femininity in favor of a more masculine affect. Time and time again, she brings up the necessity of being "one of the boys" in front of policeman. In *The Lunatic Café*, Anita arrives at a rural crime scene only to be greeted by a deputy, who promptly demonstrates that he is not only sexist and racist but also trigger-happy. After a confrontation in which potential violence is narrowly avoided, the local sheriff expresses doubt in Anita's expertise, commenting, "This little bit of a girl has over a dozen vampire kills under her belt?" And when assured that she is, in fact, the regional expert, he goes on to remark "I don't need a civilian woman to tell me my job" (Hamilton, 1996a, p. 52). It's hard to say which of those attributes angers him more: her status as a civilian or her gender, and though she attains a badge herself as a federal marshal, her gender remains an issue for many.

There are multiple incidences where Anita runs into resistance to her role first as a consultant to the police and later as a badge-carrying federal marshal.

The big guys with muscles do not want to accept her as a member of the club. As her role and her powers evolve, she makes some progress in this area but not as much as she would like. The local St. Louis authorities do value her and the assets that she brings to the team, although even that is variable particularly as new law enforcement agents join the forces. When she travels, such as in *Obsidian Butterfly* (2000) set in New Mexico and *Skin Trade* (2009) set in Las Vegas, she usually ends up having to re-establish herself with the police. In *Skin Trade* (2009), Anita is called in to deal with a particularly grisly series of murders in Las Vegas. Shaw, the man in charge of the local preternatural crimes unit, comments, "I'll be honest, Blake, I'd feel better if you were a guy. I'd feel even better if you had some military background" (Hamilton, 2009, p. 11) In a conversation with him a little later, she tells Shaw to warn his team about her, and the following conversation ensues,

"Warn them about what, that you're blunt?"

"All of it—blunt, a girl, pretty, dates vampires, whatever. Get it out of their system before I hit the ground in Vegas. I don't want to have to wade through macho bullshit to do my job."

"Nothing I can do about that, Blake. You'll have to prove yourself to them, just like any other ... officer."

"Woman, you are going to say *woman*. I know how it works, Shaw. Because I'm a girl, I gotta be better than the guys to get the same level of respect." (Hamilton, 2009, pp. 12–13)

When she meets the other officers in the unit, they challenge her in a way that causes her competitive nature to kick in. By this time, her physical and mental abilities have been enhanced due to her connection to Jean-Claude and Richard through their metaphysical triumvirate, she comes across not just as "one of the guys," but as physically and psychically superior to all of them. Her attempts to perform masculinity only make things worse.

In these exchanges, Hamilton channels Canadian feminist politician Charlotte Whitton, who once said, "Whatever women do, they must do twice as well as men to be thought of as half as good" (Ratcliffe, 2016). As the examples about her interactions with law enforcement show, Anita exists in an historically male field as a vampire executioner and federal marshal, which also sets her apart because these are highly specialized, dangerous, and selective positions. Because of her physical appearance as a petite and attractive woman, she is taken less seriously and must constantly prove herself to the agents with any new person she comes into contact. Moreover, her sexuality, specifically her multiple lovers, becomes a weapon wielded against her by the other law enforcement professionals. They sexually harass and denigrate her for her sexuality, and more, they continuously make assumptions about her sexual activities. Shaw questions Anita and her friend and colleague, Edward, asking Anita about the serial killer but asking Edward about his relationship with Anita. Edward calls Shaw out, saying he's trying to "scapegoat" Anita as the reason the serial killer is terrorizing Las Vegas. Edward tells Anita that the rumor is she is having sex with Edward and several of her other law enforcement colleagues. Despite any evidence or corroboration, Shaw can't believe that she's as good at her job as she claims, believing that she must use sex to con men into giving her credit for her work. Disputing the rumors as professional jealousy, Anita says, "That's part of the problem. I am better than the rest of the executioners. I've got more kills, and I'm a girl. They can't stand it, Shaw. They can't believe I'm just that good at my job. It has to be because I'm fucking my way to the top" (Hamilton, 2009, p. 77).

Whilst Shaw's misogynist bias against Anita apparently knows no bounds, Hamilton provides this character with a cause for his misogyny by rooting it in his personal life. It is revealed that he resents any woman he sees as being too close to preternatural beings because his wife left him for a shapeshifter (Hamilton, 2009, p. 232). In this way, Hamilton roots his prejudice in a very real conflation of his personal pain and suggests that this type of reaction to women in male situations has real psychological underpinnings. This does not excuse his behavior, or that of men like him; but it provides a doorway to allow the character to grow. Thus, Hamilton demonstrates that, as with other forms of prejudice, it takes personal connections/experiences to both create the prejudice and undo it. This is illustrated in the conversation in which the SWAT member reveals Shaw's personal history with shapeshifters, after verbally attacking Anita for "making a new friend" of one of the local weretigers, a SWAT team member tries to deflect his criticism, and Shaw responds:

> "You're defending her, Hooper?" He glared at me. "I thought you didn't do cops, Blake."
>
> "What's that supposed to mean?"
>
> "It means you visit SWAT for a couple of hours, and suddenly they're willing to trust you at their backs, and talk back to their superiors. You must be as good as they say." (Hamilton, 2009, p. 232)

While on this occasion, Hooper and the other SWAT team members try to deflect Shaw's animosity, Anita regularly hears comments about her supposed sexual promiscuity and that she uses her sexuality to gain favour and support from the men around her. Hamilton articulates the issue that many powerful women face: they are only in the position of power because someone else gave them something they did not actually deserve. She is aware she has multiple identities thrust upon her by circumstance and society and tries hard to live up to each of them. She wants to be a good and effective Marshal; she wants to be a moral person. She has come to terms with the idea that her personal life among the vampires and shape-shifters should not be a source of guilt to her but a source of comfort and security in an uncertain world. That her work forces her to conform to the masculine status quo and to keep the more unusual aspects of her powers and her relationships hidden creates a source of tension that leads her close to depression and sends her into therapy. After she learns how to live with the *ardeur*, she presents a blurred gender role that falls somewhere in between what is expected by society of either a male or a female, and this is true at work as well as in her home. She must adopt, or to be more precise, express, an aggressive, take-no-prisoners attitude on the job, where it's crucial that her male colleagues see her as "one of the boys," in order for her to properly perform her duties. She has trespassed in their gendered preserve, and this small, attractive woman must subvert expectations created by her physical body to function within the patriarchal hegemony of contemporary law enforcement. This identity crisis is a common trait among women in jobs coded as non-traditional.

Anita's gendered representation and her interactions with law enforcement return us to the earlier question of the impact her relationships and her sexuality have on her gender performance. The nature of her sex life basically serves to further complicate all of her identity markers. Over the years (and, to be more accurate, the mileage), she has realized that the violence in her life and her connection with supernatural creatures have put that idealistic heteronormative dream out of reach. And yet, she comes to find a certain accommodation to her needs combining with an unorthodox domesticity that suits her far better than a monogamous relationship would ever have done. Thus, the fluid sexuality inherent in the series coupled with Anita's ultimately polyamorous lifestyle reflects Hamilton's belief in the destructive nature of normative lifestyles for some people.[3] Through a circuitous route, she finds herself in a stable live-in relationship with two wereleopards, Micah and Nathaniel. There are other men in her life, but these two become her mainstays. Interestingly, especially in terms of gender norms, both of these men fall outside traditional heteronormative boundaries. Micah is the same height as the petite Anita, about 5' 3" and slender. His features are regularly described as "delicate," and he and Anita even share their "casual" clothes (Hamilton, 2003, p. 151). Nathaniel, while taller, wears his hair very long, works as an exotic dancer, and is a sexual submissive, who requires Anita to dominate him. In their household, Anita is the one that works most outside the home and is the primary breadwinner, fulfilling the traditionally masculine role. Micah does volunteer work, like a good affluent housewife, even if his position is running a coalition of the various were-creatures in the St. Louis area. Nathaniel is responsible for most of the cooking and cleaning, duties traditionally relegated to the female of the family. Outsiders view her, if not as an outright slut, as a player who keeps a stable of male lovers—a questionable lifestyle choice in the Bible Belt.

To the outside world, Anita Blake is a complicated individual. A tough cop, a ruthless killer, a steadfast friend, a creature with wild metaphysical talents. She is an adventurous lover to the point where she seems to be transitioning into a (literal) sex goddess, but she is also "one of the guys." She performs whatever role, gender or otherwise, that is demanded of her, and the price she pays for this multi-tasking, for her attempt to be all things to all people, is that often, her worlds clash, and she finds herself lost in between. Anita exists in the blurred grey area of gender, in which she is not the princess or the damsel or the even the wife. She is the breadwinner and the kick-ass Executioner. As the ever adorable wereleopard Nathaniel tells her, "You're not Cinderella, Anita, you're the prince. You're Prince Charming" (Hamilton, 2006, p. 34). Anita embraces her role as the Prince that comes to rescue an endless list of people. The "little bit of a girl" is big enough to stand up to the largest man present and sensitive enough to nurture and appreciate the talents— domestic and otherwise—of her lovers. She doesn't mention the swooshes on her Nikes much these days. She's too busy living a complicated life to worry about her shoes. Anita has come a long way from the young woman who secretly longed for suburban normalcy. While she acknowledges that loss, her new normal means living her life by her own set of rules, embracing loving polyamorous relationships, experiencing sexual pleasure, protecting those she loves, and saving the world on a regular basis. In Anita Blake, Hamilton has created the icon of the urban fantasy warrior.

NOTES

[1] Another element that becomes a genre trope. See Eric Northman in the Sookie Stackhouse Southern Detective Series, Adam Hauptman in Mercy Thompson, or Bones in Night Huntress.

[2] Anita is particularly squeamish about her male lovers, especially Jean-Claude, having sex with other men. Characters call Anita out on her homophobia, and at some point, she begins to recognize this as her having homophobic tendencies.

[3] Hamilton is openly polyamorous. Though married to Jonathan for many years, they are in a relationship with another couple. Hamilton regularly writes about her husband, who also co-wrote the graphic novel *First Death* with her, and the "other half" of their "fourple" on her blog, which can be found at: https://www.laurellkhamilton.com/category/blog/. Hamilton is very vocal in her writing, in interviews, and on her blog that her personal relationships have influenced her writing of Anita Blake.

REFERENCES

Abraham, D. (2010, October 29). *Why Jayne Heller won't get raped* [Blog]. Retrieved from http://www.danielabraham.com/2010/10/29/mln-on-uf-why-jayne-heller-wont-get-raped/

Butler, J. (1988). Performative acts and gender constitution: An essay in phenomenology and feminist theory. *Theatre Journal, 40*(4), 519–531.

Hamilton, L. K. (1993). *Guilty pleasures*. New York, NY: Ace Books.

Hamilton, L. K. (1994). *The laughing corpse*. New York, NY: Ace Books.

Hamilton, L. K. (1996a). *The lunatic cafe*. New York, NY: Jove Books.

Hamilton, L. K. (1996b). *Bloody bones*. New York, NY: Jove Book.

Hamilton, L. K. (1997). *The killing dance*. New York, NY: Ace Books.

Hamilton, L. K. (2001). *Narcissus in chains*. New York, NY: Berkley Books.

Hamilton, L. K. (2003). *Cerulean sins*. New York, NY: Berkley Books.

Hamilton, L. K. (2006). *Danse macabre*. New York, NY: Berkley Books.

Hamilton, L. K. (2009). *Skin trade*. New York, NY: Berkley Books.

Hamilton, L. K., & Wilson, L. (2010). *Ardeur: 14 writers on the Anita Blake, vampire hunter series*. Dallas, TX: BenBella Books.

Ratcliffe, S. (Ed.). (2016). *Oxford essential quotations* (4th ed.). New York, NY: Oxford University Press. Retrieved from http://www.oxfordreference.com/view/10.1093/acref/9780191826719.001.0001/q-oro-ed4-00011512?rskey=e12lzq&result=3885

Saintcrow, L. (2010). Ambiguous Anita. In L. K. Hamilton & L. Wilson (Eds.), *Ardeur: 14 writers on the Anita Blake, vampire hunter series*. Dallas, TX: BenBella Books.

Tiedemann, M. (Interviewer). (2003). *Laurell K. Hamilton*. Retrieved from http://archive.li/qlabY

Candace Benefiel[†]
Texas A&A University

SARAH A. SMITH

3. EMPOWERING OR FETISHIZING

Wonder Woman *Takes the Bechdel Test*

INTRODUCTION

What one does when faced with the truth is more difficult than you'd think.

– Diana (Heinberg & Snyder, 2017)

As a little girl, I would dress up as Wonder Woman and fight crime throughout the house and yard. Every Saturday morning a local television station played the Lynda Carter series reruns. I wore men's red soccer socks with the white stripes at the top; star covered panties, and a tiara and bracelets that my grandfather made me. There was even a golden lasso that I attached to my hip. No crime was going to happen on my watch! There would be no injustices in our home.

One of the things I remember fondly about my childhood heroine was that I felt powerful and beautiful. As her, I was unstoppable. I learned that women could be smart, strong, funny, compassionate, and equal, if not stronger, than men. Yet as a male driven comic, *Wonder Woman* was filled with problematic images of womanhood that perhaps only an adult would notice.

Feminist and editor of *Ms. Magazine*, Gloria Steinem, was a huge fan of the DC comics, but like many other women of second wave of feminism, she was disappointed in the ways Diana Prince's character reflected patriarchal concerns rather than celebrating strong independent womanhood in an age when women were entering the workforce in increasing numbers. At one point in the comic book series, in a moment reflective of the backlash against feminism, Diana Prince is stripped of her powers, essentially stripping her of masculine perceived, and therefore, problematic independence. Thus in 1972, Steinem fought back against the diminishing of the core character, with a vitriolic editorial in *Ms.*, lobbying DC Comics to reinstate Prince back to her old stature (Desta, 2017).

Steinem's arguments cleverly focused on the ways the world of Wonder Woman highlighted her "family of Amazons on Paradise Island, her band of college girls in America, and her efforts to save individual women" thus

© KONINKLIJKE BRILL NV, LEIDEN, 2019 | DOI:10.1163/9789004394100_003

presenting a vision of womanhood filled with "welcome examples of women working together and caring about each other's welfare" (Desta, 2017). Images of men working in harmony are accepted as 'normal' yet "women know how rare and therefore exhilarating the idea of sisterhood really is" (Desta, 2017). Despite the visually anti-feminist comics, there existed an incidental empowerment which presented multiple examples, such as Wonder Woman's mother Queen Hippolyta, who "offers yet another welcome example to young girls in search of a strong identity. Queen Hippolyta founded nations, waged war to protect Paradise Island, and sent her daughter off to fight the forces of evil in the world" (Desta, 2017). Ultimately, Steinem (1972) argues,

> Wonder Woman symbolizes many of the values of the women's culture that feminists are now trying to introduce into the mainstream: strength and self-reliance for women; sisterhood and mutual support among women; peacefulness and esteem for human life; a diminishment both of "masculine" aggression and of the belief that violence is the only way of solving conflicts.

Steinem's voice was heard, and the Wonder Woman she loved returned, providing a living example of the fictional character's concerns receiving mainstream acknowledgment and recognition. Steinem's critique was so impactful that in 1975, Wonder Woman leapt from the pages of a comic book to television, expanding her visibility to millions of girls and boys as well as women and men. This exposure helped guide the character into the modern era and Wonder Woman was brought to movie screens in 2017. Some feminists lauded the movie; others criticized it as another portrayal of fetishized womanhood. This chapter subjects the 2017 *Wonder Woman* movie adaptation to the Bechdel test in order to determine whether this film is actually feminist in its portrayal or another example of female objectification.

Being media literate, especially when it comes to gender roles, is important in contemporary research, development, and analysis creating an overall understanding of what we are viewing and how it plays a role in our paradigms and societal expectations. Analysts can take a simple three-question test to assess a medium, in this case a movie, to see if it has validity in being named a feminist piece and consider if that equals feminist construction. This doesn't mean the test is perfect, and there are plenty of movies that pass the Bechdel Test that are not considered feminist in nature, but it is an easy introduction to the process of evaluating the presentation of gender roles in today's media.

The existence of male privilege exemplified by the male gaze, consistently sees womanhood only in relation to men and motherhood. The male gaze, a term created by Laura Mulvey, addresses the way women in media and literature are viewed from a heterosexual male perspective (Sassatelli, 2011). Women are often presented as sexual objects, only existing for the male characters' and audience's pleasure. The male gaze has perspectives that influence the representation of women: the writer, the director, the person filming, the characters within the film, and the viewer. The Bechdel Test thus also provides a lens through which a viewer can explore whether or not they believe the male gaze still informs most mainstream films.

Overall, and perhaps unsurprisingly, the *Wonder Woman* comics and subsequent TV shows, so influential in my own upbringing and that of millions of young girls, would not pass the Bechdel test. The *Wonder Woman* movie, however, allegedly aligns with the original literal conception of Bechdel's comic strip. Utilized for a comic that targeted a specific population in the 1980s, the Bechdel test has found its way into the feminist media critics' toolbox. Simplistic in its format, its close-ended questions should not allow for subjective conclusions; the film either passes or it does not. However, humans are complex, and their processing of these results are not always objective. Many tend to look at critiques with shades of grey rather than black and white, making their conclusions subjective and emotional. These attributes are not considered while performing the Bechdel Test.

The following pages will introduce the audience to the Bechdel test; it's origins, with some focus on its evolutions and other newer tests to consider. The audience will be introduced to the Wonder Woman movie and that it does pass the Bechdel test. Then there will be a discussion for how passing the test does not make it a feminist film.

This is not a chapter on the comic book or the creator of Wonder Woman. There is a plethora of material about her creator William Moulton Marston, also known as Charles Moulton, including the fictionalized biographical movie, *Professor Marston and the Wonder Women* (2017). There are also many themes that complicate arguments about the relative sexist or empowering elements, such as bondage or Marston's polyamorous lifestyle. Instead, our core concerns are the ways in which artifacts like film can either oppress or empower a female audience (or do both simultaneously), and whether or not the zealous claims of feminism are exaggerated because of the limited images focused on the female rather than male gaze.

Understanding the intent of the film becomes key to understanding why it was so successful and so lauded as a feminist text despite imagery reminiscent of the highly sexualized Wonder Woman of the seventies and reflective of the overly-sexualized fetishized warrior woman found in such films as *Tomb Raider* (2018). Have we really come so far that girls now have a fictional icon they can proudly emulate, or is the 2017 *Wonder Woman* movie simply another example of females so devoid of positive images that we find empowerment where there really is none?

THE BECHDEL TEST

The Bechdel Test is not meant as a moral or ethical judgment on the strength or depth of female characters in a work. It is entirely possible for a film to pass without having pro-feminist themes, or even characterizing females positively. (TV Tropes, 2018)

In 1985, Alison Bechdel authored the serialized comic strip, *Dykes to Watch Out For,* and the Bechdel test was born (Bechdel, 1985). Alison Bechdel has consistently reiterated that the test described in the comic strip was her friend Liz Wallace's and has asked that people refer to the test as the Bechdel-Wallace Test (Gross, 2015). In this strip titled "The Rule," two female characters discuss the opportunity to see a film. One of the women explains that she only goes to a movie if it satisfies the following requirements:

1. The movie has to have at least two women in it,
2. who talk to each other,
3. about something besides a man (Bechdel, 1985).

The second character acknowledges that the idea is strict but good. Then the first states the last movie she was able to see was *Alien* (Ridley Scott, 1979), meaning it passed the test because Ripley (Sigourney Weaver) and Lambert (Veronica Cartwright) discuss their escape plan.

According to Bechdel, this strip was meant to be "a little lesbian joke in an alternative feminist newspaper" (Morlan, 2014). Twenty-five years later, the test has become a "standard by which feminist critics judge television, movies, books, and other media" (Steiger, 2011, p. 104). Neda Ulaby, an American reporter for National Public Radio (NPR), believes the test resonates because "it articulates something often missing in popular culture: not the number of women we see on screen, but the depth of their stories, and the range of their concerns" (Ulaby, 2008). With few alternatives, women have been forced to watch visual media through a consistent male gaze, which produces images of women where the focus has been on their looks and worthiness as a sexual partner as if all they can be are sexual objects. Utilization of Bechdel's test unpacks visual media in a way that enlightens audiences and ultimately creators. *Wonder Woman* is arguably the first contemporary female superhero protagonist film to pass each element of the test, suggesting its relevance to modern female audiences. Unpacking the film and passing the Bechdel Test are central to understanding the ways visual media continues to develop. Yet why did a movie about a highly sexualized superhero so positively pass the test?

A POSITIVE RESULT

Just as seeds are dispersed through the force of wind and water, movies too have the power to disperse ideas through their narratives. For many of us used to the mawkish idea of a hero 'saving' us, Wonder Woman offers a forceful rethink. – Divyani (Rattanpal, 2017)

The latest iteration of the Wonder Woman tale was the fourth DC Universe movie, following Batman *v Superman: Dawn of Justice* (2016), where we are first introduced to Diana Prince (Extended DC Universe, 2018). As part of Zach Snyder's universe, the *Wonder Woman* screenplay was written by a male writer, Allan Heinberg, but became the first ever DC movie directed by a woman, Patty Jenkins, best known for her Oscar winning film *Monster* (2003). Zach Snyder is well-known for his freeze-frame, slow motion films such as *300* (2006) and *Man of Steel* (2013) that feature seemingly strong women with a veneer of independence. Yet in these films, his female characters are seemingly there to add eye-candy to uber-masculine storylines (think Queen Gorgo in *300*) or there to humanize the male lead (i.e., Lois Lane in the DC Universe). Snyder's past films have definitively failed the Bechdel Test, featuring female characters rarely interacting or working together. Wonder Woman in *Batman v Superman* is the first female character whose primary purpose is *not* vulnerability to be protected by the male lead, while providing eye candy for the male audience.

Wonder Woman's story is set as a flashback to explain a photo depicting Diana (Gal Gadot) and a group of soldiers in World War I, featured in *Batman and Superman* (David S. Goyer, 2016). The audience is taken on a 141-minute journey from Diana's childhood, through her training as an Amazon warrior, the introduction of the first male on the island, to her leaving Themyscira focused on destroying the god Ares whom she believes is responsible for World War I.

The entire plot seems revolutionary and reflective of the new 'Woke' generation, who believe they transcend the limitations of gendered labels. This global generation has grown up in a world where, in some places, women can be anything they want from CEOs to political leaders to marines and all roles in between. In short, the film was released at a time when its audience could believe that being born female is no longer a barrier to achieving your dreams.

But was the explosive positive response reflective of the film's actual content or were the ideals it suggested, in actuality, left unfulfilled (Funny or Die, 2017)? By dissecting the Bechdel Test into its three requirements, we might be able to find an answer unrelated to the emotional responses the film garnered. Once again, the three Bechdel steps are as follows: (1) The movie has to have at least two women in it, (2) who talk to each other, and (3) about something besides a man.

Simply stated, the *Wonder Woman* movie passes the Bechdel test fulfilling each element in multiple scenes. The movie (Heinberg, 2017) takes us back to Diana's childhood on Themyscira.[1] A couple examples of female to female conversations that pass the test within this time are:

- Diana, as a young child, speaking with her mother, Queen Hippolyta (Connie Nielsen) and General Antiope (Robin Wright).

  Diana: Hello mother. How are you today?

  Queen Hippolyta: Let's get you back to school, before another tutor quits.

  Diana: But don't you think it's time to start my training? Antiope thinks I'm ready.

  Queen Hippolyta: Does she?

  General Antiope: I could begin showing her some things. She should at least be able to defend herself (Heinberg, 2017).

- General Antiope fighting with Diana during her training.

  "General Antiope: You are stronger than this, Diana. Again. Never let your guard down. You expect the battle to be fair. A battle will never be fair" (Heinberg, 2017).

- Diana and Etta Candy shop for clothes[2]

  Diana Prince: [examining a corset on display at a department store] Is this what passes for armor in your country?

  Etta Candy: Armor? Well—it's fashion. It keeps our tummy's in!

  Diana Prince: Why must you keep them in?

  Etta Candy: Only a woman with no tummy would ask that question (Heinberg, 2017).

In order for a movie to pass the Bechdel test, not every scene has to qualify. The criteria are met even if only one scene passes, and the balance do not. It is important to note that the test is not meant to be indicative of whether a movie is a "good" or "bad" portrayal of feminism based on audience evaluation. The steps measure the purpose of women in a film and whether it can be accurately called a feminist piece. While the test identifies films that project a feminist narrative, it also helps to identify those that do not and therefore, can be considered problematic due to male gaze influence. Yet, given the above examples, *Wonder Woman* is a Bechdel test success.

A FLAWED PERSPECTIVE

Be careful in the world of men, Diana. They do not deserve you.
– Queen Hippolyta (Heinberg, 2017)

The Bechdel Test only indicates whether women are present in a work of fiction, and if they speak to each other about something other than a man. A film may fail because there are no female leads. A film may pass the test and still be sexist, such as the recent *Justice League* (2017) movie. There are many examples, but the most obvious is when the audience sees a male directed film that takes Diana and the Amazon women of Themyscira's wardrobe from scantily clad to barely skimpy. The Bechdel Test, in fact, has flaws, but its use continues to dominate the media world. Supporters seem to have one voice when it comes to results, cohesive in their belief that visual media landscape is lacking in strong independent women with lives of their own distinct from the male characters. For its feminist supporters, *Wonder Woman*'s success demonstrates that a film can be considered a success even when a majority of scenes seem to reflect the male gaze.

There are several arguments for how the *Wonder Woman* movie actually fails the Bechdel Test. One of the core problematic elements is the claim to an all-female world. Themyscira is an island of scantily clad women, thus all conversation is necessarily between and about women. There are literally no men. Moreover, while it is not explained, most of the Amazons, including Diana, have never seen a man. Yet when Queen Hippolyta and General Antiope, argue about Diana's training, it is still filtered through their fears of Ares, a very masculine Greek God best known for his love of war. The discussion between young Diana and her mother about the Amazon's origin does not pass the Bechdel Test. They talk about Zeus, a male god, and the creation of Themyscira due to Ares's manipulation of men demonstrating that the movie is still really about the male gaze.

When a man, Steve Trevor (Chris Pine), crash lands on their island, all conversation shifts to be about him. Even when Diana arrives in the United Kingdom, Trevor takes her shopping with his assistant Etta Candy (Lucy Davis); she's a large woman, and hence the male writer assigns her last name as Candy. This is the only woman Diana interacts with in any meaningful way, and it is predicated on female jealousy with Etta joking about her envy for Diana's beauty and popularity with men. In short, there is surprisingly little evidence of the desires for equitable images of "strength and self-reliance for women; sisterhood and mutual support among women ... a diminishment both of 'masculine' aggression and of the belief that violence is the only way of solving conflicts" (Desta, 2017), desired by Gloria Steinem almost half a century earlier. *Wonder Woman* is all about violence as the core way to resolve conflicts, even if Diana believes that killing the God of War will end all violence at the heart of humanity.

Finally, the Bechdel test demands female comradeship, and yet *Wonder Woman* lacks any scenes in which two women as friends converse. In actuality, Diana functions in a role typical of films where the female protagonist stands in clear opposition to other female characters and finds support from a man who inevitably becomes her love interest.

However, critics presenting these arguments have taken the Bechdel Test requirements and expanded them to add subjective criteria and layers of assumption ignoring the polar functionality of the steps, which allowed for *Wonder Woman* to pass the Bechdel Test from a feminist perspective.

CONCLUSIONS

We have jobs, creative projects, friendships and struggles among many other things that are actually interesting in our lives ... so Hollywood, start writing about it! (Sarkeesian, 2009)

The limits of the Bechdel test have led to other attempts to present a more effective template for critiquing contemporary media. The Vito Russo test, for example, broadens the critique by focusing on LGBTQ+ portrayals on screen. While the Finkbeiner test focuses on portrayals of female scientists and the Furiosa Test attempts to "gauge how angry people on the internet become over a film when it is designated as feminist" (Film School Rejects. com). The latter theory reflects the vocalized desire of audiences to see films with strong and diverse female characters like the surprise hit *Mad Max: Fury Ro*ad (2015). Named after a boycott orchestrated on Twitter, the

Furiosa Test (Roach, 2016) captures the testament of men's rights activists, who declared *Mad Max: Fury Road* to be feminist propaganda. The Furiosa Test is a step in the rigorous direction, where the Bechdel Test fails. In *The Oxford Handbook of Feminist Theory,* Dean Spade and Craig Willse describe the Bechdel Test as "commentary on how media representations enforce harmful gender norms" by depicting women's relationships to men, more than any other relationships, and women's lives as important only insofar as they relate to men but the creation of so many alternatives highlights the limits of its ability to do so. (Spade & Willse, 2016, p. 556).

The *Wonder Woman* movie passes the Bechdel Test by meeting all three of its requirements: two women are present and converse with each other about something other than a man. It passes because of the simplicity of the test. The question remains, upon exploring the film in more depth, was *Wonder Woman* truly a feminist film? Or, is it just another movie which fetishizes women who are desperate to see a populist figure as empowering, thus embraced the 2017 Wonder Woman as their 21st century role model? Ultimately, a film which passes the Bechdel Test may or may not be feminist in nature, but the results can stimulate the discussions needed to remove the subtle influence of the male gaze.

NOTES

[1] The scene Themyscira begins at 0:02:43, scene one through scene two, and ends with Trevor's plane crashes, 0:16:25.
[2] The scene, number six, occurs at 0:49:14.

REFERENCES

Batman v Superman: Dawn of Justice. (n.d.). Retrieved May 14, 2018, from http://dcextendeduniverse.wikia.com/wiki/Batman_v_Superman:_Dawn_of_Justice
Bechdel, A. (1985). *Dykes to watch out for* [Comic Strip]. Retrieved April 21, 2018, from https://www.flickr.com/photos/zizyphus/34585797/in/photostream/
Bechdel, A. (1985). *Dykes to watch out for*. Itaca, NY: Firebrand Books.
Bechdel Test. (2017). *Bechdel Test movie list*. Retrieved from https://bechdeltest.com/
Desta, Y. (2017). How Gloria Steinem saved Wonder Woman. *Vanity fair*. Retrieved from https://www.vanityfair.com/hollywood/2017/10/gloria-steinem-wonder-woman
Funny or Die. (2017). *Women who didn't love Wonder Woman support group* [web video]. Retrieved from http://www.funnyordie.com/videos/aa633f74a3/women-who-didnt-love-wonder-woman-support-group
Gross, T. (Host). (2015, August 17). Lesbian cartoonist Alison Bechdel countered dad's secrecy by being out and open [Radio series episode]. In T. Gross (Host), *Fresh air*. Philadelphia, PA: WHYY. Retrieved from https://www.npr.org/2015/08/17/432569415/lesbian-cartoonist-alison-bechdel-countered-dads-secrecy-by-being-out-and-open

Heinberg, A. (Screenplay), Snyder, Z. (Story & Producer), & Jenkins, P. (Director). (2017). *Wonder Woman* [Motion picture]. Burbank, CA: Warner Bros.

Martindale, K. (1997). *Un/popular culture: Lesbian writing after the sex wars*. Albany, NY: State University of New York Press.

Morlan, K. (2014, July 23). Comic-con vs. the Bechdel test. *San Diego City Beat*. Retrieved March 16, 2015, from http://sdcitybeat.com/culture/features/comic-con-vs.-bechdel-test/

Rattanpal, D. (2017). If Wonder Woman passed the Bechdel Test is a rhetorical question! *The Quint*. Retrieved from https://www.thequint.com/voices/women/wonder-woman-is-the-feminist-movie-we-need

Roach. (2016). Astraleyedandroid asked: What's the Furiosa test? *Roach patrol* [web log]. Retrieved from https://roachpatrol.tumblr.com/post/136232752302/whats-the-furiosa-test

Sarkeesian, A. (2009). The Bechdel Test for women in movies. *Feminist Frequency*. Retrieved from https://feministfrequency.com/video/the-bechdel-test-for-women-in-movies/

Sassatelli, R. (2011). Interview with Laura Mulvey: Gender, gaze and technology in film culture. *Theory, Culture & Society, 28*(5), 123–143.

Spade, D., & Willse, C. (2016). Norms and normalization. In M. Hawkesworth (Ed.), *The Oxford handbook of feminist theory* (p. 556). Oxford: Oxford University Press.

Steiger, K. (2011). No clean slate: Unshakeable race and gender politics in the walking dead. In J. Lowder (Ed.), *Triumph of the walking dead: Robert Kirkman's zombie epic on page and screen* (pp. 100–113). Dallas, TX: BenBella Books.

Steinem, G. (1972). Introduction. In W. M. Marston (Author), *Wonder Woman*. New York, NY: Holt, Rinehart and Winston.

TV Tropes. (2018). *Useful notes/the Bechdel Test* [web log]. Retrieved April 21, 2018, from http://tvtropes.org/pmwiki/pmwiki.php/UsefulNotes/TheBechdelTest?from=Main.The Bechdeltest

Ulaby, N. (2008, September 2). The "Bechdel rule," defining pop-culture character [Radio news story]. In C. Watson (Executive producer), *All things considered*. Washington, DC: NPR. Retrieved from https://www.npr.org/templates/story/story.php?storyId=94202522

Sarah Smith
Partner in Publishing

JENNA GUITAR

4. THE VAMPIRIC NATURE OF TRANSMEDIA STORYTELLING IN THE BUFFYVERSE

On March 10, 1997, *Buffy the Vampire Slayer* (*BTVS*) premiered as a mid-season replacement show on an-at-the-time-little-known network called the WB. The show quickly garnered a cult following and went on to become highly successful and critically lauded for seven seasons. However, since the cancellation of the show, it has continued to live on through various mediums and has persistently resonated with new audiences. Part of this continued attraction to the show is the way in which *BTVS* offers empowering narratives to anyone who feels different or othered. Centered on the world of a teenage girl who has to hide her true self, problems arising from closeting one's identity and other queer issues have resonated with the show, as well as the more overt feminist themes the show encapsulates.

The sheer quality of the show has undoubtedly been one of the reasons that *BTVS* has remained so relevant. Dorothy Swanson, founder of the Viewers for Quality Television,[1] states that: "A quality series enlightens, challenges, involves, and confronts. It dares to take risks; it is honest and illuminating, it appeals to the intellect and touches the emotions. It requires concentration and attention, and it provokes thought" (Wilcox & Lavery, 2002, p. xx). *BTVS* is critically lauded for doing all of these things.

BTVS studies remain a staple in popular culture, as well as in feminist and queer studies, illustrating the show's tremendous staying power. Furthermore, the feminist and queer subjects presented by the show remain contested issues and perhaps even more so under the current Trump administration that seeks to undermine the critical strides that feminist and queer activists have made in the past decade. Part of the show's staying power is its continued political relevance, as well as its continuation in both the comic book form and fan podcasts. I will be examining and analyzing one fan podcast in particular, *Buffering the Vampire Slayer*, hosted by Jenny Owen Youngs and Kristin Russo. I have chosen this podcast as the focus of analysis because it reads *BTVS* through a queer lens, while also aligning the show with current political questions and movements.

The continuation of *BTVS* in comic book form and fan podcasts speaks to the importance of transmedia storytelling in the Buffyverse. Transmedia storytelling,

© KONINKLIJKE BRILL NV, LEIDEN, 2019 | DOI:10.1163/9789004394100_004

according to Henry Jenkins, "unfolds across multiple media platforms, with each new text making a distinctive and valuable contribution to the whole" (2006, pp. 97–98). The continuation of *BTVS* across media platforms speaks to the fan's desire for more content. The fan's urge to consume more is quite vampiric as the new content continues to revive the series, much as vampires have the power to resurrect the dead. In the case of the comics, the new text progresses the storyline from where the show ended, while the fan podcasts revive the show itself, urging listeners to rewatch the show or view it for the first time. Transmedia storytelling helps to create new fans and stoke old fan's enthusiasm by continuing conversations around both old and new content.

BTVS is an exemplar of urban fantasy and is seen by many critics as a seminal text of the genre. One of the main facets of urban fantasy is that the fantastical world of magic and supernatural creatures co-exist in the modern world. The primary focus of the first three seasons of *BTVS* is that high school is hell both literally and figuratively, as Sunnydale High sits atop the mouth of hell. The horrors of adolescence manifest as literal demons and monsters. The proceeding seasons demonstrate that these horrors are not just confined to the halls of high school, but the anxieties and pressures of adulthood also become demons that we all must learn to fight. Whether it is the horror of dealing with the death of a parent to the unglamorous life of low wage employment to the loss of autonomy, *BTVS* plays upon adult anxieties as well. While mostly employing various Gothic and urban fantasy techniques and constructions of monstrosity to play out the narrative metaphors for life's issues, the show also portrays alarmingly realist depictions of gun violence, death from illness, and rape. The honesty and self-awareness of the show continue to resonate with new audiences. Stars of the show, such as Anthony Stewart Head who plays Buffy's paternal mentor Rupert Giles, state that the fans of the show who stop him in public are in many cases quite young. This points to the fact that not only is the show held in high regard from fans who watched the show as it aired in the '90s and the early aughts but that new fans are being drawn to the series. Moreover, many of the same issues that were being addressed by the show in the '90s are still crucially relevant in new viewer's lives, for example the issue of gun control. In an eerie and uncanny fashion, the original season 3 episode of *BTVS* "Earshot," an episode that deals with a shooter on school grounds, was delayed from its initial airing due to the Columbine High School shooting that occurred on April 20, 1999. This year the *Buffering* podcast coincidentally aired their episode of "Earshot" on the same day as the school shooting in Parkland, Florida on February 14, 2018. This chillingly uncanny moment reminds and reinforces the idea that

BTVS still matters as the issues and horrors of growing up depicted still exist and resonates with contemporary audiences. This can also be coupled with the fact that *BTVS* never really went away in the first place.

While the show was canceled in 2003, *BTVS* continues to live on to this day in various mediums. Seasons Eight, Nine, Ten, Eleven, and Twelve continue in comic book form and are subsequently considered canon by creator Joss Whedon, who has said that "Canon is key, as is continuity. If you are a massive nerd, which I am, I believe there is a demarcation between the creation and the ancillary creations by different people. I'm all for that stuff, just like fanfic, but I like to know that there's an absolutely official story-so-far, especially when something changes mediums, which my stuff seems to do a lot" (Dowdell, 2016). The continuation of the series in comic book form was a somewhat unprecedented maneuver. In 2007, four years after the cancellation of the show, Dark Horse began publishing *BTVS Season Eight* with Whedon acting as both "executive producer" for the series and writer for several story arcs. The very fact that this was established as a canonical continuation of the television series was quite groundbreaking. The shifting of mediums points to the paratextual importance of the continuation of canceled shows. Jonathan Gray argues that:

> Paratexts are not simply add-ons, spin-offs, and also-rans: they create texts, they manage them, and they fill them with the meanings we associate with them … a program is but one part of a text, the text always being a contingent entity, either in the process of forming or transforming or vulnerable to further formation or transformation. (2010, pp. 6–7)

BTVS's paratextual elements help to illustrate the change in viewer habits. Viewers in the twenty-first century are used to consuming media in multiple platforms and through a myriad of sources. Mark Duffett argues that audiences and fans of shows now may "meander across the surface of different media in their quest for meaning" (2013, p. 215). The paratextual elements allow fans of *BTVS* also to occupy different readerly positions. Watching the show is a much different experience and provides the writers with much more constraints, while the comics allow for a larger scale world building.

The continuation of the show into comic book form allows the Buffyverse to quite literally expand from the show's primary location of Sunnydale, California, to a more global stage. Joss Whedon and his team of writers, unfettered from budgetary and network restrictions raise the magnitude of the Buffyverse. Special effects and fight scenes, as well as magical spells, can be played out on a massive scale, and speaking of larger scales, characters are allowed to undergo a metamorphosis that would have been impossible, such as making the character of Dawn a giant. Other spectacle-driven allowances are afforded as well, Buffy's headquarters is now a castle in Scotland. The Scooby gang easily travels to exquisite locales all over the globe. The global scale of the comics also allows a more racially and culturally diverse representation of characters. The lack of racial diversity is one of the original show's weakest spots. Characters of color[2] in the television series are severely under-utilized and often suffer untimely deaths before their characters are given a chance to be fully fleshed out.

Unconstrained by the limitations of network television, the comics are also able to explore more in-depth, non-normative desire and queer sexuality. Already groundbreaking and often cited as the first network television show to offer a fully realized depiction of a lesbian romance between Willow and Tara; *BTVS* was a progressive show of its time in regard to the representation of non-normative desire. Furthermore, the depiction of sadomasochism (S/M) displayed in the depiction of Spike and Buffy's relationship, particularly in season six, produces compelling discourse. Buffy and Spike's relationship through season six is a rocky and tumultuous one, which hinges on sadomasochistic desire. Sadomasochism is a marginalized and misunderstood lifestyle that focuses on aspects of play, which is at times sexual in nature. However, play is a complex term in the S/M community and the term "references recreation and leisure and evokes a romantic sense of innocence and freedom from encumbrances" (Newmahr, 2011, p. 8). Moreover, "S/M is more easily understood as an all-encompassing lifestyle that represents liberation from the oppressive plight of the everyman and nurtures identities of marginality" (Newmahr, 2011, p. 9). Buffy and Spike enact various forms of sexual S/M play as Buffy allows herself to enact desires she has previously denied herself, as a way in which to experience the world anew after her resurrection. She constantly worries that her secret sexual escapades with Spike will be found out by her friends, at which point she will face ridicule. Forms of desire perceived as perverse are generally marginalized or indicative of a severe character flaw because ultimately this non-normative desire threatens the hegemonic way in which society chooses to view desire. The character of Buffy may fear ridicule, but *BTVS* appeals to the fan's acceptance of diverse forms of desire, while using Buffy and Spike's unusual sexual relationship to form a safe space where non-normative desire is no longer denigrated, but instead raised up to allow the exploration of desire and the ways in which non-normative desire can be seen as an empowering agent to marginalized groups.

The show's ability to deconstruct heteronormative desire allows non-normative desire to flourish when it is not kept under the restraints of a patriarchal preoccupation of how desire should operate. *BTVS* is undermining traditional conceptions of desire and opening up a safe place to discuss non-normative desire. In season six, Buffy and Spike are unable to fit into the mainstream, instead they assume the position of marginalized outsider figures, who do not fit into the constructs of society. Spike, by this point in the show, has effectively been neutered by the government initiative. They have placed a chip in Spike's brain that does not allow him to hurt humans, but the chip still allows violence against demons. His life as a vampire is now perverse as he fights against his own kind and alongside Buffy. On the other hand, Buffy has consistently felt like an outsider as the slayer, an identity that requires secrecy and a kind of closeting. Buffy often daydreams about how wonderful it would be to have a normal life, but when faced with normalcy (minimum wage jobs, problems with the plumbing, bills, housing repairs, etc.) that season six presents to her, she longs for a break from the monotony of "normal" life, the very thing she has longed for in all previous seasons. Anne Billson adds that "Buffy had already survived death; now, Season Six featured life as the Big Bad" (2005, p. 112). The greatest fights Buffy encounters this season are internal struggles. Buffy has fought with the forces of darkness her whole life, but it isn't until this season that she is asked to battle her own personal demons. One of the biggest obstacles that Buffy must overcome is her guilt with what she views as her perverse desire in regard to Spike. The guilt Buffy feels is put upon her by a heteronormative world that demands desire follow a specific hegemonic pattern. Michel Foucault discusses in *The History of Sexuality* how in the creation of sexuality "perverse pleasure" needed to be "assigned a role of normalization or pathologization with respect to all behavior; and finally, a corrective technology was sought for these anomalies" (1984, p. 105). The process of normalizing perverse pleasure creates guilt by those members who derive pleasure from the perverse but have been taught that pleasure is something that needs to be corrected. After all we think of the term perverse as meaning doing something against one's better interests, but when Buffy states that "last night was the most perverse degrading moment of my life" (Noxon, 2001), the viewer has to wonder whether we agree with such a statement. It is after all through her relationship with Spike that Buffy discovers many things about herself and begins her recovery from her post-resurrection depression. Desire renews her, gives her life again, Willow may have brought Buffy back from the dead, but it is Buffy's perverse sexual desire that truly brings Buffy back to life.

Buffy's non-normative desire in season six, is not the only time that kinky desire is presented as standard fare but again albeit in a subtle sub-textual manner in the show. Any relationship with a vampire is after all heavily saturated in necrophilic subtext. Terry L. Spaise argues that:

> The act of necrophilia, though rare in reality, has always been linked in literature with vampirism. The embrace and bite are a parody of the sexual act, particularly because they are traditionally performed by a male character on a female victim who is passive and seems to welcome his touch. As a result of the pain of the bite and the loss of blood, she even experiences a pseudo-orgasm, which Buffy herself illustrates when she cures a poisoned Angel by letting him feed on her in "Graduation Day, Pt. II." (2005, p. 745)

Thus, Buffy's relationships with the male vampires in her life that may set a heteronormative precedent at first can be read in a queer manner. Therefore, the queering of desire in Buffy's sexual encounters must be approached with a cipher.

While much of the queerness in Buffy may stem from the subtext in the television show, the comics unconstrained by network stipulations delve more explicitly into Buffy's desires and sexuality. In one panel, from season eight Buffy is shown fully clothed wrapped in chains with her two (un)dead lovers Angel and Spike, naked on either side of her. The visualization of Buffy's erotic fantasy shows her desiring a ménage a trois and perhaps even double penetration. The look on Buffy's face, as well as the positioning of her body, makes it clear that Buffy is in control of this fantasy. The bodies of Angel and Spike are exposed and vulnerable contrasted against the clothed Buffy, as she also seems to be guiding the movements of Angel and Spike's bodies. Later in the season eight arc, Buffy explores her bisexual desire as she engages in a brief affair with Satsu, a fellow slayer, thus queering Buffy's sexuality and allowing us access into Buffy's bisexual desire that is never explored beyond subtext on the television show most notably in season three with Faith Lehane. The queer subtext between Faith and Buffy is something that Whedon decried, when fans began to invest heavily in the homoerotic content of the girl's relationship on early message boards. After investing more time into delving into fan's theories concerning the homoerotic subtext of Buffy and Faith, Whedon had to concede that indeed the subtext was there. Whedon, thus, coined the term "BYOsubtext" and admitted that fan interpretations of the subtext in his work were, while being subjective, still plausible and at times quite undeniable (Bianculli, 2009). While Buffy's relationship with Satsu does not last long, the exploration of Buffy's queer desire seems to be an express love letter to the queer fans that always hoped to have Buffy's bisexuality examined more thoroughly. The comics have opened up queer visual spaces that allow for a more nuanced exploration of female desire. While the comics have provided a queered visual space to extend the narrative from the television series, the life of the show has also continued and evolved in other paratexts, such as through the use of fandom podcasting.

Podcasting came of age in 2005, the year in which the medium skyrocketed in popularity and "podcast" was chosen as the *New Oxford American Dictionary*'s Word of the Year. According to studies from the Pew Research Center, podcast listening has been growing considerably over recent years, and the number of American podcast listeners nearly doubled between 2008 and 2015. Market research has discovered that podcast fans tend to be highly dedicated "super listeners," consuming more audio by time than listeners of AM/FM radio, streaming music, or any other form of audio. The success of *Serial* in the fall of 2014—the program that spurred nearly 77 million downloads within its first seven months of release—helped to thrust podcasting into the limelight. Suddenly, media critics were declaring it "the golden age of podcasts" (Bottomley, 2015). While media personalities and Hollywood stars are now making podcasts, many podcasts are still mostly amateur productions originating outside traditional media industries. Podcasts open up a unique space for fans to gather digitally and talk about shows, even ones that have been off the air for some time now, renewing interest in long-canceled shows. These podcasts in effect are reviving shows and giving them a second life.

Buffering the Vampire Slayer is a current weekly podcast in which the hosts Jenny Owen Youngs (professional musician and recreational Whedonverse aficionado) and Kristin Russo (professional writer and self-pronounced former goth teen, who is also a queer advocate who runs the online advocacy and support groups for "Everyone is Gay" and "My Kid is Gay") discuss *BTVS*, one episode at a time. Every installment of the podcast also includes a new original song recapping each *BTVS* episode. The podcast has received favorable attention and has been listed on *Entertainment Weekly*'s "Must List," as well as *Time*'s and *Esquire*'s lists of top podcasts of 2018.

Youngs and Russo lovingly critique the show but also do not hold back when problematic issues arise, i.e., basically anytime Xander[3] opens his mouth or, for instance, the cultural insensitivities of the episode entitled "Inca Mummy Girl," where cultural appropriation is on full display at the Bronze.[4] Youngs and Russo also make it a point to use the term "patriarchy" at least once an episode to indicate when oppression occurs that stems from patriarchal constructs. They have even created a patriarchy jingle that they play during moments of oppression. In addition, after the season two episode "Reptile

Boy" that centers on the abuses of power enacted by a fraternity against girls in order to appease a reptilian demon who bequeaths the members of the fraternity with wealth and prestige (Greenwalt, 1997), the podcasters termed the phrase "smash the demon lizard patriarchy." The phrase has become a paratextual entity in its own right as it has become emblazoned on shirts, hoodies and perhaps most importantly, a free downloadable poster meant to be printed on poster board for political marches.

Furthermore, Youngs and Russo honor a pair of characters with the sexual tension award every episode. The sexual tension award is often bestowed to the characters that display the most homoerotic desire. A few of the winners of this award are Angel and Xander, Giles and Ethan Rayne, Willow and Cordelia. Most notably in season three, the relationship between Buffy and Faith is given special attention as the podcasters emphasize the homoerotic undertones on the show. They have even gone so far as to create a new version of "Baby It's Cold Outside" that replaces the lyrics with those driven by Buffy and Faith partaking in the flirtatious banter of the redone Christmas carol. The revised song can be looked at as a form of slash fanfiction as the show never materializes more than subtle hints at the desire between the two women. Their compelling analysis of *BTVS* equals the playfulness of the podcast through the lens of two queer women. Their conversations are frank, and they do not allow their love of the show to overshadow their intellectual criticism.

The podcast not only smartly discusses each episode, but it has become a haven for the queer community as well. Youngs and Russo have had many other queer podcasters and entertainers guest star on their show. Furthermore, the use of technology, such as Facebook Live allows Youngs and Russo to participate in a "live watch" of particular episodes online. Fans from all over the world watch the episode together, while also watching Youngs and Russo provide commentary. The viewer utilizing the Facebook messaging function may live chat with one another as well. A show that has not aired "live" in essentially 20 years is being revived once more and being watched at the same time by people all over the globe.

Moreover, the inclusion of the original song at the end of each podcast also speaks to a potentiality for world building. The songs, while being an homage to the series, produce a new archive detailing the narrative and emotional trajectory of the show. Youngs performs the songs written by herself and Russo and generally produces them from the perspective of Buffy allowing us a glimpse of interiority that may not have been present otherwise.

It can certainly not be denied that much of fandom relies on the urge to collect and consume material goods. Fans can, thus, be seen as "specialist consumers, whose fandom is expressed through keeping up with new releases of books, comics and videos," and I would also add clothing, jewelry, games, action figures, prop replicas, among other ephemera related to fandom experience to this list (Hills, 2002, p. 29). Jenkins articulates a persuasive argument that relocates the perception of fans from passive consumers to active participants in that "media fans are consumers who also produce, readers who also write, spectators who also participate" (1992, p. 208). This move positions the active fan, such as Youngs and Russo, in a unique locus.

The consumption of the text is one way in which the fan becomes always already a consumer, but fandom also relies on the need to encounter the text multiple times. The act of rereading a text is considered an integral element of fandom. "Rereading is central to a fan's aesthetic pleasure. Much of fan culture facilitates repeated encounters with favored texts" (Jenkins, 1992, p. 69). Jenkins, by way of Roland Barthes, suggests "that rereading runs counter to 'commercial and ideological habits of our society' and thus books are constructed to sustain our interests only on a first reading 'so that we can then move on to another story, buy another book'" (1992, p. 67). Essentially Barthes, and, therefore, Jenkins argue that this return to the material disrupts the consumer cycle because instead of purchasing a new text you are returning to the one you have already bought, thus, not consuming more material. However, it seems that the mere act of rereading a text has lost a bit of its radical denial of the commercial with the rise of streaming services, such as Netflix and Hulu. Streaming sites with monthly subscription costs have commodified the urge to rewatch. You can easily choose to repeat your viewing of a television show, but you are always paying for that pleasure.

There may still be a way that rewatching a text can be seen as a resistant act to the formation of commercial consumerism. The act of rereading a text in the streaming age now no longer runs counter to the commercial habits of our society. However, I argue that we can read podcasts as the radical intervention that disrupts commercial capital and employs a form of resistance against industrial consumerism. Fandom podcasts, such as *Buffering the Vampire Slayer*, follow a similar structure of rewatching a television show one episode at a time. Fandom podcasts generally format their show around a chronological rewatching of a television series. For example, *Buffering the Vampire Slayer* calls for consumption of the original primary text, but Youngs and Russo, fans of the show, not only produce new material through their podcast but also through creating an entirely original song at the end of each session that summarizes the episode's central themes. The podcast itself exists as a free piece of media. I acknowledge that one must have the technology to support playing podcasts which still elevates the show into a space of economic privilege that is not able to be accessed by all classes of people, but at the same time it points to an exciting way to trace fan consumption and disruption of economic means in 2018. However, if a listener of the podcast is so inclined, they may become a patron of the podcasters by supporting them through Patreon, a company that allows independent producers to collect monthly subscription fees from fans of their show. If you become a supporter through Patreon, you choose to donate a specified amount per month to the podcaster of your choosing. Not only do fans have the ability to support only the artists that they wish, but they are also able to consume this media without any cost, if so financially constrained. Podcasters can also, of course, make money off their podcasts by soliciting advertisements for their show and creating fan merchandise. Fans can efficiently make a living off of their fandom pursuits and have been dubbed "fan-trepreneurs." However, while this still inculcates the fan as a part of the consumer culture that has plagued the image of fans, it concurrently motions to a radically new formulation of the commodity. In the example of *Buffering the Vampire Slayer*, the fan may choose to support two queer women by becoming a Patreon supporter and also by purchasing their extensive line of t-shirts, CDs, and enamel pins. Many fans, dismayed by the recent allegations lobbied against Joss Whedon by his ex-wife as a philanderer and gaslighter, have opted out of buying licensed merchandise and instead support podcasts like *Buffering* and other independent artists that also create fan related merchandise to sell on such platforms as Etsy. Furthermore, if podcasters (such as Youngs and Russo) operate from a place of social justice, the power of the fan's capital can also have a positive charitable effect. For example, each month, Youngs and Russo sell five handwritten lyric sheets for $100 each and donate 100% of the proceeds to a different charity. Additionally, they recently had an exclusive promotional T-shirt where 100% of the proceeds went to support the #TimesUp movement, which has established a Legal Defense Fund that provides subsidized legal support to those who have experienced sexual harassment, assault, or abuse in the workplace. I find these examples to be encouraging ways in which fandom can disrupt the typical capitalist ensnarement of consumption that has traditionally plagued fans. Fandom's relationship to merchandise is undoubtedly complicated, but podcasts like *Buffering* provide a new and potentially fruitful way to think about fandom and consumption.

Through rewatching Buffy in the twenty-first century alongside the *Buffering* podcast, Buffy proves that she is the hero we still need today when we have a president and a government that threatens women's reproductive rights and the rights of LGTBQ+ folks. Buffy helps to empower people to stand up to oppressive forces. After all, at the end of the series, instead of gaining more power for herself, Buffy changes the entire future of the slayer line by sharing her power, allowing all 'potentials' to become slayers. After the election, Youngs and Russo offered statements of solidarity, as they mourned with the queer community and much of America about the events that transgressed that fateful November 8th. The podcast was gearing up for the season one finale, wherein Buffy faces the Master—the ancient vampire who has been prophesied to rise from his underground prison, kill the slayer and unleash literal hell upon Sunnydale. When Buffy learns she is fated to die, she tries to run away from her responsibilities. Only to be confronted with the horror of the Master's vampire minions slaughtering numerous high school students on campus. Buffy's best friend Willow sits beleaguered on her bed as she explains to Buffy that the vampires had made our world theirs. Buffy, determined to no longer run from her doomed fight, meets the Master in his underground lair where he drowns her, and Buffy momentarily dies. Luckily, her friends find her, and Xander revives her with CPR. Once alive again, Buffy knows the fight isn't over and proceeds to track the Master down and properly stake him (Whedon, 1997). Buffy's urge to "just keep fighting" becomes an anthem that songwriter Jenny Owen Youngs picks up on. The song that Youngs performs for the last episode of season one of the podcast resonates with Buffy's final trials against the Master, but more importantly crystallizes the mournful but impassioned pleas that so many felt during the last days of 2016 … to just keep fighting. The following is a verse from Youngs' song "Prophecy Girl":

What will come, what will come
If our world belongs to them
What will come, what will come

Just keep fighting, just keep fighting, that's what I'm supposed to do
If I just keep fighting, just keep fighting, know that I'll believe it too.
(Youngs, 2016)

The probing question of "what will come if our world belongs to them" relates back to Willow's fears of the vampires making our world their own, but even more so in light of the election night news, the fear that gripped the hearts of those who saw a hate mongering tyrant win the election. This caused many to fear what would come from the Trump administration. Many queer folks and allies were left terrified and immobile at the thought of how the world would change now that hate had seemingly been allowed to win the election. The immobilization didn't last long as the women's march galvanized those to take action and stand for the rights of all marginalized people. Youngs' song became an anthem for many in the Buffering fandom to unite and gain strength from both Youngs' words and the images of a slayer standing against seemingly insurmountable odds. Youngs' ventriloquial use of Buffy's determination to "just keep fighting" illustrates the staying power of *BTVS* and the ability to imbue the show with new meanings and new connotations as it is consumed by new audiences or re-watched by old fans in new political contexts.

Elana Levine and Lisa Parks, editors of *Undead TV*, state that "the industrial structure of commercial television lends itself to the constant recovery of used, terminated, canceled, expired material for maximum return" (2007, p. 5). Thus, the life of a rich television show can virtually live forever and continually be resurrected. I see both fan podcasts and the comics as opening up queer spaces and a means of resistance to mainstream, heteronormative media. The comics have become freed from the shackles of television studio constraints, while the podcast is free from any overarching constraints to shape its discourse and format in whatever way the hosts deem suitable. Ultimately, we do not live in a post-Buffy world, and we still need our favorite vampire slayer to remind us to "just keep fighting."

NOTES

[1] Viewers for Quality Television is a now defunct non-profit organization that operated from 1984–2000, whose goal was to rescue critically acclaimed shows that were in danger of being cancelled and which *BTVS* won the Founder's Award in 2000.

[2] For example, Kendra the vampire slayer is a woman of color from Jamaica who is depicted in stereotypical fashion and is also easily dispatched by the vampire, Drusilla in the season two finale. Kendra is portrayed as socially awkward, owning only one set of clothes, and is mocked by Buffy concerning her language and dialect—undoubtedly troubling stereotypes at play.

[3] Xander can be seen as symbolically embodying the problematics of patriarchal boyhood on into manhood. His comments frequently represent offensive misogynistic policing of women's bodies and sexuality. While he is coded as the good "guy," he still expresses problematic views stemming from toxic masculinity.

[4] "Inca Mummy Girl" (S2 E4) concerns the cultural exchange event at Sunnydale High. Buffy houses an exchange student from Peru—Ampata. Ampata is actually a mummy brought back to life who must sustain herself with the life force of other humans. The episode ends with a dance at the Bronze where the students are dressed in highly culturally insensitive costumes. The dance and furthermore the episode as a whole is full of problematic stereotypes.

REFERENCES

Bianculli, D. (Host). (2009, February 12). *Joss Whedon: Slayers, dolls and singing villains* [Radio broadcast episode]. Retrieved from https://www.npr.org/templates/story/story.php?storyId=100601869

Billson, A. (2005). *Buffy the vampire slayer: A critical reading of the series*. London: British Film Institute.

Bottomley, A. J. (2015). Podcasting: A decade in the life of a "new" audio medium. *Journal of Radio & Audio Media, 22*(2), 164–169.

Dowdell, A. (2016). *A brief history of Buffy the vampire slayer comics*. Retrieved January 25, 2018, from https://www.completeset.com/a-brief-history-of-buffy-the-vampire-slayer-comics/

Duffett, M. (2013). *Understanding fandom*. New York, NY: Bloomsbury.

Foucault, M. (1978). *The history of sexuality: Volume one*. New York, NY: Vintage Books.

Gray, J. (2010). *Show sold separately: Promos, spoilers and other media paratexts*. New York, NY: New York University Press.

Greenwalt, D. (Writer/Director). (1997, October 13). Reptile boy [Television series episode]. In J. Whedon (Producer), *Buffy the vampire slayer*. Hollywood, CA: The WB.

Hills, M. (2002). *Fan cultures*. New York, NY: Routledge.

Jenkins, H. (1992). *Textual poachers: Television fans & participatory culture*. New York, NY: Routledge.

Jenkins, H. (2006). *Convergence culture: Where old & new media collide*. New York, NY: New York University Press.

Levine, E., & Parks, L. (2007). *Undead TV: Essays on Buffy the vampire slayer*. Durham, NC: Duke University Press.

Newmahr, S. (2011). *Playing on the edge: Sadomasochism, risk, and intimacy*. Bloomington, IN: Indiana University Press.

Noxon, M. (Writer), & Solomon, D. (Director). (2001, November 27). Wrecked [Television series episode]. In J. Whedon (Producer), *Buffy the vampire slayer*. Hollywood, CA: UPN.

Spaise, T. L. (2005). Necrophilia and SM: The deviant side of Buffy the vampire slayer. *The Journal of Popular Culture, 38*, 744–762.

Whedon, J. (Executive Producer & Creator). (1997–2003). *Buffy the vampire slayer* [Television Series]. Hollywood, CA: The WB & UPN.

Whedon, J. (Writer/Director). (1997, June 2). Prophecy girl [Television series episode]. In J. Whedon (Producer), *Buffy the vampire slayer*. Hollywood, CA: The WB.

Wilcox, R. V., & Lavery, D. (2002). *Fighting the forces: What's at stake in Buffy the vampire slayer*. Lanham, MD: Rowman & Littlefield Publishers.

Youngs, J. O., & Russo, K. (Hosts). (2016). *Buffering the vampire slayer* [Audio podcast].

Jenna Guitar
Department of English
University of Rhode Island

AMANDA JO HOBSON

5. BEWITCHING BODIES

Sex, Violence, and Magic in Urban Fantasy

"Wouldst thou like to live deliciously," Black Phillip, a devil in the form of a goat, asks burgeoning witch, Thomasin, in Robert Eggers's brilliantly creepy *The Witch: A New England Folktale* (2015). The temptation of witchcraft and the seductive powers of the witch incite our imaginations and our sexual impulses. Popular culture tells us that women can be seduced to darkness and that men must beware the seductress, who induces unsuspecting men to give in to their baser sexual needs and be mindful of the siren calling sailors to crash their ships upon the rocks sending them to death in the murky depths of the sea. The messages from mythology to contemporary popular culture are that you must avoid the witch, and if you cannot, she must be destroyed before she wreaks havoc upon you. Yet there is a counter image in popular culture of the witches and wise women of mythology and fairytales represented by characters like Glenda the Good Witch, the Halliwell Sisters, Meredith Gentry, Anita Blake, and Willow Rosenberg, all wielders of magic that have captured our cultural imaginations. Though there have been male magic users, it is the perceived witchcraft of women that has had lasting historical and cultural implications. Historically speaking, Anne Llewellyn Barstow (1994) writes, "Having a female body was the factor most likely to render one vulnerable to being called a witch. The sexual connotations and the explicit sexual violence utilized in many of the trials make this fact clear" (p. 16). With few exceptions, these factors hold firm in urban fantasy engagement with magical beings as well: it is women, their bodies, and their magic that become tools to drive the narrative story arcs of these tales. The witch embodies power and strength just as often as they demonstrate how insecure women's bodies can be in popular culture and the real world.

Throughout fiction, film, and other types of art and media, portrayals of witchcraft and magic play a key role in the construction of our cultural understanding of ourselves. Humans have been enthralled with the icon of the witch often leading to violent manifestations of fear of those perceived as wielders of magic, as evidenced by the European witch hunts and Salem Witch Trials. Our modern fascination with the witch and magic illustrates not only the

© KONINKLIJKE BRILL NV, LEIDEN, 2019 | DOI:10.1163/9789004394100_005

continual allure of witchcraft but also the shift in our perception of the witch in western culture. Because while the witch is still an icon of mystery, she is also an alluring and enduring figure. Urban fantasy fictions rely heavily upon the use of magic as a core driving force of the narrative. In television series, such as *Buffy the Vampire Slayer*, *Charmed*, and *The Magicians*, and novels by authors, such as Laurell K. Hamilton, Karen Marie Moning, and Deborah Harkness, we see these images of magic practitioners that demonstrate an endless fascination with our (in)ability to control the world. One of the key factors of historical and fictional witch narratives is the prevalence of violence enacted upon the specifically female body and often in undeniably sexualized acts. This chapter will address the constructions of magic and witchcraft, the use of sexuality to fuel magic, and the production of gender within urban fantasy narratives. In examining the intersections of sex, magic, and violence in the urban fantasy, I will pull from historical and fictional accounts and the Wiccan treatise on ritual practice to address the portrayals of magical bodies.

The genre of urban fantasy has been steeped in magic since its inception. As discussed in the introduction to this book, urban fantasy is a hybrid genre that grew out of necessity to categorize one series—Laurell K. Hamilton's *Anita Blake, Vampire Hunter Series* (1993–present)—that defied conventional genre boundaries. When I discovered Hamilton's novels in 1997, trying to find copies of those first six novels was like conducting a scavenger hunt through every bookstore. Each individual bookstore shelved the series in different locations, sometimes in science fiction, sometimes in horror, sometimes in mystery, and later, as the series grew more sexual and more based in the relationships of Anita and her men, in romance. But shelving issues aside, the ways Hamilton unraveled the ideas of stable genre constructions allowed her to create complicated narratives that often surprised the reader who relied on the established patterns of genre to predict the narrative.[1] When Hamilton began the *Merry Gentry* series in 2000, she continued her bending and blending of generic practices and built another complex and complicated set of characters and metaphysical constraints. With these two series, Hamilton has continued to shape and redefine the genre and reconceptualize portrayals of the magic wielding woman.

Urban fantasy establishes that women can gain real, usable power through their bodies via sexual and non-sexual physical and emotional behaviors or rituals. In the contemporary fictional explorations, supernatural powers can take the form of inherent abilities, salient identity factors, or a combination of both for the wielder. For many paranormal novels, the engagement with magic comes with ingrained codes and practices. The core construction of magic and witchcraft within paranormal fiction is the use of ritual, which allows for the creation of energy through symbolic or real actions. These practices can either be draining or invigorating practices and can be achieved by accident, through intentional invocation, or through ritual ceremony. Urban fantasy blends the fantasy and science fiction worlds of magic users and preternatural beings with detective and mystery plots and adds in significant romance tropes with love stories and a happily-ever-after (HEA)[2] for main characters and often supporting ones. It is this unsettling of the orthodox notions of fixed genre that makes urban fantasy so appealing to many readers but often maligned by critics and scholars. Outside of the urban setting, one of the core traits of the genre is the presence of magic and, moreover, those who wield it. The magic at the heart of urban fantasy can be a wide range of identities and powers, such as necromancy in *Anita Blake* and Fae (fairy) magic in *Merry Gentry*, and witchcraft as in *Charmed*, Druidry as in Jim Butcher's *Dresdan Files Series*, shamanism as in C.E. Murphy's *The Walker Papers Series*, and sorcery as in Jordan L. Hawk's *Whyborne and Griffin Series*.[3]

Another aspect of urban fantasy is the explicit engagements with issues of gender and character constructions. In its early days, urban fantasy as a literary genre was predominantly written by women, and as the genre proliferated and moved to the screen, men began to write in the genre more frequently. In a genre whose inception grew from women authors trying to find a home for their amorphous fictional creations, there is a significant predominance of female protagonists. These protagonists have skills and abilities that lend themselves to solving mysteries and taking on dangerous foes, and they are often mortal, in worlds filled with extremely long-lived—sometimes immortal, nearly indestructible beings. The higher percentage of women shaping the genre meant that narratives featured explorations of gender and featured characters that are complicated, complex, flawed, and powerful. These characters often struggle with very real-world issues, such as sexual harassment and violence, pregnancy scares, being taken seriously in the work place, imposter syndrome, and so much more. The inclusion of complex women characters is not surprising in a genre that blends aspects of romance, which has consistently engaged in examinations of gender roles. Authors of urban fantasy, such as Hamilton and Karen Marie Moning, do more than show that women characters, and by extension living women, are complicated and intelligent but also show women breaking gender norms and people that can defeat any paranormal threat. As urban fantasy has continued to grow, trans and non-binary authors, such as Jordan L. Hawk, delve into discussions of gender exploring the ways in which dualistic constructions of gender present limited options and representations.

The ability for people who are gender diverse to write and see themselves reflected in urban fantasy is a direct result of its foundational engagement with upending gender dichotomies. When urban fantasy authors write about magical characters, they offer both reevaluations and reaffirmations of the stereotypes about witchcraft and gender. Urban fantasy foregrounds historical and cultural representations of gender norms and constructions, often demonstrating the ways in which misogynist and patriarchal societal structures inhibit women as well as other marginalized people, using the icon of the witch as a solid foundation for these gender explorations.

THE CRAFT IN THE MATERIAL WORLD

Our cultural and fictional representations of magic wielding witches have roots in contemporary witchcraft and Wicca, in historical midwives and healers, and the recorded histories of witch trials. There is a great deal of the theoretical and metaphysical underpinnings of Wicca and historical witchcraft in these fictional depictions. These novel and celluloid accounts often expound on, react to, and/or reject Wiccan ideals. Some of this tendency grows out of the normal research that artists and writers undertake when creating their stories. In part though, the reliance on tenets of Wicca develops from the fact that at least some of the authors and producers are pagans, wiccans, or other earth-based religious practitioners.[4] The United States has not experienced a witch trial, since the end of the Salem Trials in 1693, but there is a never-ending cycle of news reports that incorrectly link witchcraft to stories of ritual murders and religious cults. Witchcraft and paganism have a long history of popular cultural and socio-political portrayals, and these fictional works engage in the process of simultaneously supporting and rejecting stereotypes about Wicca, even if the practitioners of magic in these novels very rarely identify as Wicca or even as pagan.

In our contemporary popular engagement with magic, the exercise of supernatural powers plays a core role, and our belief in paranormal abilities grows out of a long historical tradition. Throughout a great deal of human history, people have sought out wielders of magic and providers of herbal medicines to help them when they were sick or afflicted by other misfortunes. They also decried those same healers as witches, shamans, or sorcerers, blaming them for the fallowing of fields, the death of animals, their ill-health, and the withering of their children. The supernatural is a key to an on-going strong belief in not only witches but also vampires and the existence of demons working among us, and more importantly, these supernatural explanations were the only available ones for a great deal of history. The witch, in the guise of the wise woman or healer that was imbedded into their communities as neighbors and relatives, was denounced as the cause when the community faced a crisis. Though we can look back from the modern era and understand that none of the people named, condemned, and killed were actually witches or wielders of any supernatural power, it was the invocation of witchcraft and in the name of protecting the predominant religion—Christianity in most cases—that spurred on the horrors of the witch trials.

As mentioned earlier in the chapter, those accused of witchcraft throughout the witch trials were predominantly women. The European Witch Trials lasted from 1450 until 1750 with most of the accusations and executions occurring between 1500 and 1727. The records are not complete from the European trials, and therefore, we have only estimates of the number of accused, with the best estimation being two-hundred thousand people accused and approximately half of those killed by the state and/or mob executions or were tortured to death in the effort to gain a confession. In discussing the trials, Barstow relays that eighty percent of the accused and eighty-five percent of the executed were women (Barstow, 1994, pp. 22–23). In the context of the United States, the demographics of the accused were similar. The American cases of witch accusations ran from 1620 until 1725, and during that time, witchcraft was a capital crime, meaning that it was consider a crime against the state and, therefore, punishable by death. According to records, three hundred and fifty-five people were accused of witchcraft, and seventy-eight percent of them were women. Overall the American trials had far fewer executions than the European trials with only thirty-five executions total with twenty-eight of those women (Karlsen, 1987, pp. 47–49). Additionally, scholars note that most of the men accused were related to one of the accused women.[5] What these outbreaks of witch accusation had in common was, indeed, the prevalence of women being accused and condemned to death. This is equally true in the fictional universes, as the witches are predominantly women and are consistently at the center of the fictional witch hunt narrative.

As an example of the representation of the witch trials in urban fantasy, The *Penny Dreadful* episode "The Nightcomers" blends the historical presentation with the urban fantasy depiction of witches and witch hunts (Logan, 2015). The episode is essentially a flashback, in which the audience discovers Vanessa Ives's (Eva Green) connection to witchcraft and an earlier encounter with the Nightcomers. Believing she is under a curse, Vanessa seeks out Joan Clayton, known as the Cut-Wife (Patty LuPone), a Daywalker meaning an herbal healer whose name derives from her services as an abortion provider. Joan teaches Vanessa the art of witchcraft only to be faced with the Nightcomers, who are witches that have traded their souls to the devil for more magical power. With the accusations of the Nightcomers, the town turns against the Joan, burning her at the stake as a witch. This episode relies on two tropes of witchcraft: harmful, devil-worshiping, evil witches and the compassionate, benevolent, and healing witches. Unfortunately, the town falls prey to the "bad" witches, and, in the process, destroy the "good" witch. Joan is sacrificed as much for the townspeople's manufactured fear of witches as for her knowledge and skills as a healer, potion maker, and abortionist. She knew too many of their secrets, and when they feared that knowledge could be used against them because of the accusations of the Nightcomers, the town turns on Joan. This scene is indicative of the witch trials, and it builds an opposition between the two types of witch. All of the witches in *Penny Dreadful*—either good or evil—are women.

GENRE, GENDER, MAGIC, AND BEING CHARMED

That urban fantasy centers both magic and explorations of gender is no coincidence. By drawing on the figure of the witch (or other magic user), urban fantasy writers connect to long-standing myths, iconography, and stereotypes of women coded as dangerous and seductively influential, taking the historical ideas about the witch and incorporating concepts that their powerful characters can control the elements, influence nature, and possess ritual and herbal skills that increase their strengths. They seem to have embraced the slogan seen on many protest signs in the last few years, "We are the granddaughters of the witches you couldn't burn."[6] The difference in urban fantasy is that the creators postulate a world in which women have access to preternatural power that allows them to overcome their enemies and those that would threaten the very fabric of the universe, because the stakes are always high in the urban fantasy world. For instance, in the Anita Blake novels, the Mother of Darkness wants to swallow the world whole; in Moning's *Fever* series, the Unseelie Fae have invaded the human world, and the *Sinsar Dubh*—a sentient book filled with the darkest and most dangerous magics of creation and destruction—seeks to unmake the world and destroy humanity. Though vampires, lycanthropes, Seelie Fae, and so many more paranormal beings populate these urban fantasy worlds, it falls to women with magical powers and ritual skills, a necromancer and a Sidhe-Seer respectively, to save the world. This reliance upon the woman magic-wielder to save, rather than annihilate, the community upends the historical narrative that witches sought the destruction of their neighbors. In these tales, the women actually have the power to save the world, and they do it regularly.

A crucial example of this connection between genre, gender, and witchcraft is the television show *Charmed*, which ran from 1998 until 2006 on the WB. *Charmed* was created by Constance Burge, who at the time was known for her work on *Judging Amy* and *Ally McBeal*, and produced by Aaron Spelling, well-known for his hip and drama-fueled television shows like *Charlie's Angels* and *Beverly Hills 90201*. *Charmed* introduces audiences to the world of the Halliwell sisters—Prue, Piper, and Phoebe originally with the addition of Paige in 2001. These sisters, also known as the Charmed Ones, grow over time both in their powers and their characters, dealing with everyday mundane life to major life crises. They are strong, independent, and complex characters that have been widely embraced by young women as feminist heroes, even beyond the ending of the series with its continued syndication and the ability to binge-watch on Netflix. The show also demonstrates that magic and witchcraft are not solely about innate mystical power; it shows that magic takes effort, experience, and most importantly ritual. Though the Halliwell's have innate magical powers passed to them through the female line of their family, they cannot vanquish their weekly demon, warlock, and creature foes without a spell and/or potion drawn either from their Book of Shadows or created by one of the sisters, who then memorialize it in the Book. The show relies consistently on a gendering of magic; in *Charmed*, witches work for the good of the world and are women, though there are a few exceptions to this. Warlocks, though, are always seeking destruction and are evil, and they are predominantly men. The vast majority of the Charmed Ones' enemies of all ilk are men. Almost every week during the show's original broadcasts, the audience witnessed the powerful "good" witches battle the forces of evil in male bodies. Episodes of *Charmed* are quite often literally a battle of the sexes, for instance dueling with their inverse the Evil Charmed Ones—three warlock brothers (Swenson & Feigenbaum, 1999)—and actually wrestling with demons for the fate of a soul—complete with *World Championship Wrestling* (WCW) professionals playing the roles of the demons (Anderson & Inch, 2001). The Halliwell sisters defeat these enemies through wit, teamwork, and martial arts as well as their magical abilities, spells, and potions. Their bond as sisters is one of their most important tools because "The Power of Three" is one of the most formidable spells in their arsenal. They also frequently use their sexuality in order to get information and befuddle their opponents.

The Charmed Ones' power is inextricably linked to their gender and the individual sisters' performance of their femaleness, especially as romantic subplots are staple features of the show. The episodes center the ways in which these women navigate their romantic lives, which play key roles in the way their magic often functions. Magic, for the Halliwells, is linked to emotion: the stronger the emotion the more powerful and potentially volatile their magic could be. This representation draws upon stereotypes of women's emotionality and unpredictability, which are commonplace in contemporary popular culture as well as in historical records of the accusations directed toward alleged witches during the witch trials. This capriciousness was often historically assigned to women because of the myths surrounding female sexuality.

AROUSING POWER

Episodes of *Charmed*, like many urban fantasy narratives, feature some moment of conversation or a lingering on at least one of the female protagonists' sexuality, which is in line with the historical narrative of the witch, and just as with the Charmed Ones, the witches of urban fantasy have a deep connection to sexuality. The historical accounts revolve around the absolute belief that witches possessed power that they could use over others, and moreover, their power was harnessed and manifested through sexual energies.

One of the repeating images of the testimonies used in the trials centered upon the idea that accused witches cavorted with the devil. These images are so ubiquitous across time that we see the same images of witches romping with the devil in a sexualized rite of magic to the horrification and titillation of the viewing audience from Francisco Goya's "*Witches Flight*" (1797) to Robert Eggers's *The Witch: A New England Folktale* (2015). In the *Malleus Maleficarum* (also known as The Hammer of Witches, 1486)—a legal and theological text that created a foundation for the trials—Heinrich Kramer and James Sprenger write, "To conclude. All witchcraft comes from carnal lust, which is in women insatiable" (2002, p. 114).[7] For Kramer, Sprenger, and their devotees, women's sexual natures made them more vulnerable to seduction by the devil and was also a tool through which these women harnessed their magical will to do harm. The sexualized natures of the accused behaviors of the women and the testimonies demonstrated a cultural anxiety about female sexuality. These fears grow out of the concern that women's sexuality was simply too uncontrollable and too voracious. Barbara Creed (1993) writes, "All human societies have a conception of the monstrous-feminine, of what it is about woman that is shocking, terrifying, horrific, abject" (p. 1). That abjection often rises out of a sense that female sexuality must be harnessed, in part to assure bloodlines but also in part to reify the cultural institutions and normative structures of gendered ideals. These perceived sexual proclivities meant that women were set up to be monstrous even without adding a sexual relationship with the devil. Women's perceived weakness and susceptibility to being recruited by evil stemmed from these notions that women could not control their own desires, especially older unmarried or widowed women because they had no other potential outlets. Many accused witches were in fact older single or widowed women, who were no longer under the visible regulation of male figures that could temper their impulsive sexualities. The testimonies during the witch trials often pointed to a hypersexuality of this group of women in particular.[8] These cultural foundations influenced the witch trials and the manner in which testimony was given and sought, as women were questioned under torturous methods and also their verbal evidence was afforded less credence by the court than men's testimonies. Moreover, these historical accounts demonstrate an already visible and pervasive link between female sexuality and witchcraft.

The tenor of the contemporary narrative has continued to reinforce some of these cultural concerns about women's hypersexuality. Controlling female sexuality via state and church sponsored physical torture, such as the witch trials, has not recurred in that specific form, but the cultural, emotional, spiritual, and physical control mechanisms created in the period have had lasting impact. This control has manifested in ostracization, criminalization, and institutionalization of women perceived to step outside the boundaries of the sexual norm. Though these attempts to control women's sexuality have remained pervasive, women have been prompted to believe that in the era after the introduction of the birth control pill they have access to power through their sexuality, but this cultural conception of female sexuality can be as dangerous. This phenomenon of supposed female empowerment through an individual's sexual activity can be deeply problematic because as Jaclyn Friedman (2017) argues this approach postulates an individual solution to the cultural problem of oppression. Said differently, the cultural issues facing women, for instance the lack of representation in positions of power, the wage gap etc., cannot be unraveled by individual women engaging in sexual relationships as their sole cultural place of power (pp. 8–9), particularly in a political era in which protections for reproductive rights have been consistently rolled back and shaming of women for their sexual activities is rampant. Only specific types of sexual behavior under specific circumstances and with culturally approved sexual partners allow women to gain access to cultural power through their sexuality, and here again only a culturally accepted certain type of woman—white, cisgender, conventionally attractive, thin, etc. These seemingly oppositional ideas of female sexuality—the out-of-control hypersexual woman that must be constrained and the culturally-empowered-through-sex woman—are interwoven and create the basis for much of our current imagining of the witch, especially in the world of paranormal fiction.

Using sexuality as a type of power is translated literally in urban fantasy. Stories consistently use narrative arcs in which a witch's sexual behaviors can be used to increase their metaphysical power through both ritual and non-ritual sex magic. Ritual sex magic requires preparation, a magical circle, and other magical tools, and non-ritual sex magic does not.[9] In some ways, these urban fantasy creators draw upon contemporary neo-pagan and Wiccan beliefs that sexual acts raise emotional, spiritual, and physical energy and, therefore, can provide energy to fuel magic. Pagan scholar, Starhawk, outlines some of the core values for witchcraft as honor, sexuality, life, and magic. Writing about sexuality, she argues, "In Witchcraft, 'All acts of love and pleasure are My rituals.' Sexuality, as direct expression of the life force, is seen as numinous and sacred" (1999, p. 37). While the sexual act itself can be used as a way to honor pagan ritual practices, the energy derived from sexual activities and especially from an orgasm can act as a powerful source for a spell or ritual. As Fiona Horne writes in her text intended for the education of Wiccan practitioners, "The energy of an orgasm can be the most powerful fuel to help propel a spell along to fruition; in fact, virtually all power raising in a Circle is based on the build-up/release/wind-down pattern of the orgasm. Orgasm can also be used as a tool to achieve transcendental states" (2000, p. 233). These conceptions of sex magic are at the heart of paranormal fictions. The use of sex magic in urban fantasy structures sex as a magical "booster" that can be an isolated event or sustained behavior to enhance magical power.

An example of an urban fantasy university that uses sex magic in isolated incidents is Syfy Channel's series, *The Magicians*,[10] which features magic wielding graduate students at Brakebills University. The use of isolated acts of sex magic as spell boosters plays a regular role in the narrative. In "Homecoming," Quentin Coldwater (Jason Ralph) and Alice Quinn (Olivia Taylor Dudley) learn a spell that is powered by sex magic from an otherworldly traveler (Jonathan Scarfe). The spell is the only way to send a beacon to one of Quentin and Alice's friends—Penny Adiyodi (Arjun Gupta)—who is stuck in a place of dimensional portals because he does not know which doorway will send him home (Myers, 2016). In order to send the beacon to him, Quentin and Alice must reach orgasm simultaneously. The problem, as Alice confesses, is she has not been able to climax in her sexual interactions with Quentin, and the necessity of a simultaneous climax seems impossible. Though this revelation is both challenging and embarrassing for Quentin, it leads to a conversation about women's bodies and their sexual pleasure. The spell means that Quentin and Alice, as a couple, must build a healthy approach to their sexual communication, and it centralizes women's sexual pleasure as a necessary and important factor in sexual interactions. While the dialogue creates a sense of humor around this conversation, the narrative centers women's pleasure as essential for the sex magic to fuel the beacon. In *The Magicians*, women are fundamental to sex magic, as their bodies are the conduits for the mystical energy.

The show also contradicts the idea that orgasm or women's pleasure is important for successful sex magic. In the episode "Have You Brought Me Little Cakes," Quentin receives a gift from the god, Ember (Dominic Burgess), to help the students defeat the Beast (Charles Mesure); that gift is the god's "essence" (Gamble, McNamara, & Deed, 2016). When Ember hands Quentin the jar of his essence, it is clear that it is full of the god's semen. Though Quentin is willing to consume the essence, he is not the strongest or most skilled magic wielder: Alice is. The moment Alice swallows revolves around her personal disgust but also the ribald jokes of her friends about her imbibing the essence of Ember. Alice gains increased magical energy through a sexual activity, but there is no joy or pleasure in it. *The Magicians* articulates the ways urban fantasy shows isolated incidents of sex magic are useful fuel to mystical energy. As in all urban fantasy narratives, emotion is central to magic use and energy creation and manipulation, which is evidenced in these scenes of *The Magicians* as well as the other uses of sex magic.

On the other hand, urban fantasy often features structures in which characters use sex magic as a continuous way to build and maintain their mystical powers. Sexual tension, activities, and behaviors act as a magical battery for the characters in these narratives, and that battery can be recharged endlessly. There are two key trends in this type of prolonged sex magic in urban fantasy: the pairing and the initiator models. These models differentiate the way in which the characters engage in sexual behaviors for the purpose of raising metaphysical power. Within both of these models, the characters' power grows over time, increasing exponentially through sexual contact.

In the pairing structure, the writer constructs a pair bond, typically a predestined duo that can create power together. In Shannon Butcher's *Sentinel Wars Series*, the male in the pair holds the energy or capacity for magic within his being as a natural talent. He must find the woman with whom he is compatible in order to wield the magic that overloads his body, which can lead to the death of his soul if he does not find his predestined soulmate in time. Most often in this series, the woman does not know that she can wield the power until the man draws her into his world through the completion of a ritual bond. Their bond is made through a spoken vow, the use of ritual jewelry (the *luceria*—a thick collar-like necklace—and a ring), and engaging in penetrative sexual intercourse. It is the pairing that brings mystical power to the woman, but once she has access to magic, her power is more formidable.

Another branch of the pairing is one in which the bond can amplify preexisting power, for instance Jessica Andersen's *Final Prophesy Series*. For the mages of this series, their power is inherent in their being and readily at their access through blood sacrifice, often in the form of a small cut made by the mage. When they find their "Gods-destined" mate, the pairing amplifies their magic. A core aspect of this pairing trend is that the couple must maintain a functioning and healthy relationship in order to ensure the proper functioning of their magic. Once they have paired, disruptions to their relationship can destroy or impede the couples' magical capabilities.

In both of these examples and in other pairing bond models, the couples must engage in a healthy relationship with regular physical and sexual contact in order to strengthen their bond but also to build and control their magic. These pairing models consistently also have strong and capable women who are predestined to be the mate for a damaged and troubled—albeit physically and magically powerful—man. In this way, these urban fantasy narratives rely heavily upon genre conventions of romance.

Unlike the pairing model, the initiator trend encompasses the notion that an individual with power can enhance the power of others as well as their own, generally through sex magic. We could also call this trend "the Kingmaker," as the power the individual builds for self and others often skews the magical dominance dynamic within the plot granting the individual and her group an advantage over the other groups within the universe of the tale. The best examples of the initiator are from the works of Laurell K. Hamilton. Both Anita Blake and Merry Gentry have core internal magical abilities through their talents as a necromancer and Fae princess respectively. Possibly their most valuable assets are their abilities to increase, enhance, revitalize, restore, and bring new power to their sexual partners. Because while Anita and Merry are deeply powerful within their own right, their abilities ensure their faction's capacity to overcome their adversaries. Merry, for instance, brings back long-dead powers to the Fae but also to the fairy mound and the world of the Fae through her sexual encounters with her men, and this also aids her by drawing more power through alliances with those who see Merry's abilities as assets to themselves as well as the Fae as the whole. For Anita, over the course of the series, her power grows more firmly rooted in her sexuality when Jean-Claude's mystical power the *ardeur* transfers to Anita as well through the bonds of their triumvirate of power with werewolf Richard. The *ardeur* is an ability to feed on the energy of others, specifically sexual energy,[11] making Jean-Claude and Anita an incubus and a living succubus respectively. The vampire council and many vampires fear the magical capabilities of Jean-Claude and Anita because of her too voracious sexuality, particularly as Anita must feed her *ardeur* regularly or she drains the lives of the men to which she is connected through magical bonds. While this use of sex magic is not sanctioned within the tenet of Pagan practices or in Anita's own moral code, it demonstrates the manner in which the raising of power within the series can frequently be "accidental"—outside of an intentional ritual—as Anita seeks to understand and constrain her ever growing powers. For Anita and Merry, sex magic grants them power while also building the strengths of those in their core group. Neither sets out to use sex magic specifically to gain power, but once they recognize the power of that magic, they use sexual activities to build mystical power to protect themselves and their loved ones. The core of their magic is emotionally based, as it is for much of urban fantasy's engagement with sex magic, but such power can come at a price.

ON THE DARK SIDE OF SEX MAGIC

Sex magic grants an enormous amount of power in urban fantasy narratives, aiding characters in strengthening their positions, building stronger magic, and helping others. However, the reliance upon sexual energy as a fuel for magic has a dark side. Sexualized violence is pervasive in these narratives. This is not particularly surprising given the historical intersections of gender, sexuality, violence, and witchcraft. The accused witches faced allegations during the witch trials that frequently centered upon perceived abnormal sexual behaviors and the belief that witches cavorted with demons, and the torture of many accused witches was also sexual in nature. Barstow writes, "Women were seen as overassertive sexually, even to the point of wanting to be raped, a belief widely held in the medieval period. The later idea that women wanted the devil to seduce them was based on the medieval literary formula in which women seek and enjoy rape" (p. 136). These perceptions continue to underlie literature and film, including an overarching threat of sexualized violence that populate all urban fantasy narratives, especially the witch stories within the genre. This notion that women desire sexual violence carries into contemporary popular culture, and it underpins the widespread myth that women invite sexual violence through their own behaviors. These tales frequently feature actual on page or screen acts of rape and other types of sexualized and gendered violence as methods for control and to create power for the perpetrator.

Urban fantasy narratives are truly haunted by the threat of sexual violence, as evidenced by some of the most popular examples: *Buffy the Vampire Slayer*, *Charmed*, *Fever Series*, *Anita Blake, Vampire Hunter Series,* and *Meredith Gentry Series*. The predominance of sexualized violence in urban fantasy reflects the pervasiveness of sexualized violence in contemporary culture, and therefore, writers draw on the seemingly commonplace experiences of sexual violence that women encounter, which is demonstrated by the tidal wave of revelations through the #MeToo movement, which began in Fall of 2016. Moreover, the ubiquity of sexual violence narratives makes sense given urban fantasy's prevalence of women-identified creators and audience members. It is a cathartic experience to write about or read about (or watch) a character experiencing and coping with sexualized trauma because it allows the individual to grapple with difficult material from a distance, offering an emotional outlet for the day-to-day violence and harassment many women face in contemporary society. The catharsis, though, does not negate the emotional impact of reading or seeing sexual violence in popular culture narratives. It can be jarring, triggering, and emotionally wrecking, especially for individuals that have experienced sexual assault in their lives.

Sexual violence creates a foreboding pall over many witch stories, where witches experience an underlying widespread threat. In *Midnight, Texas*,[12] Fiji Cavanaugh (Parisa Fitz-Henley) is a witch, who has the ability to control the elements, and the demon Colconnar (Derek Mears) is stalking her. He wants Fiji because she is a powerful witch, and she is also a virgin. The mythology relies on the idea that virginity is a more powerful fuel to magic, based in the notion that sexuality is a well of power to draw from and that the untapped magical well of virginity is a stronger energy source. In order to save her from Colcannar, Fiji and Bobo Winthrop (Dylan Bruce), the best friend with whom she is in love, have sex so that she is no longer a virgin, and therefore, saving her from being raped by Colcannar (Owusu-Breen, 2017). Though her virginity would strengthen her power in sex magic, Fiji is also threatened with sexual violence because of that same potential power. These types of narratives around the threat of sexual violence are omnipresent, especially in magical tales. Moreover, danger to virginity has been long used as a control mechanism to keep women and girls relegated to the home. Virginity has been given cultural power because it assumes that a woman's sexuality has been constrained and, therefore, the paternity of progeny can be guaranteed.

To return to *The Magicians*, its philosophy about magic is articulated by Elliot Waugh (Hale Appleman), "Magic doesn't come from talent. It comes from pain" (Gamble & Smith, 2016). Since emotion fuels magic, and pain can be a powerful tool in mystical power creation and use. All of urban fantasy narratives discussed in this chapter would agree with this ideology, but there is a danger lurking in the application of this philosophy in *The Magicians* and many of the other magical tales that feature sexualized violence prominently. For most characters in *The Magicians*, it is the pain of heartbreak or the death of a loved one that drives their power, but for one character, her road to magic is based in being sexually assaulted on multiple occasions. Julia Wicker (Stella Maeve) is not accepted to the magical graduate school along with her best friend, Quentin, even though she does have magical powers. In a bar bathroom during her birthday party, a hedge witch, Pete (David Call), attacks her, stripping her clothes off, tying her up, and threatening rape. Because of that violence, Julia is able to access her abilities for the first time to fight against Pete's magical hold. While the visual portrayal on-screen was jarring and difficult to watch, it is the description from the full-recap of the episode on Syfy.com that is even more dismissive and ultimately more dangerous and damaging:

> Meanwhile, you know who's not doing great? Julia. She's been searching for magic things on the Internet, and when James, Julia's boyfriend, tells Quentin to come to her birthday party, she tells him she remembers Brakebills and wants in. Quentin, however, refuses to help her because he doesn't want to get kicked out. Later, Julia has a tricky time in the bathroom when a magician turns up, sexually aggresses her and then says he was just trying to make sure she was really magic. Looks like she has found her way in to the world of mysticism ... just not through the University. (Syfy.com, 2015)

This description shows a lack of care or compassion about victims of sexual violence and demonstrates the pervasive nature of sexual assault in urban fantasy texts as a call to magic. With this occurring in the first episode of the series, it establishes that Julia's path to magical power comes through sexual pain. Julia becomes a hedge witch in the aftermath of this assault, but her victimization does not end. Twelve episodes later, a minor deity—Reynard the Fox (Mackenzie Astin)—tricks Julia and her coven of hedge witches, taking possession of one of the members of the group. When he becomes corporeal, he kills almost all of the coven. Julia intervenes, saving the life of one member, but Reynard then rapes Julia (Gamble, McNamara, Deed, & Smith, 2015). This leads Julia on a revenge plot, in which she increases her powers any way that she can. In this way, Julia embodies two trends for urban fantasy witches and sexual violence: rape as instigator of mystical power for women and rape-revenge narratives as plot devices. Her sexual assaults allow her to gain power but at a great cost, as she literally loses her soul as an outcome of Reynard's assault. Julia's path to revenge against Reynard causes Quentin to nearly die and kills Alice, and there are other consequences as well to Julia and those around her.

Many urban fantasy series incorporate all of the sex magic tropes, including the reliance upon sexual violence. As the originator of urban fantasy, Hamilton's *Anita Blake, Vampire Hunter Series* develops many of these trends. Anita is under constant sexualized threats from a wide range of individuals and frequently has to use her magical skills to ward off sexual assault. *Anita Blake* is also an exception in the world of urban fantasy, as it is Anita who is sometimes the sexual aggressor wielding her magical powers to assault others, almost exclusively men. When Anita receives the power of the *ardeur*, she cannot control the power, yet it is also a weapon that she is able to use against her enemies. The *ardeur* brings an individual under her thrall through sex and subsuming their own decision making, but the *ardeur* acts like alcohol or drugs, meaning that the person cannot consent to the sexual acts because their will has been overridden by her power. Therefore, Anita sexually assaults her victims with them unable to consent to either sex or to be a booster for her magical power. Anita uses it to help gather more power for herself and her circle.

There are multiple incidents of her uses this power against various lycanthropes and lower level vampires. When she rolls Augustine (Auggie), Master Vampire of the City of Chicago, who is one of the most powerful vampires in the United States, under her vampiric power of the *ardeur*, she demonstrates how daunting her power has become. Because she was unwilling to back down from Auggie's threat of force when he purposely uses his vampiric powers to raise Anita's *ardeur*, she and Jean-Claude feed on his desire, bringing Auggie under their power (2006, pp. 88–90). Through Auggie, Anita and Jean-Claude also feed on the energy of all of the people that had sworn loyalty to him, giving them a major power boost. Richard accuses, "You [Anita] helped him [Jean-Claude] rape the Master of Chicago." Anita responds, "It wasn't rape, Richard. You know that. You felt some of what Auggie was feeling. Hell, Richard, Auggie started the ball rolling He raised my *ardeur* on purpose, picked a fight with me" (Hamilton, 2006, p. 103). Anita's justification echoes quite closely the cultural responses to rape victims, which are based on long-standing rape myths, such as that they invited the assault through their actions, and that if they had a physiological response of arousal or orgasm, then, they were not raped. Though Auggie begs for the sexual activities and for them to feed on him, he is under their sexual thrall, and therefore, the question about whether he could legitimately consent remains. Once Auggie has been rolled by Anita's power, he becomes a formidable ally. Hamilton inverts the statistics on sexual violence perdition and victimization with Anita, the woman, as the perpetrator and Auggie and other men as her victims. In the series, Hamilton clearly centers sex and sexual violence, as fuel to magic through the introduction of the *ardeur* and the traits she imbues her paranormal characters—especially Belle Morte's vampire line and all of the lycanthropes—with the need for touch and sex. The use of sexualized violence to raise magic is in direct opposition to the tenets of Wiccan and neo-Pagan practices because the central ideology of these faiths is "And ye harm none, Do what ye will."

CONCLUSION

Contemporary urban fantasy narratives rely on witches and other magic wielders as central figures, allowing a foregrounding of gender and sexuality based in the long history of women's connection to the witchcraft narrative. Sex magic plays a key role in urban fantasy whether in subtle forms, such as the exchange of blood for power in typical vampire tropes to the more blatant witchcraft and ritual uses. The intersection of gender, sexuality, and magic provides fodder for our long-standing cultural examinations, the historical witch trials, and contemporary forays into paranormal fiction. The use of sex in order to build power for magic is a core strategy in paranormal tropes. The construction of these images has ensured a narrative structure that at least on the surface grant the female protagonists a great deal of power over themselves, their circumstances, and the protection of their loved ones. The examples in this chapter are a mere fraction of the urban fantasy narratives that focus on witches, sex, and violence, and there will continue to be new instances of these intersections.

NOTES

[1] In the later parts of Hamilton's *Anita Blake, Vampire Hunter Series* and her *Merry Gentry Series*, she establishes her own authorly patterns, meaning the series become yet again predictable for the readers, but her rebellion against the norms in her early work created a foundation for other authors to innovate and continue to stretch urban fantasy further.

2   In longer running urban fantasy or romance series, there is sometimes a happily-for-now (HFN) at the end, as the story will continue in subsequent installments.

3   All of these forms are distinct types of magic. Witchcraft, Druidry, sorcery, necromancy, shamanism, and Fae magic are all different not only in name but in culture and in the ritual practices necessary for power evocation.

4   For instance, Laurell K. Hamilton is an open practitioner of Wicca, which influences her writing of both her *Anita Blake* and her *Merry Gentry* series. Some of the authors' personal engagement in witchcraft come via a family member.

5   For more on this topic, see Barstow and Karlsen's texts and also John Putnam Demos's *Entertaining Satan: Witchcraft and the Culture of Early New England* (1982/2004).

6   I first remember seeing this message on a plaque for sale in a store that sold items for both tourists and practitioners of witchcraft in Salem, Massachusetts, in 2001. This slogan is wildly popular at the women's marches across the globe since the presidential election of November 2016, and it has also made an appearance in Tish Thawer's *The Witches of BlackBrook* (2015).

7   *The Malleus Maleficarum* exists in the public domain, which means that there are a plethora of versions and copies available. As the Reverend Montague Summers has had significant influence on the study of the paranormal and the occult, I have chosen to use the text of his translation published in 1928, which has also fallen into the public domain.

8   For more, see Anne Llewellyn Barstow's *Witchcraze: A New History of the European Witch Hunts*.

9   These descriptions of ritual and non-ritual sex magic apply also to standard ritual and non-ritual magic. For more on ritual magic and pagan and Wiccan practices, I recommend Starhawk's *The Spiral Dance: A Rebirth of the Ancient Religion of the Goddess 20th Anniversary Edition* (1999), Margot Adler's *Drawing Down the Moon: Witches, Druids, Goddess-Worshippers, and Other Pagans in America* (1979/2006), Scott Cunningham's *Wicca: A Guide for Solitary Practitioners*, and River and Joyce Higginbotham's *Paganism: An Introduction to Earth Centered Religions* (2013).

10 Syfy's *The Magicians* is based on the trilogy by Lev Grossman: *The Magician* (2009), *The Magician King* (2011), *The Magician's Land* (2014).

11 Over time, Anita learns that she can also feed off of the anger of others.

12 *Midnight, Texas*, the television show, is based on the novel series of the same name written by Charlaine Harris. Harris, best known for her *Sookie Stackhouse Southern Vampire Mysteries Series*, conceived of *Midnight, Texas*, as a trilogy and published the three novels between 2014 and 2016, beginning with the book *Midnight Crossing*.

REFERENCES

Andersen, J. (2008). *Nightkeepers*. New York, NY: Berkley Books.

Anderson, S. (Writer), & Feigenbaum, J. (Director). (2001, February 2). Wrestling with demons [Television series episode]. In C. Burge & A. Spelling (Producers), *Charmed*. Los Angeles, CA: The WB.

Barstow, A. L. (1994). *Witchcraze: A new history of the European witch hunts*. New York, NY: HarperCollins.

Butcher, S. K. (2009). *Burning alive: The sentinel wars*. New York, NY: Berkley Books.

Creed, B. (1993). *The monstrous-feminine: Film, feminism, psychoanalysis*. London: Routledge.

Eggers, R. (2015). *The witch: A New England folktale* [Motion picture]. New York, NY: A24.

Friedman, J. (2017). *Unscrewed: Women, sex, power, and how to stop letting the system screw us all*. New York, NY: Seal Press.

Gamble, S., McNamara, J., & Deed, D. (Writers), & Smith, S. (Director). (2016, April 11). Have you brought me little cakes [Television series episode]. In S. Gamble, D. Cadena, M. Cahill, M. Engel, L. Lieser, M. London, J. McNamara, H. A. Myers, & J. Williams (Producers), *The magicians*. New York, NY: Syfy.

Gamble, S., McNamara, J. (Writers), & Cahill, M. (Director). (2015, December 16). Unauthorized magic [Television series episode]. In S. Gamble, D. Cadena, M. Cahill, M. Engel, L. Lieser, M. London, J. McNamara, H. A. Myers, & J. Williams (Producers), *The magicians*. New York, NY: Syfy.

Gamble, S. (Writer), & Smith, S. (Director). (2016, January 25). The source of magic [Television series episode]. In S. Gamble, D. Cadena, M. Cahill, M. Engel, L. Lieser, M. London, J. McNamara, H. A. Myers, & J. Williams (Producers), *The magicians*. New York, NY: Syfy.

Hamilton, L. K. (2006). *Danse macabre*. New York, NY: Berkley Books.

Horne, F. (2000). *Witch: A magical journey*. London: Thorsons.

Karlsen, C. F. (1987). *The devil in the shape of a woman: Witchcraft in colonial New England*. New York, NY: Vintage Books.

Kramer, H., & Sprenger, J. (1486/2002). *The malleus maleficarum* (M. Summers, Trans.). Retrieved from http://www.malleusmaleficarum.org/downloads/MalleusAcrobat.pdf

Logan, J. (Writer). (2015). The nightcomers [Television series episode]. In J. Logan (Producer), *Penny Dreadful*. New York, NY: Showtime.

Owusu-Breen, M. (Writer), & Solomon, D. (Director). (2017, September 18). The virgin sacrifice [Television series episode]. In M. Owusu-Breen, E. Charmelo, B. Finnigan, T. Good, C. Harris, D. Janollari, B. Johnson, M. Kruger, B. Malone, C. Markey, A. McGintee, T. Meyer, T. Roman, L. Sagal, A. Septien, N. Snyder, & D. Solomon (Producers), *Midnight, Texas*. New York, NY: NBC.

Starhawk. (1999). *The spiral dance: A rebirth of the ancient religion of the great goddess*. San Francisco, CA: HarperCollins.

Swenson, E. (Writer), & Inch, K. (Director). (1999, April 28). When bad warlocks go good [Television series episode]. In C. Burge & A. Spelling (Producers), *Charmed*. Los Angeles, CA: The WB.

Amanda Jo Hobson
Women's Resource Center
Indiana State University

LAUREN ROCHA

6. FIGHTING AND FEMINIST EXPRESSION

The Argent Family and the Limits of Female Agency in Teen Wolf

MTV's popular television series *Teen Wolf* (2011–2017) focuses on the fictional town of Beacon Hills and the supernatural creatures that reside there. The show primarily centers on teenager-turned-werewolf Scott McCall (Tyler Posey) and his friends as they navigate the realities of the coexistence between humans and non-humans. Scott's life is complicated not only by the bite that turns him into a shapeshifter but also by his attraction to Allison Argent (Crystal Reed). At the beginning of the series, Allison is seen as the new girl in town and Scott's love interest; however, soon Scott discovers that her family hunts supernatural creatures, especially werewolves. Armed with guns and other weapons, Allison's parents are shown as constantly disciplined and strategic in their behavior. This includes their control over Allison as she is repeatedly manipulated and used by the Argent family to achieve their goals. Even when she is trained in combat, her agency is largely limited in favor of spotlighting the dominance and agency of the male characters. Allison thus illustrates the problematic gender dichotomy still prevalent in today's society whereby female identity is restricted to traditional patriarchal roles enforced by her family. This chapter explores the portrayals of the women in the Argent family on *Teen Wolf*, specifically that of Victoria Argent and her daughter Allison. In highlighting the mother-daughter pair, the chapter aims to question gender subversion in familial power structures and the show's treatment of anxieties surrounding female empowerment and deviant femininity.

From the onset of the show, Allison is treated, not as an individual, but as an object for male characters to use, particularly as an object of Scott's romantic and sexual desire. Played by actress Crystal Reed, Allison's physical appearance is typical of the MTV stereotype, evocative of a fairytale figure with pale skin, long, flowing dark hair and feminine clothing. She instantly becomes part of the popular clique in school due to her fashion sense and beauty and is initially seen only through Scott's fetishizing gaze that focuses on the female body as object. For example, in the pilot episode of the series, she knocks on the door of the animal clinic after hours that Scott works at

© KONINKLIJKE BRILL NV, LEIDEN, 2019 | DOI:10.1163/9789004394100_006

(Davis, 2011). Her hair and shirt are drenched from the rain, showing off her body, and she pleads for Scott to help her with a dog she accidentally injured. That she enters the scene in such a way highlights the sexual tone, as Allison is shown as a body not as an individual. They go out back, she shivers, and he offers her a shirt to change into. Watching her undress from the doorway, despite this being for a young adult audience, the camera focuses on the exposed skin of her back and Scott's eyes staring at her, his gaze symbolically penetrating her. When she comes back into the room, she sheepishly admits that she "freaked out like a girl … a girly girl," to which Scott points out "You are a girl" and teases her that he probably would have cried in that situation and "not like a man either." This conversation, marked by definitive statements, is indicative of the gender dichotomy of the series and establishes the relationship dynamic between Scott and Allison. She states that she is "tougher than that," but the scene undermines that statement; in doing so, the scene associates weakness with female characters, while male characters possess the strength to handle situations. The scene furthers the portrayal of femininity on the show as one characterized by the traditional norms of dependency on men and objects of their gaze (Davis, 2011).

This characterization continues when, on her birthday, Scott mocks her concern over getting detention for skipping school, asking her "do you always follow [the] rules?" pointing out her obedience. When Allison throws her arm across Scott's chest to protect him while driving, he says, "I'll pick up my masculinity on the way back," equating her gesture with emasculation. Later in the woods, he catches her when she stumbles, and she assures him, "I think you just earned your masculinity back." The positioning of these two statements regarding Scott's masculinity demonstrates the show's treatment of femininity and masculinity with women expected to allow men to protect them; any underscoring of that, even a minor one, necessitates a return to the traditional dichotomy (Macer, 2011).

Kimberley McMahon-Coleman and Roslyn Weaver (2012) elaborate on the relationship between Allison and Scott, particularly regarding his werewolf identity:

> Scott's love interest Allison is his 'anchor' (1.06); she helps him maintain control over his anger and thus his shifting (yet, contrarily, provokes him into shifting in their romantic scenes). Her last name is Argent, which means silver … the Argent name encapsulates the broader theme of women as a softening effect on these violent males. (p. 60)

While the first episode of the series marks Allison as an object of Scott's romantic and sexual desire, the second episode builds on the first with a transformed Scott scaling the roof of Allison's house to spy on her through her window in werewolf form (Davis, 2011). Just before this, the camera narrows in on a printout of a muscled werewolf holding a fainted woman in his arms. The indication, once again, being that Allison is meant to be an object of Scott's sexual, animalistic desire. In doing so, the series both limits Allison's character as well as reducing Scott's masculinity to that of an animalistic, base nature. He, later, dreams that he kills Allison in a fit of passion on a school bus, and when the bus is found with claw marks and blood the next day, he believes his dream was a reality until an encounter with Allison in the hall proves otherwise. The scene is problematic in its depiction of Scott's sexuality, casting it as predatory. His reaction likewise demonstrates McMahon-Coleman and Weaver's point since it forces him to confront and restrain his sexuality.

Allison's limited agency is illustrated through her relationship with weapons. Armed with a bow in hand, Allison reveals to Scott that she is a skilled archer and that her family is in the firearms business (Sinclair, 2011). He asks her if she is going to go into the family business, and she coyly answers, "Depends. Do you think I'd look hot with a gun?" pinning the proposed skill as a fetishized accessory rather than as a defensive skill. His response, "I think you'd look hotter without one," further devalues her defensive abilities, not only again fetishizing it but implying that a defenseless Allison is a more attractive one. Scott is not the only character who prefers Allison without a weapon, however; later, her father would break her bow out of disapproval of Allison's use of weaponry (Davis, 2012). The message is clear: girls are not supposed to have weapons. She is instead supposed to be seen as the love interest and the daughter who needs to be protected from potential danger.

Allison's father, Chris, embodies the traditional role of the overbearing patriarchal father figure through his interference in Allison's life. He is first seen in the woods in his role as hunter where he shoots Scott in the arm with an arrow, asserting his role as the dominant male through puncturing Scott with the phallic weapon; thus, threatening Scott's physical and sexual body, a recurring theme on the show (Davis, 2011). One of the earliest scenes of the second season portrays Scott's flashback to him and Allison kissing in his car only to be forcibly interrupted by Chris pulling him out through his windows, throwing him on top of the car with a gun pointed to his face. Allison, frantic, intervenes saying she'll do anything to stop her father from killing sixteen-year-old Scott, promising that she'll never see him again. Chris echoes her promise, saying "Never" (Davis, 2012). Chris's excessive use of force in relation to Scott compromises Scott's masculinity in addition to weakening Allison's independence. Like a fifties stereotype, her father does not want her to engage in a romantic relationship; rather, he wants her to enact the role of a passive, submissive daughter regardless of her desires. Later, he runs over Scott, when Scott is jumping from his roof after having spied on Allison, upholding his role as Allison's protector (Vlaming, 2011). While Scott lurks to watch Allison (itself a problematic endorsement of stalking), Chris does not need to resort to such measures; as her father, he believes he has the right. He freely enters her room without knocking, invading her personal space and informing his daughter that she cannot out that night (Vlaming, 2011). Allison, however, defies him, sneaking out her window in order to go on a date (Vlaming, 2011). These acts of teenager rebellion are ultimately irrelevant since her family continues to dominate her life. Throughout the second season, the Argents continue their invasiveness into Allison's and the other teenager's lives by placing patriarch Gerard as school principal and Allison's mother Victoria as secretary to monitor the security cameras they placed throughout the premises (Cochran, 2012). The Argent's invasiveness constantly puts Allison on display, causing Allison to be the subject of surveillance. The Argents are not simply trying to protect her, however; rather, they are trying to control her through monitoring her behaviors and movement, thus reflecting the young adult theme of unwarranted parental interference.

This control is also exercised by her mother, Victoria, when she takes on the role as a substitute teacher in one of her daughter's classes. She stops Allison after class, when they are alone, and the following conversation takes place, regarding Allison's romantic interest in Scott:

Victoria: I know how hard it is, sitting here, trying not to look at him [Scott]. Think of how strong it makes you. Especially when all these other girls are just letting their entire high school lives be defined by some boy they are just praying will take them to senior prom.

Allison: Can't I be strong and go to prom?

Victoria: Of course. But with someone else. Remember, so long as you stay strong, we won't have to kill a sixteen-year-old boy. (Davis, 2012)

Victoria utilizes coercion in convincing her daughter to stay away from Scott, threatening to kill him if she does not, a shocking thing to say to your child and indicative of the belief that all parents are oppressive. For Allison and thus all girls to be "strong," then, is to be obedient and passive rather than independent and assertive. Although Victoria has seemingly empowering reasons for her decisions, encouraging her daughter to excel in her studies and not be defined by a relationship, in reality her interference negates her daughter's decision to be her own person.

Victoria's support of this oppressive patriarchal system is so complete she is willing to give up her own life. She is bitten by Derek Hale and would thus turn into a werewolf on the next full moon (Davis, 2012). Rather than become the creature she, but more importantly, her patriarchal family rejects, she chooses to commit suicide. Chris believes that she will choose to kill herself using prescription pills, since "According to gender statistics, most women …" (Davis, 2012). He is not able to finish his sentence as Victoria picks up the butcher knife, showing her preferred method: a modern-day equivalent of a phallic stake to the heart, death by male dominance. Gerard reminds Chris of his role in the ritual, as the dutiful hunter husband helping his wife choose death over becoming a werewolf, directing him to "help your wife die with dignity. Because if she doesn't fall on her own sword, one of us is gonna have to run her through." At this point, Victoria is no longer thought of as an individual; instead, she is a problem, "that thing over there," "a cocoon waiting to hatch." The emphasis is not placed on the difficult choice Victoria is making; rather, her suicide is coldly treated as protocol, a fact that Gerard reaffirms in saying "we all have our roles to play." For Victoria, that role is the self-sacrificing woman to ensure the patriarchal paradigm stays in place, evidenced through the conversation she has with Chris before her death:

> Victoria (watching the full moon rise): I can feel it. It's happening. You know what to do. You know what to tell people. Tell them I had a history of depression. Promise me.
>
> Chris: I will. Even though I haven't seen you depressed once in twenty years.
>
> Victoria: Allison needs to say it too … She'll hear things. People will say I was weak. They'll say I took the easy way out.
>
> Chris: I'll tell her it was the hardest thing you ever did.
>
> Victoria: They'll ask, how could I do this to my family?
>
> Chris: She'll know you did it for us. (Davis, 2012)

The conversation points to the dismissal of concern about female characters' wellbeing, both Victoria's and Allison's. His candid response that she is choosing suicide "for us," refers to her choice as one to uphold the family's patriarchy; in becoming a werewolf, her power would threaten to surpass that of her human husband. Her constant questioning throughout the dialogue hints at her doubts surrounding the decision. This is again demonstrated when she pauses, unable to push the knife into her own heart. She says, "I can't do this myself. Chris, help me," before going into his arms as he pushes the knife into her heart. This scene can be read as both Victoria's need for Chris to stake her through her heart to prevent her from becoming a monstrous werewolf, and thus an abject woman, and as a continuation of the show's traditional values that favor men's power over women.

Even when theoretically attempting to empower her through training to be a hunter, her family undermines and controls Allison's agency. In the episode "Ice Pick" (Passmore, 2012), Allison's training begins via kidnapping from her father and fellow hunters. She is taken to the former home of alpha werewolf Derek Hale, tied up in a chair across from her similarly tied up father, while a voice recording taunts her about what would happen if she or her father were bitten. Chris finally breaks free of the restraints and answers, "Everything changes," exposing the orchestrated charade to his terrified daughter, informing her that such exercises are how they are going to train her. He then reveals the following truth about the Argents:

> See, our family has a surprisingly progressive tradition. Knowing wars and violence are typically started by men, we place the final decisions, the hard ones, with the women. Our sons are trained to be soldiers and daughters, leaders. Training starts now. (Passmore, 2012)

Chris's speech clearly establishes the gender dichotomy of the family: despite alleging that women are the ones who play an active role in the family, they remain largely passive while it is the men who take action, who are "soldiers." Women are given the vague title "leaders," not a military one, while it is the men who are featured fighting and taking action against supernatural creatures. Although Chris's speech may, in fact, suggest a "progressive" view of gender, in reality, it is conservative. Sons are soldiers and leaders while daughters are meant to be supporters and followers. This is seen when Gerard kills a lone werewolf, casting aside the family code of ethics in lieu of his declaration:

> No code. Not anymore. From now on these things [supernatural creatures] are just bodies waiting to be cut in half … I don't care if they're wounded and weak, or seemingly harmless, begging for their life with the promise that they'll never, ever hurt anyone. Or some desperate lost soul with no idea what they're getting into. We find them. We kill them all. (Davis, 2012)

It is Gerard, the patriarch, who makes this declaration; not one of the female members of the family. His statement contradicts Chris's, revealing the limitations of female agency in the Argent family and the prevailing patriarchal structure.

In addition to coercing Allison into training, her family manipulates her to keep her in a constant state of fear. Gerard uses his position as high school principal to call Allison into his office to interrogate her about the whereabouts of Jackson Whittemore, the shapeshifting kanama behind the murders in Season Two (Davis, 2012). He hovers over her, putting his fingers on the pulse on her neck while the camera focuses on the wide eyes of the scared Allison. He tells her to think of his questioning "as a game," as the camera shows her bare neck with his fingers on it and alternates to her neckline, lips, and his fingers. As he continues his questioning, he increases the pressure, saying "Your pulse jumped." She finally tells him that he's scaring her, and with that response, he backs away, smirking, telling her "I'm sorry, sweetheart. That was definitely going way too far. It wasn't right for me to use tactics like that, I'm sorry." The scene has sexual undertones to it with Gerard's fingers pressing on her neck symbolically penetrating her skin. Her physical space violated, as she exits his office, she notices the new security cameras he installed throughout the school in order to visually violate her space and continue to control her. The viewers are reminded of Allison's limited expression and role as an object of others' desire for power.

While Allison's parents seek to keep her in a manipulated state of fear and ignorance, it is Allison's aunt Kate who aims to empower her niece. Allison's potential as a hunter coincides with the arrival of Kate, a hunter and a character, cast as a deviant, dangerous woman as she orchestrated the deaths of the Hale bloodline in order to extinguish a werewolf family. Kate gives Allison the family crest necklace for her birthday, which features a wolf in the middle, in order to lead her to learning the family history of hunting supernatural creatures; that she is the one to do so establishes the relationship between empowering women through knowledge and villainy (Sinclair, 2011). Kate holds her brother, Chris, accountable for keeping Allison ignorant of the supernatural world, and at one point he admits to her, after realizing the threat of the alpha werewolf is even more dangerous than previously imagined, "Yes, I underestimated the danger. Yes, I should have listened to you" (Macer, 2011). Kate comments about her brother's hesitation in teaching Allison self-defense skills, skills that could translate into being a hunter, telling him that his "extra skills" are something he could be teaching her (Vlaming, 2011).

When Chris realizes that Kate told Allison the truth about their family, Kate defends her position, saying that Allison needs to know in order to be prepared for the realities of the world they live in (Davis, 2011). Even after Allison's parents are aware of what she knows, they try to restrict her knowledge. Victoria yells at Allison when she questions what will happen to Scott, saying, "What you want doesn't matter. What you need is to stay quiet! You're catching a glimpse of something you're not quite ready to see and there are others outside of this family that are not ready for you to see it. Staying quiet is the best protection" (Davis, 2011). Victoria's language reduces Allison's self-defense to "staying quiet," connoting passivity and submission rather than action. That Allison is "not quite ready" to see and know what she already does transcends parental concern and instead reveals the larger patriarchal society she is a part of, the "outside of [the] family." Yet Allison chooses not to remain a passive female; rather, she and Kate go into the woods to attempt to capture Scott and Derek, Kate mentoring Allison as she takes aim at the werewolves (Davis, 2011).

Kate is also teaches Allison how to use a stun gun to defend herself after Allison and her friends were locked in the high school with the monstrous alpha werewolf (Macer, 2011). In an episode aptly entitled "Wolf's Bane," the following conversation occurs between Allison and her aunt:

Kate: What do you want, Allison?

Allison: I want to not be scared. That night in the school I felt utterly weak, like I needed someone to come in and rescue me. I hate that feeling. I want to feel stronger than that. I want to feel powerful.

Kate: I think I can give you exactly what you want. (Roessler, 2011)

Kate fulfills her promise, leaving clues for Allison to lead her to the truth about the supernatural inhabitants of Beacon Hills and about her family, such as when she leaves the other half of a light explosive for her to reattach and try out on her own with her crossbow. After Allison does so, she accidentally shoots Scott with the stun gun as he attempts to sneak up on her; no longer able to surprise her, she is ready for him.

Kate is aware of the precarity of her situation as a female hunter in a largely male-dominated hierarchy. In one scene, Chris and two other male hunters are plotting their next move when Kate walks in with a gun in her hand (Macer, 2011). While the men talk, Kate adjusts her gun, an assault rifle, and sarcastically remarks to the men, "You're the expert, you tell me." Although her position as a powerful female, handling a deadly phallic object with expertise, comes across, so too does her exclusion from the active conversation as evidenced by her flippant comment. Allison's mother, Victoria, walks in with a plate of cookies, instructs them that if they find alleged murderer Derek, to kill him and cut him in half. She ends her graphic instructions by asking the group "Anybody want a cookie?" Victoria's appearance at first undercuts the male dominance with her ultimately instructing the men what to do, but her offering of a cookie positions her back into the traditional female role of the housewife entertaining her husband.

Kate is very much the opposite of her niece: first introduced driving to her brother's house in the dark, early morning hours, she is attacked by a werewolf (Sinclair, 2011). She is not damsel-in-distress, however; instead, she grabs a nearby gun and wards off her attacker. She, then, reveals her steady supply of ammunition in the trunk of her car, loads an even larger rifle, and screams into the air "Come on!" an open invitation for her attacker to try again, this time with much more deadly aim. (Sinclair, 2011). McMahon-Coleman and Weaver emphasize Kate's importance in the series:

> Kate's introduction to the series in the Buffy-esque terms: a beautiful blonde is a stalked by a monster only to pull out a weapon and shoot it (1.04). Kate tortures werewolf Derek in a sadistic manner, taking pleasure in his pain and mocking their earlier romance, but her treatment of protagonist Scott is seen as a betrayal of the code, which Chris Argent describes as 'We hunt those who hunt us' (1.12). (p. 52)

In an ironic twist, the events that culminate in Kate's murder by Alpha Peter, take place in an episode titled "Magic Bullet" (Sinclair, 2011), a name that both refers to the bullet Kate uses to shoot Derek Hale and lethally infect him as well as to the female sex toy often described as a replacement for male penetration. Given the heavy phallic symbolism with all the weaponry, the title points to female empowerment through combat training, becoming women who can save themselves.

Allison is frequently marginalized in scenes involving combat, in favor of interactions between male characters. In "Restraint," Allison enters the boys locker room after hearing strange sounds from within (Antosca & Vizzini, 2012). She finds a nude Jackson who corners her, calls her a "bitch," and invokes fears of sexual assault when he pins her to the wall with his hands. He teases that the werewolves will kill her and with a clawed hand caresses her neck, saying "I hope your dad's been teaching you moves to protect yourself," the line reminding viewers that her father is her protector. She pushes Jackson off and he takes her with him, pinning her to the floor. The positioning of the characters—distressed, scared Allison and Jackson's nude body over hers as he threatens her—implies that the threat in this scene is not the reptilian kanama, the creature Jackson shifts into, but sexual assault from the human Jackson reminding the audience that the monsters come in many forms.

It is Scott, not Allison, who ends Jackson's threat. Hearing Allison's panic from afar, Scott rushes into the locker room and fights Jackson. During the fight, Allison is not featured at all, causing the viewer to wonder if she is still in the locker room, escaped into the hall, or somewhere else altogether. The absence of Allison is important as it not only seemingly erases her from the scene but erases her suffering in favor of two male characters fighting for dominance over her body. Only after the fight is broken up by a teacher, the boys' lacrosse coach, another symbolic figure of masculinity, does she emerge, the saved maiden in distress. Allison's absence from combat is again shown when confronting the kanama and Gerard (Davis, 2012). After shooting werewolf Isaac in the shoulder with an arrow, she disappears into the shadows, leaving the primary fighting to Chris, Isaac, Derek, and Scott. When she does reappear, it is with knives, attacking Isaac again with them. Her moment of power is short-lived, however, as the kanama grabs hold of Allison. Gerard, in control of the creature, allows it to choke Allison, therefore choking her power. This is again used as motivation for Scott to do as Gerard wants, with Gerard's declaration that "He (Scott) knows that the ultimate prize is Allison. Do this small task for me and they can be together … There is just no competing with young love." Upon being free from the kanama's control, Allison and Scott hold hands, and she profusely apologizes "for what [she] did, for what [she] said, for everything." Scott, Chris, Gerard, and the other men do not apologize, nor do they have to; in the series' gender paradigm, they were the ones in the right while Allison's disobedience and deviance threatened to derail the proper order.

Even when Allison is aware of the truth about her family and takes her place as a hunter, she is still kept ignorant to preserve male authority. When the hunters gather in the basement of her home, she is not shown as one of them; instead, she is sitting off excluded in a corner on the stairs like a child (Davis, 2012). Afterwards, Gerard says, "As willing a participant as your young protégé seems to be, she seems under the impression that we're planning a trap." Chris's answer, "She doesn't need to know any more than that," limiting her knowledge and thus her agency while the men assume the authoritative stance. Gerard clarifies, "For the rest of us then, let's be perfectly clear: you don't trap a creature this dangerous. You kill it." He makes this declaration while holding a pocketknife next to his face, the phallic dominance of the scene reaffirmed.

Allison hallucinates seeing a hooded figure of herself, shooting her in the stomach with a crossbow (Davis, 2012). As she calls to Scott for help, the double mocks her, saying "Look at you, yelling for help. Always yelling for help. It's pathetic. You have no idea how much I've been looking forward to this," before taking aim to shoot Allison in the head, forcing the real Allison to break the illusion. The appearance of this figure harkens Freud's notion of the double or *Doppelganger*:

> A person may identify himself with another and so become unsure of his true self, or he may substitute the other's self for his own. The self may thus be duplicated, divided and interchanged. Finally there is the constant recurrence of the same thing, the repetition of the same facial features, the same characters, the same destinies, the same misdeeds, even the same names. (2003, pp. 141–142)

The placement of Allison's vision with that of her mother's suicide is intended to show that with Victoria's death, Allison will rise as a hunter; indeed, in the next episode "Fury," Allison now appears as the one who Gerard and Chris turn to for authority, awaiting her orders to act (Davis, 2012). The reality, however, is that Gerard has a plan of his own, one that posits him in a position of even greater power as the kanama's master. Allison's empowerment, then, is an illusion just as her double was at the party; in truth, she is still manipulated and controlled by the men around her. When her father stops her from further torturing teenage werewolves Erica and Boyd, he reproaches her for her methods, reminding her "That's not the way we do this," even though he and others have used similar, if not worst, means to achieve their ends (Davis, 2012). She is again treated as a prize to be won, with her grandfather using her as motivation to coerce Scott into his bidding, stating "You give me Derek and I'll let you have Allison" (Davis, 2012). Allison is not portrayed as an individual; rather, she is an object for the men to use, manipulate, and shape to fulfill their needs and desires. Chris reminds her that Gerard is using her to his ends, saying "Allison, you're doing exactly what he wants. We all are" (Davis, 2012). He likewise makes sure that she does what he wants, breaking her crossbow to take away a venue of power for her and using his daughter's rage and newfound confidence to redeem his character through questioning his family's morality. His break from the actions of his family marks Chris as a hero since, as Lynette Porter notes, "Audiences still seem to want their heroes to know the difference between what is morally ideal and what isn't, even if they don't always follow the ideal" (2010, p. 35).

Allison is now cast as the deviant woman, allowing Chris and Scott to be portrayed as saviors as exemplified by Chris's speech to Scott: "Gerard has twisted his way into Allison's head, the same way he did with Kate. I'm losing her, and I know you're losing her, too" (Davis, 2012). The language he employs suggests that the Allison he is losing is the ideal image of his daughter, the passive, submissive female, just as Scott is losing his passive, submissive girlfriend. Upon learning of Gerard's betrayal, Allison once again reverts to her original self in saying "I'm sorry … for what I did, for what I said, for everything" (Davis, 2012). Allison realizes that she was acting as a deviant woman and thus makes amends to the men she undermined.

Even in her death, Allison's agency remains limited. After forging a lethal silver arrow that would be able to kill the Oni, demon warriors, she, herself, is killed by one of the creatures. Scott rushes to her, and she dies in his arms, saying "You were my first love" (Davis, 2014). Show creator Jeff Davis said in an interview with *Entertainment Weekly*:

> I said if Allison is going, we're going to have her go out with a bang. And one of the great things about her death is that we want to give it meaning. It's one of those great heroic deaths that I love, and I love that she dies in her first true love's arms. It's the first person she loved. She may have dated others but Scott was the one. And it doesn't mean that they wouldn't have fallen in love with other people, but as she says in the episode, 'It's perfect; I'm glad in your arms.' (Gonzalez, 2014)

As Davis himself states, the meaning behind Allison's death is not that she dies a hero, despite his claims that her death is "heroic," but that she dies in Scott's arms. The scene thus echoes the overall treatment of Allison in the series: as a romantic interest and sometimes warrior. She is remembered most not as a hunter, not as a fierce female character, but as an object of Scott's affections.

Ultimately, *Teen Wolf* expertly, yet unintentionally, explicated contemporary attitudes towards gender in a package that cleverly focuses on young adult themes of agency and parental control. With the show aimed at a young audience, its lessons become more pertinent because of the ways such shows, like *The Vampire Diaries*, *The Originals* etc., inculcate ideas about patriarchy and accepted roles for girls. By offering a contradictory set of examples about how females can be and demonstrating that women who transgress are always punished, the show reinscribes existing sexist attitudes that prevent girls from reaching their full potential. Finally, as a contemporary urban fantasy text, *Teen Wolf* illustrates the idea that the monster is inside us rather than a creature that can be destroyed by a silver bullet.

REFERENCES

Antosca, N., & Vizzini, N. (Writers). (2012, July 9). Restraint. In T. Andrew & J. Geiner (Producers), *Teen wolf* [Television series]. Beverly Hills, CA: MGM Television.

Cochran, A. (Writer). (2012, June 4). Shape shifted. In T. Andrew & J. Geiner (Producers), *Teen wolf* [Television series]. Beverly Hills, CA: MGM Television.

Davis, J. (Writer). (2011, June 5). Wolf moon. In T. Andrew & J. Geiner (Producers), *Teen wolf* [Television series]. Beverly Hills, CA: MGM Television.

Davis, J. (Writer). (2011, June 6). Second chance at first line. In T. Andrew & J. Geiner (Producers), *Teen wolf* [Television series]. Beverly Hills, CA: MGM Television.

Davis, J. (Writer). (2011, August 15). Code breaker. In T. Andrew & J. Geiner (Producers), *Teen wolf* [Television series]. Beverly Hills, CA: MGM Television.

Davis, J. (Writer). (2012, June 3). Omega. In T. Andrew & J. Geiner (Producers), *Teen wolf* [Television series]. Beverly Hills, CA: MGM Television.

Davis, J. (Writer). (2012, July 2). Frenemy. In T. Andrew & J. Geiner (Producers), *Teen wolf* [Television series]. Beverly Hills, CA: MGM Television.

Davis, J. (Writer). (2012, July 16). Raving. In T. Andrew & J. Geiner (Producers), *Teen wolf* [Television series]. Beverly Hills, CA: MGM Television.

Davis, J. (Writer). (2012, July 23). Party guessed. In T. Andrew & J. Geiner (Producers), *Teen wolf* [Television series]. Beverly Hills, CA: MGM Television.

Davis, J. (Writer). (2012, July 30). Fury. In T. Andrew & J. Geiner (Producers), *Teen wolf* [Television series]. Beverly Hills, CA: MGM Television.

Davis, J. (Writer). (2012, August 13). Master plan. In T. Andrew & J. Geiner (Producers), *Teen wolf* [Television series]. Beverly Hills, CA: MGM Television.

Davis, J. (Writer). (2014, March 17). Insatiable. In T. Andrew & J. Geiner (Producers), *Teen wolf* [Television series]. Beverly Hills, CA: MGM Television.

Freud, S. (2003). *The uncanny*. New York, NY: Penguin Books.

Gonzalez, S. (2014, March 17). 'Teen Wolf' post-mortem: [Spoiler] talks about leaving the show. *Entertainment Weekly*. Retrieved from http://ew.com/article/2014/03/17/teen-wolf-post-mortem-crystal-reed-interview/

Macer, M. (Writer). (2011, June 27). The tell. In T. Andrew & J. Geiner (Producers), *Teen wolf* [Television series]. Beverly Hills, CA: MGM Television.

Macer, M. (Writer). (2011, July 18). Lunatic. In T. Andrew & J. Geiner (Producers), *Teen wolf* [Television series]. Beverly Hills, CA: MGM Television.

McMahon-Coleman, K., & Weaver, R. (2012). Wolf boys and wolf girls. In K. McMahon-Coleman & R. Weaver (Eds.), *Werewolves and other shapeshifters in popular culture: A thematic analysis of recent depictions*. Jefferson, NC: McFarland.

Passmore, L. (Writer). (2012, June 11). Ice pick. In T. Andrew & J. Geiner (Producers), *Teen wolf* [Television series]. Beverly Hills, CA: MGM Television.

Porter, L. R. (2010). *Tarnished heroes, charming villains, and modern monsters: Science fiction in shades of gray on 21st century television*. Jefferson, NC: McFarland.

Roessler, J. (Writer). (2011, July 25). Wolf's bane. In T. Andrew & J. Geiner (Producers), *Teen wolf* [Television series]. Beverly Hills, CA: MGM Television.

Sinclair, D. (Writer). (2011, June 20). Magic bullet. In T. Andrew & J. Geiner (Producers), *Teen wolf* [Television series]. Beverly Hills, CA: MGM Television.

Vlaming, J. (Writer). (2011, June 13). Pack mentality. In T. Andrew & J. Geiner (Producers), *Teen wolf* [Television series]. Beverly Hills, CA: MGM Television.

Vlaming, J. (Writer). (2011, August 1). Co-captain. In T. Andrew & J. Geiner (Producers), *Teen wolf* [Television series]. Beverly Hills, CA: MGM Television.

Lauren Rocha
Department of English
Merrimack College

ANA G. GAL

7. TOUGH WOMEN, PATRIARCHAL VIOLENCE, AND THE PROBLEM OF NON-INTERSECTIONAL FEMINISM IN LES WISEMAN'S *UNDERWORLD SERIES*

Urban fantasy has become the ideal setting for monsters and supernatural creatures, especially in the film of the new millennium, but its hybridized nature or partial overlapping with other genres—such as horror, science fiction, romance, and even adventure—has made it rather difficult to define or recognize it as a self-standing genre. Thus, urban fantasy inhabits a liminal space in which representational elements of other genres amalgamate quite successfully to articulate brand new narratives. As recent scholars have shown, while some relevant distinctions exist between the (sub)genres that compose it, taking into account the artificiality of the frontiers that separate them is crucial, as they should be constructed as categories that are mutually reliant or dependent.[1]

According to Carol J. Clover (2015), the trademark of cinematic horror/ science-fiction/fantasy is the movement away from stereotypical female images, especially perpetuated by slasher films, and the introduction of full-fledged heroines who at the end of a perilous journey annihilate the main villain(s). Clover calls such heroines "Final Girls" or "tortured survivors," who for the entire duration of the film are "being chased and almost caught, hiding, running, falling, rising in pain and fleeing again" (p. x). The five urban horror films in the *Underworld* franchise (2003–2016)[2] in particular feature this kind of resourceful female warrior who "kicks ass," despite having to navigate a space dominated by the violent decisions and actions of male assailants. By examining the gender, race, and class dynamics operating within the series, I will primarily discuss how the films deconstruct and criticize masculine violence, but in the process only legitimize one strain of femininity (i.e., white and mainstream). The franchise narativizes, almost myopically, Selene's liberation from a toxic patriarchal order, but in its centering of this (white) female protagonist as the norm and representative of the female experience, it ends up antagonizing and ultimately erasing alternate (non-white and Lycan) femininity, which is mainly relegated to the margins as absence.

© KONINKLIJKE BRILL NV, LEIDEN, 2019 | DOI:10.1163/9789004394100_007

The racial and class connotations in the filmmakers' treatment of vampires and werewolves have been extensively addressed by scholars who have taken an interest in the films. As Kimberly Frohreich (2013) argues, the figure of the vampire has become the ideal "destabiliser of the category of race" (p. 33), and in particular *Underworld*'s vampire-werewolf dynamic exposes views on miscegenation (p. 37). In a similar vein, David Magill (2015) analyzes the first film in the series in terms of "an allegory of American multiculturalism played out through a Gothic vampire-werewolf civil war" (p. 82). The whole franchise is in fact a macro-narrative that creatively re-inscribes the history of race relations in the United States from the pre-Civil War era to the civil rights movement of the 1960s to contemporary debates about white fragility. *Underworld* presents a world fractured by the violent schism between two racialized patriarchal systems that compete for hegemony: the privileged vampires seeking to eradicate the Lycan culture and the marginalized werewolves fighting to retain their identity. The hierarchical relations between the two male-led societies are evident in each group's material conditions. Vampires' aristocratic heritage and access to capital is featured throughout the series. For example, in *Underworld* (2003), Selene's coven of vampires resides in a historic mansion with a refined décor and luxuriously furnished. As Magill notes too, vampires "drink fine wine [in crystal glasses] and listen to music" (p. 84). By contrast, the Lycans lurk in murky sewers and engage in gory bare-chested fights, reminiscent of proletarian entertainment—often seen as mindless or uncultured.[3]

The vampiric social order is thus depicted as more civilized, elitist, and progressive than the Lycan one. The first three films in particular—*Underworld* (2003), *Underworld: Evolution* (2006), and *Underworld: The Rise of the Lycans* (2009)—complicate this vampire-werewolf dynamic by emphasizing the Lycans' initial status as slaves serving vampires during the day. It is clear vampires not only perceive the werewolves to be racially and culturally inferior but also assign to them a series of negative "innate" traits (i.e., resistant to civilization, savagery, and primitive barbarism). In addition, derogatory qualifiers are constantly used to describe Lycans, such as "mangy animals," "pack of rabid dogs," "raging monsters," and "beasts." This defamatory language is especially propagated by vampire leaders to incite racial hatred by targeting the werewolves' difference in terms of physical appearance and metamorphic abilities. The race and class implications are hence inescapable here; as both Frohreich and Magill contend, vampires can be coded as "white" while werewolves as "black" (pp. 37, 84); to this, we can add the contrast between upper-class sophistication and working-class crudeness.

Much of the scholarship focuses on this racially-motivated (male) conflict or binary, but I would also argue that both male-led groups share significant ideological commonalities, more specifically the adherence to patriarchal mandates that entail the systematic devaluation of femininity and that perpetuate a culture that rewards male aggression. In addition, both societies are ruled by a coalition of alpha males (either the oldest or most muscular). *Underworld*'s female characters, vampire and Lycan alike, inhabit a profoundly oppressive and hyper-masculine world. When the first film in the series opens, Selene's vampire coven is structured around the centralized authority of three elders—two male (Viktor and Markus) and one female (Amelia). The existence of a female elder is a distraction, however, or a façade of gender equality, as she seems to function more as an illusory token of female emancipation. She is not only featured quite minimally in the series, but she is the only elder (out of the three) without a full-fledged backstory or whose government is placed under the temporary supervision of an interim male leader, Kraven (assigned by Viktor before he goes into his cyclical hibernation). In fact, the scene that introduces her character for the first time cements her diminished power and failed management. As vampires are preparing for the Awakening, a sacred ritual that can be performed only by an elder, Amelia is viciously attacked and killed by a horde of male werewolves trying to prevent the resurrection of Markus, the next-in-line scheduled to rule the coven for the next one hundred years. The scene featuring her death is disturbingly violent, the camera lingering on her maimed and fang-penetrated body acting as a graphic reminder of female fragility and powerlessness in a world dominated by men. The scene also serves to re-inscribe Amelia's body as a target of male hostility or a "battlefield," a concept theorized by Susan Books Thistlethwaite (2015) in relation to the prevalence of physical and sexual violence against women in Western culture. She states:

> All day long, all night long, every day and every night, the bodies of women and girls are turned into battlefields. Their bodies are penetrated against their will; they are burned, maimed, bruised, slapped, kicked, threatened with weapons, confined, beaten with fists or objects, shot, and knifed […] They are terrorized and they are killed. (p. 1)

A similar pattern of devaluing women's political and intellectual labor (symptomatic of a patriarchal society) can be observed in the fifth film *Underworld: Blood Wars* (2016) as well. When the female elder (and antagonist) Semira petitions the Eastern Coven's Elite Council to implement her proposed measures against the new Lycan leader Marius, she cannot do so without privately seeking the support of a male peer, despite being an experienced Council member.

Male vampires in the *Underworld* universe are almost compulsively beset by a fear of female disobedience. For example, Kraven, the leader of the Budapest Coven and a bureaucrat, repudiates women in active or traditionally male roles. He is depicted constantly attempting to domesticate Selene, who is a "death-dealer" or a fierce warrior trained to fight werewolves. When she refuses to exchange her latex dominatrix costume for more conventional (feminine) attire and defies his orders by fleeing the mansion to rescue Michael Corvin (a descendant of Alexander Corvinus, the Father of both bloodlines), Kraven asserts his masculine privilege by manhandling her and locking her in a room under the supervision of a more compliant female subordinate, but not before decrying that "you take this warrior business far too seriously" (*Underworld*, 2003). His retaliatory aggression toward Selene stems not only from sexual jealousy, understood here as anxiety compounded by male competitiveness, but also a fear of emasculation. Selene's interest in Michael is perceived by Kraven and other male vampires as a dangerous, if not a capital, transgression, and as Frohreich notes, she is "fought over and depicted as in need of protection," more specifically from being polluted by werewolves (p. 39). Selene's surrogate father in particular, Viktor, is protective of the female body. As a patriarch, he wants monopoly over his daughters' (Selene's and Sonja's) reproductive choices and reduces their bodies to a commodity that is intimately tied to the (vampire) family's honor. His fear of miscegenation[4] is so visceral and uncontrollable that he even commits filicide when Sonja is impregnated by Lucian (a Lycan), despite his restrictive paternal control. As he tells Sonja before savagely executing her: "You have betrayed me to be with an animal [...]. That thing inside you is a monstrosity" (*Underworld: Rise of the Lycans*, 2009). Thus, it is clear that he perceives the female body and sexuality as a vehicle for potential racial contamination which, if not suppressed or carefully surveilled, could lead to the eradication of the vampire culture.

In addition, as the purveyor of (white) male power, Viktor understands that not only violence but also censorship is necessary to maintain both racial and gender supremacy. Immediately after deceptively assuming control over the Old World Coven (the "original" coven in Europe), Viktor's first step toward securing hegemony is to implement a state-based regulative censorship system that not only deems "digging into the past" illegal, but also enforces drastic penalties against anyone who attempts to research historical truth.[5] In the *Underworld* universe, memories can be retrieved and transferred through blood ingestion—a practice that is forbidden by law on the grounds that such transmission of information can be lethal to non-elders. Viktor tampers with historical knowledge and collective memory by mandating Tanis, the official chronicler of the Coven, to erase or alter facts as well as restrict access to any authentic documents. In *Underworld: Evolution* (2006), Kraven tells Selene:

> Let me tell you a little something about your beloved dark father ... Never could follow his own rules. Said he couldn't abide the taste of livestock, so every once in a while, he went out and gorged himself on human blood. I kept his secrets, cleaned up his mess, but it was he who crept room to room dispatching everyone close to your heart.

This is a turning point in the narrative, as it exposes the sinister deception behind the practice of censorship: to promote a sanitized, alternative truth about vampire society and to disseminate propagandist material construing the Lycan culture as savage, bestial, and unevolved, and the vampire (especially male) as civilized and restrained (i.e., able to practice moderation). Thus, it is clear the male vampires' performance of racial superiority is but a façade perpetuated over centuries as a means of subjugating non-vampires. In addition, Selene learns from Tanis that Viktor's motivation for constructing racial hybridity as polluted is self-serving, in that Viktor's documented genealogy is a fabrication. Ironically, he is not an Original vampire as his propagandist machine has promoted for centuries, but a fifth-century Hungarian human lord who was sired by Markus in exchange for political favors. His dismissal of the "original mythos" founded on the sameness of vampires and Lycans (i.e., both species originating from the same source) serves not only to maintain an ideology of racial difference but also to conceal his own hybridity as a marker of inferiority and racial contamination.

As previously argued, Lycan society operates in analogous ways, especially in terms of gender relations and the extent to which masculine values dictate norms. However, there is a significant hierarchizing distinction. Following the same white-black racial dichotomy that posits Lycan-ness (or blackness) as pre-civilized and animalistic, werewolves are presented perpetuating a patriarchal structure that is very backward (if not prehistoric) and thus at a much lower level of social development than the vampire one. As a warrior society, werewolves are so restrictive that women do not have a recognized place; it is a social system primarily founded upon the radical excision of femininity from the visible (public) sphere and at times even the domestic one (especially childbearing). The five films feature very few female werewolves. The fifth installment, *Underworld: Blood Wars* (and boasting the creative contributions of director Anna Foerster), includes only a couple of scenes portraying female Lycans—all lacking a character arc and mostly serving as nameless soldiers or casualties in the vampire-werewolf conflict. The series takes on a new direction in the fourth film, which includes an entirely new cast of characters (except for Selene and Michael) and which propels the plot twelve years into the future, after Lucian's and the vampire elders' deaths. *Underworld: Awakening* (2009) presents a post-apocalyptic world where both vampires and werewolves are on the verge of extinction due to two distinct purges, and where experiments are conducted on them in sophisticated laboratories by a pharmaceutical company called Antigen. Lycan and vampire fangs alike are commercialized in convenience stores as trophies and the last survivors of each species live hidden from view, either in sewers or underground covens. The writing remains consistent, however, in its erasure of alternate (Lycan) femininity, as the new order of Lycans is under the authority of a father-son duo (Dr. Jacob Lane and Quint), the mother having been completely erased from the narrative. Another female werewolf is Lucian's mother in *Underworld: Rise of the Lycans*, who is afforded less than a minute of screen time, and whose body is entirely reduced to a receptacle of male seed. As Viktor's caged slave, her worth lies solely in the ability of her womb to replicate slave labor for vampires. Once she gives birth to her son—the first werewolf capable of shapeshifting at will and maintaining his human form—her body is killed and discarded. Capitalizing on Lucian's back-and-forth metamorphic abilities that the descendants of the Original werewolf (William) do not exhibit, Viktor switches to a more effective system of Lycan slave reproduction that is fully devoid of female participation and that relies on replication through the act of male-on-male biting. This enables vampires to manufacture a perfected, exclusively male slave force, that can tap into the werewolf's bestial strength to perform labor in the mines but whose human form can be more easily surveilled and subjugated. While Viktor's motivation for eradicating the female Lycan element is never explicitly addressed in the films, I would argue that the narrative implies that a productive labor force, especially one that is forced to face hostile working conditions, is dependent on the rejection of female bodies, seen not only as too delicate but also as germinating vessels threatening to revert Viktor's procreative experiments.

The perpetuation of Lycans through aggressive male-on-male biting suggests a sort of dangerous reciprocity. The act of werewolf-making is penetrative and physically debilitating for the "receiver" of the bite, and while no sexual ecstasy seems to be derived from the exchange of fluids (blood and saliva), it can be argued that the interaction is largely modeled after patterns of sexual behavior. The series is replete with images of half-naked male werewolves living together in very close quarters, which contrast heavily with the vampires' preference for heterosexual practices. While vampirism can be replicated through biting as well, all vampire characters (both male and female) are shown engaging in sexual relations with members of the opposite sex, which serves to a great extent to promote the divide between the vampire and Lycan societies—the former normalized by heteronormativity, the latter perverted by hereditary male bonding and the lack of hetero-genital sex. It is worth mentioning here that while Lucian is afforded an on-screen a romantic relationship with Sonja, his desire to mix the bloodlines and his persistent apologetism only further the narrative of the werewolves' degenerative reproductive practices. More specifically, as Frohreich argues, Michael's mixed race or hybridity—facilitated by Lucian himself—enables Lucian to "replace" the child Sonja would have borne or that would have ended the vampire-Lycan conflict (p. 39). In addition, he constantly berates the other male Lycans for their uncivilized behaviors. In one instance, he calls them "'a pack of rabid dogs'" (p. 37), asking them to act like "gentlemen" and "put some clothes on." In another instance, when one of his subordinates brutalizes Michael, he exclaims in frustration: "He's in desperate need of a lesson in manners" (*Underworld*, 2003). The subtext is, of course, that Lycans (or at least those who have benefited from their close proximity to elite vampires, just like Lucian) accept their inferior status and to some extent even repudiate their racial identity.

As previously argued, female Lycans too are portrayed as victims of patriarchy. It is important to emphasize here, however, that they face a double discrimination: on the one hand, they are systematically oppressed and silenced by their own men, and on the other hand, they are devalued (even criminalized) and killed by vampires, including Selene. Also, a probable reason for female werewolves being *almost* entirely absent from the franchise may be related to the fact that female werewolves in general are relatively rare occurrences in popular culture. Yet, in an MTV interview from 2006, when asked about the overall marginalization of female werewolves in the series, Len Wiseman and Kate Beckinsale (Selene) explained their exclusion from the viewers' gaze in terms of an aesthetic choice:

MTV: Why don't we see Lycan women?

Beckinsale: Because that could be really horrifying. Hairy, thuggish women.

Wiseman: And you don't actually want to see little furry children. I've seen furry women.

Beckinsale [Laughing]: Not here! (L. Carroll).

It is clear both Wiseman and Beckinsale situate Lycan women outside of conventional femininity, which contrasts with an aggressive (or "thuggish") masculinized femininity. As Zoë Newman notes in her discussion of Barbara Creed's concept of the "monstrous feminine," a masculine woman is "a woman whose behavior [...] and actions suggest that she is a man 'trapped' in a woman's body" (2012, p. 73). This observation complements Elizabeth Clark's argument that the female werewolf is "a kind of gendered border crossing: a female body expressing characteristics labeled both masculine and male by the dominant culture (power, strength, rage, aggression, violence, and body hair)" (p. 2).

I would argue that this absence of Lycan female bodies also attests to the systematic erasure of black female bodies from narratives that are centered around the emancipation of a desirable white female character. Lycan bodies, when fully metamorphosed, are only flesh and slick muscle, black-skinned and subhuman, and always lurking in or attacking from the shadows. Such representations are familiar, as they replicate images of black corporeality perpetuated by the media and Hollywood on a loop. We are also quite accustomed to black female characters in films and television shows dying for comedic or dramatic effect or acting as hollow dummy figures written solely to prop up white characters. As Sherrie Inness (2004) writes, "a fierce kick-ass black woman is more likely read as hyper aggressive, wild, untamable, and vicious rather than an admirable warrior woman breaking down age-old stereotypes that white women invoke." She adds: "Standing up for herself, fighting back, is not in the name of the same virtuosity [...] portrayed by the white kick-ass woman" (p. 111). The interview with Wiseman exposes then the implicit bias that is involved in the exclusion of alternate femininity in the series: black women are perceived as too "thuggish," too hairy, not feminine enough and therefore unaesthetic (or visually unappealing) to be afforded a central/pivotal role. Like their male counterparts, Lycan women are all hair (especially on portions of the body that our culture is conditioned to associate with male virility). As Merran Toerien, Sue Wilkinson, and Precilla Choi contend, women's routine depilation in Western culture is intimately shaped by hairlessness as a staple image of ideal femininity (2005, p. 334). To this, we can add the most visible symbols of womanliness—large, round breasts and a small waist—both denied to the female werewolf, whose muscular frame becomes instead a signifier of grotesque and (sexually) deviant femininity. *Underworld: Blood Wars* includes only one scene that puts Lycan women's bodily transformation on display, this sort of censorship most definitely echoing Wiseman's claim that such images of non-normative femininity would be too "horrifying" and uncanny. By contrast,

Selene's white, smooth-skinned, and hairless body is positioned in a way that allows her to maintain her erotic capital, despite her adoption of masculine characteristics, such as physical strength and stamina. More specifically, her physical attractiveness is featured in on-screen sex scenes and highlighted by close camera angles that spectacularize her female form.

The franchise has been enthusiastically praised by film critics for its feminist approach, but I would argue that while such a claim makes sense to some extent, it is a bit shortsighted. Indeed, the series focuses only on Selene's character arc, and what draws attention immediately is that she does not fulfil the familiar horror film trope of the screaming damsel in distress. On the contrary, she is what Inness (2004) defines as an "action chick," i.e., a heroine who "can physically power [her] way out of dangerous situations using any combination of weaponry and martial arts, all the while maintaining traditional signs of femininity" (p. 97). Selene fits this formula perfectly, given that she is a sexy female warrior who masterfully wields swords and guns as well as engages in close, kung-fu-style combat against powerful male enemies. In addition, she flips the damsel-in-distress female archetype, as she constantly faces hordes of angry werewolves in her mission to rescue the male protagonist and her romantic interest (Michael). She takes on the absolute Patriarchs (Viktor, Markus, etc.) and wins, the triumph being depicted in very graphic or gory detail, with the camera lingering almost fetishistically on the sliced, decapitated (castrated), or shredded bodies of her male opponents.

This seems to position Selene's character within a discourse of female empowerment; yet, her attempt to decentralize patriarchal values is sabotaged by the filmmakers forcing her female body into reductive categories that solely serve to recode her as an object for male consumption (both visually and sexually). Despite being unusually athletic, she is hyper-sexualized. Her tight black one-piece cleavage-baring PVC suit, high-heeled boots, and body language during fighting sequences speak to the strategic rise in the "pornification" of female bodies in a contemporary market that often caters to male tastes or fantasies. Her body seems written for a male fetishist audience and constantly subject to an objectifying male gaze or what psychoanalytical film theorists call "a spectatorial desire" or "a [male] pleasure in seeing what is prohibited in relation to the female body" (Doane, 1991, p. 20). Thus, while on a surface level Selene's portrayal as a butt-kicking warrior does seem to suggest that the *Underworld* films have operated a revolutionary shift from previous, less flattering, cinematic representations of women, in the end it is just an attractively pre-packaged product masquerading as progressive and cleverly camouflaging its adherence to more traditional gender roles for women. As Angela McRobbie (2008) notes, contemporary texts in particular should be regarded with a dose of skepticism for their tendency to employ seemingly feminist strategies "for the re-securing of patriarchal law and masculine hegemony" (p. 58). This is because despite their more positive treatment of female characters, many films engage in what Ken Gelder (1994) calls a "process of ideological and cultural 'remodeling' of old formulas" (p. 92), or superficial innovation of familiar feminine tropes.

In conclusion, the key here is that the polarized depiction of female vampire and Lycan bodies in *Underworld* is symptomatic of a culture that rejects intersectionality and that is rooted in a long history of pitting white and black women against each other. This is the same conclusion Clark reaches when she notes that when cultural texts narrativize more than one typology of femininity threatened by male hegemony, "they are often shown in competition or contrasted in terms of good versus evil" (p. 34). We can see how the female Lycans' absence-presence or erasure is primarily used as a boost to Selene's character, who seems to have been written primarily to fulfill the function of a white heroine and champion of feminism—of course, a feminism that benefits and empowers primarily women who share her whiteness and privilege. Her inability to view Lycan women beyond their racial difference or as beings who are burdened by gender, race, and class divisions simultaneously mirrors to a great extent the dominant culture's failure to recognize how various systems of oppression intersect. As Leslie McCall (2005) posits in "The Complexity of Intersectionality," there is danger in operating with the assumption that gender is the only dimension that shapes a woman's lived experience, as this unilateral approach neglects the existence of "multiple and conflicting experiences" located at the intersection of gender, race, sexuality, nationality, and especially class (p. 1780). The consequence of non-intersectionality is first and foremost that it ends up pulling non-white women's "loyalties into two directions, that is, feeling the need to either choose between being loyal to feminist ideas or being loyal to their racial or ethnic communities" (Potter, 2012, p. 57). Selene's (white) supremacist ancestry and the depiction of female werewolves as bestial bodies defined either by their reproductive function or violent nature showcase not only white feminism's failure to treat intersectionality as essential to the understanding and construction of womanhood but also its participation in maintaining its own privilege.

NOTES

[1] Joyce G. Saricks (2014), for example, notes that both fantasy and horror capitalize on cultural anxieties as well as feature "alternate universes" and a feeling of "otherworldliness"

(p. 266). Roz Kaveney (2012) theorizes paranormal romance as a subset of urban fantasy (or "dark fantasy"), in that both genres feature erotic or romantic elements (p. 215). See Saricks's *The Readers'Advisory Guide to Genre Fiction* and Kaveney's "Dark Fantasy and Paranormal Romance" in *The Cambridge Companion to Fantasy Literature.*

[2] The five films in the franchise are as follows: *Underworld* (2003, directed by Len Wiseman), *Underworld: Evolution* (2006, directed by Len Wiseman), *Underworld: The Rise of the Lycans* (2009, directed by Patrick Tatopoulos and written by Len Wiseman et al.), *Underworld: Awakening* (2012, directed by Mans Marlind and Bjorn Stein, and written by Len Wiseman et al.), and *Underworld: Blood Wars* (2016, directed by Anna Foerster; Len Wiseman is credited for his creation of characters).

[3] These observations are supported by several scholars as well. Both Magill and Frohreich discuss the socioeconomic power that vampires and werewolves possess. See Frohreich's "Sullied Blood, Semen, and Skin, Vampires and the Spectre of Miscegenation" and Magill's "Racial Hybridity and the Reconstruction of White Masculinity in *Underworld*." In addition, Peter Hutchins (2012) argues that *Underworld* is a narrative about "a vampire aristocracy threatened by a proletariat werewolf rebellion" (p. 21); see his article "The Limits of European Horror" in *European Nightmares: Horror Cinema in Europe Since the 1945.*

[4] According to Frohreich, the term "miscegenation" was coined by David Goodman Croly in 1864 to induce anxiety into the white male population about the threat to the white man's electoral, racial, and cultural power posed by "the blending of races" (p. 34).

[5] Sue Curry Jansem (2004) defines regulative censorship as "a legally constituted form of censorship practiced by church or state ... [enforcing] sanctions against those who cross the boundaries, canon, or law" (p. 150). See "Censorship" in *Routledge International Encyclopedia of Women: Global Women's Issues and Knowledge.*

REFERENCES

Beckinsale, K., & Wiseman, L. (2010, January 10). *Blood, sweat, and fur—'underworld: Evolution' mysteries explained.* Retrieved from http://www.mtv.com/news/1520474/blood-sweat-and-fur-underworld-evolution-mysteries-explained/

Clarke, E. (2008). *'Hairy thuggish women:' Female werewolves, gender, and the hoped-for monster* (Unpublished master's thesis). Georgetown University, Washington, DC.

Clover, C. J. (2015). *Men, women, and chain saws: Gender in the modern horror film.* Princeton, NJ: Princeton University Press.

Doane, M. A. (1991). *Femmes fatales: Feminism, film theory, psychoanalysis.* New York, NY: Routledge.

Foerster, A. (Director), & Wiseman, L. (Writer). (2016). *Underworld: Blood wars* [Motion picture]. Beverly Hills, CA: Lakeshore Entertainment.

Frohreich, K. (2013). Sullied blood, semen and skin: Vampires and the spectre of miscegenation. *Gothic Studies, 15*(1), 33–43. doi:10.7227/gs.15.1.4

Gelder, K. (1994). *Reading the vampire.* London: Routledge.

Hutchins, P. (2012). The limits of European horror. In P. Allmer, E. Brick, & D. Huxley (Eds.), *European nightmares: Horror cinema in Europe since the 1945* (pp. 13–24). New York, NY: Wallflower Press.

Inness, S. A. (2004). *Action chicks: New images of tough women in popular culture.* New York, NY: Palgrave Macmillan.

Jansem, S. C. (2000). Censorship. In C. Kramarae & D. Spender (Eds.), *Routledge international encyclopedia of women: Global women's issues and knowledge* (pp. 147–151). New York, NY: Routledge.

Kaveney, R. (2012). Dark fantasy and paranormal romance. In E. James & F. Mendleshon (Eds.), *The Cambridge companion to fantasy literature* (pp. 214–223). Cambridge: Cambridge University Press.

Magill, D. (2015). Racial hybridity and the reconstruction of White masculinity in underworld. In M. Anyiwo (Ed.), *Race in the vampire narrative* (pp. 81–90). Rotterdam, The Netherlands: Sense Publishers.

Marlind, M., & Stein, B. (Directors), & Wiseman, L. (Writer). (2012). *Underworld: Awakening* [Motion picture]. Beverly Hills, CA: Lakeshore Entertainment.

McCall, L. (2005). The complexity of intersectionality. *Signs: Journal of Women in Culture and Society, 30*(3), 1771–1800. doi:10.1086/426800

McRobbie, A. (2012). *The aftermath of feminism: Gender, culture and social change*. London: Sage Publications.

Newman, Z. (2012). Bodies, genders, sexualities: Counting past two. In D. Brock, R. Raby, & M. P. Thomas (Eds.), *Power and everyday practices* (pp. 61–85). Toronto: Nelson Education Ltd.

Potter, H. (2013). An argument for Black feminist criminology: Understanding African-American women's experiences. In M. Chesney-Lind & P. Lisa (Eds.), *Girls, women, and crime: Selected readings* (pp. 53–66). Thousand Oaks, CA: Sage Publishers.

Saricks, J. (2009). *The readers' advisory guide to genre fiction*. Chicago, IL: American Library Association.

Tatopoulos, P. (Director), & Wiseman, L. (Writer). (2009). *Underworld: Rise of the lycans* [Motion picture]. Beverly Hills, CA: Lakeshore Entertainment.

Thistlethwaite, S. B. (2015). *Women's bodies as battlefield: Christian theology and the global war on women*. New York, NY: Palgrave Macmillan.

Toerien, M., Wilkinson, S., & Choi, P. Y. (2005). Body hair removal: The 'mundane' production of normative femininity. *Sex Roles, 52*(5–6), 399–406. doi:10.1007/s11199-005-2682-5

Wiseman, L. (Director). (2003). *Underworld* [Motion picture]. Beverly Hills, CA: Lakeshore Entertainment.

Wiseman, L. (Director). (2006). *Underworld evolution* [Motion picture]. Beverly Hills, CA: Lakeshore Entertainment.

Ana G. Gal
Department of English
The University of Memphis

CAIT COKER

8. THE PROBLEMATIC FAN-GIRL

Cassandra Clare's Gendered Revisions in the Mortal Instruments Series

Cassandra Clare's multivolume Young Adult series *The Mortal Instruments* features Shadowhunters, demon-hunters who roam the "Downworld" of contemporary New York City and come across vampires, werewolves, and angelic and demonic hybrids on a regular basis. In addition to the novels, the series has spawned several graphic novel adaptations, a feature film, and a television series. Readers might find it a hormone-fueled derivative of the *Harry Potter* megafranchise … and they would be more right than they would necessarily think. Clare began her writing career as a fanfic writer online, sharing numerous highly popular stories that were read by thousands if not millions of readers, including a *Harry Potter* series entitled "The Draco Trilogy" that consisted of three novel-length stories focused on the characters as teenagers, though written and shared online before the release of Rowling's novels during that time period.

Of particular interest here is how an excerpt from one of the Draco stories, featuring an emotionally charged scene between Hermione Granger and Draco Malfoy, appears largely intact in Clare's novel *City of Bones*, repurposed to fit her characters Clary and Jace. Clary and Jace have other similarities to the *Harry Potter* characters, with Clary as a young woman raised as a "mundane" despite having fantastic magical powers and Jace coming from a respected and wealthy family of magic-users himself. Functionally, in Clare's writing, Hermione becomes the heroine of the series, rather than the sidekick she often remains in Rowling's work. This essay examines *The Mortal Instruments*' origins within *Harry Potter* fandom and how Clare's revising of elements from her fanfic serve as a postfeminist response to Rowling's more traditional iterations of gender roles.

FROM *HARRY POTTER* TO *SHADOWHUNTERS*

The popularity of the *Harry Potter* (hereafter abbreviated to HP) book franchise was at its height in the early 2000s, concurrent to the release of the fourth volume (with its sudden "dark" turns) and of the first film. Early online mega-fandoms like HP (and *Buffy the Vampires Slayer* and *Lord of the Rings* aka LOTR) came of age in a unique intersection of technology (the new omnipresence of the Internet), popular culture (multiple big-budget genre films and television shows), and political anxiety (the Bush administration and 9/11). They seeded the roots of a new fannish norm of fan work creation and dissemination, such that most textual consumers could functionally come of age reading fan work, in contrast to previous generations of fans who usually discovered fan writing and fanzines by happenstance as adults. For better or for worse, for non-fans this solidified the picture of the average fan writer as a teenage girl writing reams of unreadable "fic" in her room—an image that hasn't altered in recent years despite the revelation that runaway bestseller *Fifty Shades of Grey* (2012) had its origins in fan fiction. The ties between fan writers, genre, and gender intertwined to create the image of the problematic fan girl, iterations of whom would appear on episodes of *Supernatural* (as "Becky the Fan Girl" who is sometimes helpful to the heroes but who also roofies and rapes one of them) and in novels like Rainbow Rowell's 2013 *Fangirl* (where the heroine uses fandom to retreat from her problems but ultimately "emerges" successfully in college with original fiction writing and a real boyfriend).

The literary legacy of mega-fandoms like HP and LOTR go beyond dubious acknowledgement in popular culture. Anne Jamison notes in her collection *Fic: Why Fanfiction is Taking Over the World* (2013) that access to and involvement in online fan fiction communities has helped shape both future writers and the changing economics of fiction publishing itself; she writes that the "influence of these fansites and the networks, systems, and cultures they help put in place has been enormous—and it isn't likely to fade any time soon" (152). Numerous professional writers have their ties to and origins in fan fic, including Lois McMaster Bujold, Naomi Novik, and Meg Cabot, among others.[1] In general, most writers try to distance themselves from their fannish origins, largely because of the attitude of popular disdain that has historically been aimed at fannish writing. While attitudes towards fan writing are slowly changing, there are several popular writers in the HP fandom who have made the shift to pro writing, like Holly Black (*The Spiderwick Chronicles*), Sarah Rees Brennan (the *Demon's Lexicon* trilogy), and Cassandra Clare.

"Cassandra Claire," the fan pseudonym for Judith Rumelt, who now publishes as Cassandra Clare, emerged first as a BNF (Big Name Fan) in LOTR fandom. The author will hereafter be referenced as "Claire" when discussing her fan writing and "Clare" when discussing her professional writing. From 2001–2002, she wrote a series of "Very Secret Diaries" from the perspectives of different characters in the style of *Bridget Jones*; their popularity garnered them unusual media attention for the time, including a brief dramatization in the 2005 documentary *Ringers: Lord of the Fans*. From 2000–2006, Claire and several of her friends, who would become known (not altogether ironically) as "The Inner Circle" shared their HP fanfiction first on a members-only Yahoo listserv Paradigm Of Uncertainty[2] and later posting on Fanfiction.net. In particular, Claire's three fan novels of the "Draco Trilogy" were exceptionally popular and influential in fandom. Altogether, they encompass some 895,000 words; though they have officially been taken offline by now, a Google search will often provide stashed PDF copies that include fan art as well as the novels themselves, which were made available by Claire for download prior to the series removal at the end of 2006. The first "book," *Draco Dormiens*, was posted serially through 2000, and the second, *Draco Sinister*, was posted throughout 2000 and 2001, with a chapter appearing roughly once a month. The final part of the series, *Draco Veritas*, was posted over a much longer period, from 2001 through 2006, while Claire began work on her original series, *The Mortal Instruments*.

In Claire's fan novels, teenaged versions of Hermione Granger and Draco Malfoy joined Harry Potter as protagonists. The series began after the events of *Harry Potter and the Goblet of Fire* (2000), the then-most recent volume in the HP series. Claire's iterations of the HP characters took what we would think of as more conventionally young adult (YA) genre approaches to character development and plot twists: unlike Rowling's novels, romance and sexual tension (and even, eventually, actual sex) are character concerns, reminding many of *Buffy the Vampire Slayer*, and indeed, the characters periodically "quoted" lines from *Buffy* (see below). The series revolves primarily around a love triangle between Hermione, Harry, and Draco (or a quadrangle, with Ginny added) in addition to the war against Voldemort and other events both magical and soap operatic. When Clare's first pro novel, *City of Bones*, appeared in 2007, fans noted that one chapter appeared largely word-for-word from *Draco Dormiens*, ascribing Draco's characteristics to Jace Wayland and Hermione's to Clary Fray, though Clary's bright red hair could also be interpreted as a revision of Ginny instead. I think that Clary can be best read as an amalgam of Hermione and Ginny, with Hermione's background—she is a Mundane (rather than a Muggle) who has been raised without knowledge of the magical world—and Ginny's physical appearance, but for the purpose of this essay I will focus more on the character of Hermione in my arguments, particularly given her status as a primary character in the original HP novels.

City of Bones was followed by further novels in Clare's series; to date, *The Mortal Instruments* series consists of six volumes, along with a second trilogy and other volumes that add an additional six books to a wide-spanning sequence known as *The Shadowhunter Chronicles*: At this point, Clare has outpaced Rowling by word count and by book. *City of Bones* was also adapted into a film titled *The Mortal Instruments: City of Bones*, in 2013, which failed commercially at the box office, cancelling any possible sequels. Nonetheless, a television show called *Shadowhunters* debuted in 2016 and ran for three seasons, concluding in 2019. Hour for hour, Clare has again outpaced the HP franchise, though with less critical acclaim. Fanworks are also limited, with not quite 7000 fan fictions for *The Shadowhunter Chronicles* listed on Archive of Our Own. This is all to say that the textual relationship between Rowling and Clare, *Harry Potter* and *Mortal Instruments*, is fascinating: mega-franchise begets mega-franchise.

REWRITING HERMIONE?

Scholarly criticism of the HP novels has covered a variety of topics, but popular criticism of the series has focused on two aspects particularly loudly: the dual problems of gender and race. What made the series so approachable to British readers, seemingly, was the familiar tropes of the boarding school novel (aspects that to many American readers came off as equally exotic), with its emphasis on institutions and sport. Though purposefully raised as an outsider, Harry finds that he is, indeed, *the* ultimate insider to Wizard culture: connected to respectable "pureblood" (more on that in a minute) families like the Blacks, with Sirius even willing him the family mansion; his father's sporting trophies on display in Hogwarts; a celebrity before he even starts school. It doesn't matter how much Harry says he doesn't want or like these privileges: as a white male wizard, he has all of them nonetheless. Indeed, much like Katniss Everdeen of *The Hunger Games,* his protests against celebrity come off as rather hollow, given their necessity to the plot and, of course, his own life.

In contrast, Hermione Granger has none of these enviable traits. She is born a "mudblood," as Draco Malfoy and others repeatedly remind her; she is a Wizard child to distinctly non-magical parents. Even through the friendly eyes of Harry, her physical appearance is critiqued, as is her knowledge (which she often can't help from sharing with the class to the dismay of students and teachers both). Her adolescence is distinguished by her interest in social justice, when she wants to free the slavish House Elves in the fourth book, *Harry Potter and the Goblet of Fire.* Hermione creates the fledgling Society for the Promotion of Elfish Welfare, with its unfortunate acronym of S.P.E.W. She and the Society are mocked by the other students (and even real-world readers), even as she makes a donation box and tries unsuccessfully to recruit members beyond Harry and Ron. S.P.E.W. can be read as an analog to numerous causes, but most especially the abolitionist societies of the nineteenth century. However, it and much of Hermione's interest disappears from the latter books. Readers can analyze and get more from Hermione's personal growth and interests than, it sadly seems, J.K. Rowling.

As Melanie J. Cordova (2015) notes in her essay "Because I'm a *Girl*, I Suppose!" Gender Lines and Narrative Perspective in *Harry Potter*," by the final book in the series, Hermione is a "young woman of seventeen who can reasonably be assumed the agent and speaker of her own destiny. She has been interpreted as capable, knowledgeable, and fairly self-assured … [but Harry's] myopic perspective of Hermione relegates her to stereotype and either ignores or misunderstands her full potential" (p. 19). In contrast, Dan Dalton of Buzzfeed created an explosive meme/critique of the series when he wrote a photo-essay on "If Hermione Were the Main Character In "Harry Potter"" and then subtitled it "Hermione Granger and the Goddamn Patriarchy." In it, he noted that, among other things, "Without Hermione, The Boy Who Lived would be dead as shit" (Dalton). Throughout Rowling's novels, Hermione is written as incredibly heroic, with a keen sense of justice and a knack for identifying important clues and information, but not as a hero herself.

Enter fan fiction. Fan fiction is commonly accepted to be a transformative and derivative work written for pleasure and without monetary compensation by a fan of a text; I say "commonly accepted" as the term has been in existence for the better part of a century with shifting meanings and usage. Foundational Fan Scholar Henry Jenkins wrote in his 1992 book *Textual Poachers* that fan texts could be of interest to scholars because of "the ways the ambiguities of popularly produced meanings mirror fault lines within dominant ideology, as popular readers attempt to build their culture within the gaps and margins of commercially circulating texts" (p. 35). Jenkins's approach was sociological and media-heavy rather than literary, but nonetheless both heavily influential and successful in elevating fan texts as being "worthy" of study. Karen Hellekson and Kristina Busse's (2014) collection, *The Fan Fiction Studies Reader*, collected a wide variety of influential approaches to the topic through differing methodologies, with the editors concluding in their introduction "that readers were interested in *the stories themselves*, so that one might read a story for a show one wasn't necessarily fannish about simply because the story was enjoyable or because the reader liked the author. In effect, fan fiction had established its own fandom" (p. 7, emphasis added).

Most recently, Francesca Coppa's *The Fanfiction Reader: Folk Tales for the Digital Age* (2017) has printed both full-length fan fiction stories alongside descriptive and analytical work to present a genuine praxis of study in which texts can be considered *as texts* rather than as theoretical or sociological demonstrations of one kind or another. What we should ultimately take from this ongoing and evolving field of study is that fan fiction is not only worthy of scholarly study and interest, but that it provides intriguing textual by-ways to the reception and critique of texts—including, and perhaps especially, the Harry Potter franchise.

Further, the dual behemoths of HP fandom and HP fanfiction ultimately changed the very landscape of online fan and producer relationships. In her 2013 essay "How Harry Potter Fanfic Changed the World (or at Least the Internet)," Heidi Tandy, writer and founder of the now defunct HP fan site FictionAlley, described in detail the shifts she saw in media, from the regular cease-and-desist letters that Warner Brothers would send to fan sites in the early 2000s to the literal "growing up" of fans as they became young women and then librarians, teachers, and published writers. For her, fandom and fan fiction were positive forces for change; the creative outlet of fan fiction allowed writers to explore sensitive topics like queerness, which was slammed as immoral in 1999, became part of the official text via Rowling's revelations of Dumbledore's identity in 1997, and was if not normalized at least broadly *legalized* through gay marriage in the US and UK in 2015. And what Warner Brothers—and Rowling—ultimately found was that fandom and the fan fiction machine simply could not be stopped.

This was not to imply that fan fiction was altogether a bed of roses. Anne Kustritz's (2015) article "Domesticating Hermione: The Emergence of Genre and Community from WIKTT's Feminist Romance Debates" analyzed as a case study a single collection of Hermione/Snape fic created as part of a HP community's writing challenge prior to the first film's release and just after the 9/11 attacks. These stories take a dark turn, including examining the psychological aftermath of rape and war, and often leaving Hermione faced with the loss of her personal and scholarly potential to become a wife and mother. And while these stories at the time were, as Kustritz notes, heavily criticized, I would note that in effect they were not that different from the "real" endings Rowling devised for the epilogue of *Harry Potter and the Deathly Hallows* or *Harry Potter and the Cursed Child*, sadly.

But what above all must be emphasized is that while various fan fiction communities create interesting tropes, motifs, and sometimes even a consensus on characterization or events (called "fanon" as in "fan canon"), each community is a world unto itself. The rest of this essay is going to be concerned specifically with the community that Clare created and was a part of, and the fanons and characterizations that were considered the norm within it. Clare's version of Hermione is as a main character and a hero; the stories are told from her point of view as well as Harry's and Draco's, but the bulk of the action is still on the boys—a sort of blueprint for the further shift through to Clary in *The Mortal Instruments* books.

PROBLEMATIC INTERTEXTUALITY, A NECESSARY ASIDE (THE PLAGIARISM CONTROVERSY)

Before proceeding further, it is necessary to acknowledge and at least briefly discuss one of the more problematic aspects of Claire's fannish writing: accusations of plagiarism. In academia, plagiarism is a fraught topic that usually involves students; the current definition of "plagiarism" used by the Modern Language Association in their Statement of Professional Ethics reads thus:

> Using another person's ideas or expressions in your writing without acknowledging the source constitutes plagiarism .... [T]o plagiarize is to give the impression that you wrote or thought something that you in fact borrowed from someone, and to do so is a violation of professional ethics .... Forms of plagiarism include the failure to give appropriate acknowledgment when repeating another's wording or particularly apt phrase, paraphrasing another's argument, and presenting another's line of thinking. (6.1; see also Gibaldi, MLA Handbook, ch. 2)

It should be noted that fanfiction by itself is *not* plagiarism; it is recognized legally as acceptable Fair Use under the American Copyright Act. There have been several notable examinations of the legal status of fanfiction, with Rebecca Tushnet's (1997) article "Legal Fictions: Copyright, Fan Fiction, and A New Common Law" perhaps proving the most influential. Tushnet emphasizes that fan works are created and disseminated in a non-monetary capacity that does no damage to the "real" rights holders, and that "Copyright's purpose, after all, is to encourage creativity for the public interest, not only to ensure monopoly profits" for the vast corporate entities that produce popular media (p. 684).

A more recent essay by Lauren Lewis, Rebecca Black, and Bill Tomlinson, "Let Everyone Play: An Educational Perspective on Why Fan Fiction Is, or Should Be, Legal," argues that fan fiction should further be a protected form of creative writing because of its pedagogical uses, particularly for creative writing. "There is a great deal of anecdotal evidence that writing, editing, and reading fan fiction has led to the honing of skills sufficient for fan fiction authors to become bona fide, published writers," they write (p. 76). "Fan fiction communities can serve as a complementary and supplementary tool for students who need extra help with their literacy and composition skills. ... The peer reviewing and editing process is a learning exercise for all participants, as writers benefit from the pointed feedback, and readers benefit from heightened attention to rhetorical purpose and conventions" (pp. 76–77). This aspect is particularly pertinent as increasing numbers of authors both bridge the gap from fan to professional writer and are also open about doing so.

In 2006, fan critic Avocado wrote a lengthy exposé on what became known throughout fandom as the The Cassandra Claire Plagiarism Debacle. Avocado provides lengthy evidence through quotes and analysis of Claire's writing to point to what are indeed at best unattributed borrowings and, at least in one section, what is word-for-word copying of another author's text (in this case Pamela Dean's 1986 novel *The Hidden Land*). As chapters were posted serially on listservs, Claire claimed that the quotes and other borrowings were a "game" for close readers, and after a time attributions began to appear at the conclusion of chapter posts. However, the Dean quote was not included in this "game," which forced Claire to eventually apologize when this particular point of evidence led to the removal of her stories from Fanfiction.net, the largest fan fiction aggregator at the time. As Avocado noted, "Cassandra Claire thought incorporating material was acceptable in fanfiction—and being blacklisted had made her realize it was not" (The Cassandra Claire Plagiarism Debacle Part VIII).

The same day Avocado's exposé appeared, the final chapter of the Draco Trilogy was posted. In a short period spanning several weeks, the stories were removed from Fanfiction.net and Claire also encouraged fans to download pdf copies of her work as she was going to take them offline prior to her debut as a professional author in 2007; the ParadigmOfUncertainty listserv, which by then held a vast quantity of related fan art and fan discussion, was deleted altogether. While many of the elements of the Debacle are problematic, they are nonetheless interesting in demonstrating the evolving norms of online fan productivity and interactions, as well as illustrative of the spectrum of textual usage that spans from genuine plagiarism to fair use to transformative work. Further, it is one of the best known examples of community policing, in which standards and norms of behavior that had been silently assumed were revealed and subsequently articulated directly. For better or for worse, the Debacle is itself now the go-to example of acceptable usage in fan writing and communities.

CLARY-IS-CLARE-IS-HERMIONE? THE "POSTFEMINIST" HEROINE AND REVISING THE AUTHORIAL SELF

I mentioned at the start of this essay that I would like to examine the textual shifts of Claire's version of Hermione to her character of Clary as a "postfeminist" heroine. I recognize that the term "postfeminist" is incredibly loaded and, therefore, want to examine it a bit closer before going further. Postfeminism is a direct reaction to and recognition of the contradictions and absences in feminism (specifically the equally loaded "white feminism"); despite its common popular usage as an adjective to describe feminism as "over," it can be useful in dissecting and analyzing lacunae in popular culture. In this specific case, I want to look at Hermione/Clary as a postfeminist heroine in that she both subverts and conforms to established contemporary gender norms both in Rowling's work and in Claire's.

Rowling's iteration of Hermione emphasizes her as a bookworm, incredibly knowledgeable and helpful to Harry and Ron, but—as mentioned above—limited through the lens of Harry's point of view (and his/Rowling's interpretations of traditional male heroism). In the decade since the publication of the final book, Hermione's "happy ending" with Ron was rejected by many fans, and Rowling has admitted that in hindsight she regrets that pairing. In a 2014 interview she stated that "I wrote the Hermione/Ron relationship as a form of wish fulfillment. That's how it was conceived, really. For reasons that have very little to do with literature and far more to do with me clinging to the plot as I first imagined it, Hermione ended up with Ron" and adding "that Hermione and Ron would probably need relationship counseling" (Stedman). Despite fan criticism, Rowling apparently doubled-down when characterizing Ron throughout *Harry Potter and the Cursed Child* as a sexist bumbler with what appears to be a drinking problem. Though problematic in itself, this official epilogue-after-the-epilogue demonstrates why many people often want more from their beloved texts, as well as something more empowering (and less depressing).

Claire's interpretation of Hermione, in contrast, is of a confident, powerful, and attractive young woman, albeit one still less powerful than Harry or Draco, who are revealed to be "Magids"—incredibly powerful wizards with access to additional abilities and wandless magic. She is also caught in a love triangle between Harry, whom she has had a seemingly hopeless crush on for years, and a sympathetically-written and redeemed Draco Malfoy, who is revealed to be less loathsome than Rowling has presented him largely through being a victim of abuse and control by Lucius Malfoy all his life. This was not an unusual characterization of Draco: in fact, far from it. Fan renderings of Draco Malfoy during this period of time frequently took this approach, often specifically to present him as a romantic interest to either Hermione or Harry. Romantic entanglements in most fan fictions transformed the genre from children's literature to Young Adult or even purely adult fare, reflecting the broader audience of the books themselves as well as their authors.

Finally, it is the aspect of the author herself that should be examined in these various iterations. A common accusation against fan writers is of writing "Mary Sues," or female characters that are obvious stand-ins for the fan author herself. The term first emerged in the 1970s from *Star Trek* fandom to describe the common appearance of a female character who is attractive and youthful, highly skilled in her area of expertise, often with an unusual background (in *Star Trek* fan fiction this usually manifested as being half-Vulcan), and the romantic interest of one of the main characters. Camille Bacon Smith noted that despite much of the criticism, which "may be a self-imposed sexism … most fans will readily admit to having written at least one Mary Sue story" (p. 97). While the direct identification of an author with a character should be treaded upon lightly, J.K. Rowling has said several times that she based at least the eleven-year-old version of Hermione on herself (Trombetta).

Cassandra Clare, on the other hand, has stated that her character Clary is not based on herself, but rather on two friends of hers (Clare). However, her icons on her Livejournal and social media sites are often images of Clary, and at more than one book signing she has worn a yellow dress like that of Clary shown in the cover art for her books. The yellow dress gains additional significance when rereading *Draco Dormiens*, in which a yellow dress has significance to Hermione and Harry when she asks him when he started having romantic feelings for her:

> Harry looked flustered. He obviously hadn't been prepared for questioning. "I-I guess, I mean, I've known it for about two years. Before that it was probably true but I just didn't know it. I remember when I first realized. We were on holiday with your parents and you were wearing that yellow dress—it's not as pretty as the dress you have on now, but—" He gave her a worried smile. "You were so beautiful."

> Hermione remembered. She'd worn the yellow dress because it was the first time she would be seeing Harry after two months of vacation, and she'd hoped he would like it, but he hadn't said anything, anything at all. (p. 147)

The yellow dress that links Clare, Clary, and Hermione is a small detail, and yet one that clarifies the connections between the author and these texts. In revising the characters from her writing, Clare has also revised her authorial self: from Claire to Clare, and from fan writer to professional writer.

CONCLUSIONS

In 2013, Heidi8/Tandy wrote on her Tumblr about the fannish origins of Claire's series in a post entitled "Things that are not true."[3] First and foremost on this post was the charge that "Her books are reworking of her own fanfiction." Heidi8 argued that this was inaccurate:

> This is not true. You may think it's true because Tumblr repeats this lie over and over, but *it is absolutely not true.* Her books are original and, with the exception of a 3-page word-for-word recycled backstory for Draco—>Jace, do not contain plot points used in the DT. ... I don't know how many other ways we can say it; it's not fucking true.

While undoubtedly written with the best of intentions for Claire and her books, it is less accurate than Tandy, Claire, or others would like to believe. As this essay has shown, ties between creative works go well beyond "word for word" text; further, the original context of a composition, even if only in part, will *always* remain. To argue otherwise is naive at best and obfuscatory at worst. While a cultural stigma remains attached to fan works, perhaps such arguments cannot be avoided, but in the interest of textual history I would argue that these origins are valuable for a variety of reasons beyond the purely creative. There is a long tradition of women's social reading and writing, of which fan practices are only the most recent iteration. By acknowledging and preserving knowledge of these social contexts, scholars (and fans!) can trace the evolution of an author's work while still interrogating how we read both "texts" and "authorship."

Cassandra Claire's gendered revisions of Hermione and Clary, and Draco and Jace, speak to more than just intertextuality or the revision of a fan text into a professional one. Instead, her writings provide print (and electronic) records of the reception and interpretation of the *Harry Potter* novels—and characters—in a specific period and by a specific community of readers. By transforming the texts of these stories first in the Draco Trilogy and later in *The Mortal Instruments*, as an author Claire is able to talk back to the genre norms that were both met and subverted by Rowling in the first place. Readers of either text can appreciate how the emphases shift to include and empower heroines as well as heroes.

NOTES

[1] For example, journalist Aja Romano was herself a member of the HP BNF "Inner Circle" with Clare and Black. She is herself a sometimes contentious figure who has written for *The Mary Sue* as well as *The Daily Dot.*

[2] The ParadigmOfUncertainty listserv and its archives were deleted sometime in 2006, as were a number of relevant posts related to the listserv and the community there. Additional commentary and resources can be found in the "Cassandra Claire" entry at Fanlore.org

[3] Archived online at https://archive.is/9955p

REFERENCES

Avocado. (2016, August 4). *The Cassandra Claire plagiarism debacle.* Retrieved from http://web.archive.org/web/20131022155458/http://www.journalfen.net/community/bad_penny/8985.html#intro

Bacon-Smith, C. (1992). *Enterprising women: Television fandom and the creation of popular myth.* Philadelphia, PA: University of Pennsylvania Press.

Busse, K., & Hellekson, K. (Eds.). (2014). *The fan fiction studies reader.* Iowa City, IA: University of Iowa Press.

Cassandra Claire. Retrieved from http://fanlore.org/wiki/Cassandra_Claire

Clare, C. (2007). *City of bones.* New York, NY: Simon & Schuster.

Clare, C. (2012, April 22). *FAQ: Where do the names of characters and places in your books come from?* Retrieved from http://cassandraclare.com/?qa_faqs=name

Coppa, F. (2017). *The fanfiction reader: Folk tales for the digital age.* Ann Arbor, MI: University of Michigan Press.

Cordova, C. (Director). (2005). *Ringers: Lord of the fans.* San Francisco, CA: Stormcrow Entertainment.

Cordova, M. J. (2015). Because I'm a girl, I suppose! Gender lines and narrative perspective in Harry Potter. *Mythlore, 33*(2), 19–33.

Dalton, D. (2015, January 16). *If Hermione were the main character in "Harry Potter": Hermione Granger and the goddamn patriarchy.* Retrieved from https://www.buzzfeed.com/danieldalton/boss-witch

Decter, E., McG, Viola, M., Dale, J. M., Kulzer, R., Lynne, M., Shaye, R., & Reisz, M. (Executive producers). (2016–2019). *Shadowhunters* [Television Series]. Burbank, CA: Freeform.

Heidi8. (2013, September 2). *Things that are not true.* Retrieved from https://archive.is/9955p

James, E. L. (2012). *Fifty shades of grey.* New York, NY: Vintage Books.

Jamison, A. (Ed.). (2013). *Fic: Why fanfiction is taking over the world.* Dallas, TX: BenBella Books.

Jenkins, H. (1992). *Textual poachers: Television fans and participatory culture.* New York, NY: Routledge.

Kustritz, A. (1992). Domesticating Hermione: The emergence of genre and community from WIKTT's feminist romance debates. *Feminist Media Studies, 15*(3), 444–459.

Lewis, L., Black, R., & Tomlinson, B. (2009). Let everyone play: An educational perspective on why fan fiction is, or should be, legal. *International Journal of Learning and Media, 1*(1), 67–81.

Modern Language Association. (2017). *Statement of professional ethics.* Retrieved from https://www.mla.org/Resources/Research/Surveys-Reports-and-Other-Documents/

Staffing-Salaries-and-Other-Professional-Issues/Statement-of-Professional-Ethics/Read-the-Statement-Online

Romano, A. (2012, August 30). 10 famous authors who write fanfiction. *The Daily Dot.* Retrieved from https://www.dailydot.com/parsec/10-famous-authors-fanfiction/

Rowell, R. (2013). *Fangirl.* New York, NY: St. Martin's Griffin.

Rowling, J. K. (2007). *Harry Potter and the deathly hallows.* New York, NY: Scholastic Books.

Rowling, J. K. (2016). *Harry Potter and the cursed child, parts 1 & 2, special rehearsal edition.* Crawfordsville, IN: R.R. Donnelly & Sons.

Stedman, A. (2014, February 2). *J.K. Rowling regrets pairing Hermione with Ron instead of Harry Potter.* Retrieved from http://variety.com/2014/film/news/j-k-rowling-regrets-pairing-hermione-with-ron-instead-of-harry-potter-1201083320/

Tandy, H. (2013). *How Harry Potter fanfic changed the world* (or at least the internet). In A. Jamison (Ed.), *Fic: Why fanfiction is taking over the world* (pp. 165–174). Dallas, TX: BenBella Books.

The Cassandra Claire plagiarism debacle. Retrieved from http://fanlore.org/wiki/The_Cassandra_Claire_Plagiarism_Debacle

Trombetta, S. L. (2015, August 26). *9 real-life people who inspired Harry Potter characters.* Retrieved from https://www.bustle.com/articles/105610-9-real-life-people-who-inspired-harry-potter-characters

Tushnet, R. (1997). Legal fictions: Copyright, fan fiction, and a new common law. *Loyola of Los Angeles Entertainment Law Journal, 17,* 651–686.

Zwart, H. (Director). (2013). *The mortal instruments: City of bones* [Motion picture]. Munich: Constantin Film Produktion.

Cait Coker
Texas A&M University

U. MELISSA ANYIWO

9. A MONSTROUS NARRATIVE

Unraveling Gender and Ethnic Archetypes
in Showtime's Penny Dreadful

I have always loved monsters. Not so much because they frighten me,
but because they move me; their terrible loneliness, their stumbling
search for acceptance. (John Logan, 2015, p. 6)

Writer and creator John Logan reflects on the writing of Showtime's *Penny Dreadful* (2014–2016) underscoring the central intent of this short lived urban fantasy (UF): to reposition the multiplicity of monstrous faces that existed at the end of the nineteenth century, thus giving them a "certain empowering uniqueness" (Logan). As with *True Blood* (HBO, 2008–2014) another show created by a white, gay man Allan Ball, *Penny Dreadful* grapples with an urban fantasy landscape with a diverse yet intolerant society much like our own, where the monstrous is present inside all of us, by exploring a range of Othered figures, this time from gothic literature including Dorian Gray, Mina Harker, Abraham Van Helsing, Dr. Seward, Renfield, Count Dracula, Victor Frankenstein and his creature(s), Dr. Henry Jekyll/Lord Hyde.[1] In short, Logan makes monsters of us all; even the landscapes function as monstrous spaces ready to consume and destroy. In this way, *Penny Dreadful* appears to create a beautifully complex and enlightened version of the Victorian Age, informed by Logan's own position as a marginalized body. Yet, when you look a little closer, it becomes clear that this very repositioning of monsters as protagonists and making all of the characters flawed actually reinforces limited and marginalizing gender and ethnic stereotypes, providing simplistic archetypes rather than true diversity. Thus, the one Irish character is a drunken whore, the one Native American is a wise medicine man filled with secrets of the other world, and the only black character is a former slave trader and the first character of the primary cast to die and stay dead. While there are multiple images of womanhood, they all ultimately function as cautionary tales about what society does to those who transgress, just as with the original penny dreadfuls. Monstrosity on the show, despite showing the horror in all of us, actually reflects and reinforces our ideas of difference. This paper illustrates the ways Logan thus unintentionally

© KONINKLIJKE BRILL NV, LEIDEN, 2019 | DOI:10.1163/9789004394100_009

highlights the contradictions of diversity in the contemporary world, where we show enlightenment by punishing any who transgress, and ensuring that ethnic portrayals are diverse only in their monstrous appearance.

AN URBAN FANTASY

London is a character in Penny Dreadful, *and it's also really important for the audience to feel like the world of* Penny Dreadful *is all of these various places—it's the low end and it's also high society and everywhere in between.* (Logan, 2015, p. 6)

Penny Dreadful takes the fictional and makes it 'real' by rewriting the classic tale of *Dracula* and placing its characters alongside other horror protagonists of a 'real' 1890s London. As with the genre itself, the show relies on both the suspension of disbelief and the rebooting of the literal past, creating a text where "fantasy and the mundane world interact, intersect, and interweave throughout a tale which is significantly about a real city" (qtd in Blakemont, 2017). There is enough pseudo-factual content to make a believably historical image, making it an excellent example of the contemporary Americanized version of the Victorian Age, one focused on progress and change at all costs. As a pseudo-historic text, it therefore lays claims to a confusing verisimilitude that presents an imagined past as fact. Logan was careful to use historic events, 'real' locations (despite shooting in Dublin and Eastern Europe), and as a true UF text, overlays them with the fantastical. For example, core settings, such as The Grand Guignol and the Mariner's Inn, actually existed. The episode "The Day Tennyson Died" (Logan, 2016) focuses on the day the world lost a poet best known for his concerns about the legacies we leave when we die, grounding the increasingly otherworldly action in a tangible reality. Thus, while the audience suspends their disbelief, the story has a seeming authenticity that convinces the audience that, whilst the characters may be fictions, the world they inhabit is not.

In successful urban fantasies, the urban environment functions as a secondary character, used to tap into and build on our knowledge and understanding of particular cityscapes, it is of course what puts the 'urban' in fantasy.[2] But the existence of a cityscape alone is not enough to make something UF nor is the addition of magic to a story enough to make it fantasy. Clearly, writers believe that both elements are vital to create the complex landscape that reflects the world building of the genre. Yet, UF rarely functions entirely in a single city or metropolis. Even *Penny Dreadful* exists in multiple spaces, from Vanessa's upbringing in the country to Ethan's life in the Old West. Yet when it does utilize the metropolis, it does so in a way that exposes "urban life with its contrasts and paradoxes" (Blakemont, p. 15).

The *Penny Dreadful* landscape falls squarely in the category of Horror London, tales that are "frequently 'extremely vague about the actual geography' of the city. They dwell instead on a set of tropes to invoke a particular mood" (Louttit, p. 3). We recognize this archetypal image of Victorian London, inspired by Dickens, Sherlock Holmes, Jack the Ripper, and ceaseless versions that have embedded this ultimately fictional landscape in our consciousness in a way that actually places it out of time so that Diagon Alley in the *Harry Potter* Series (2001–2011) is as evocative as *Harlots* (2017–present) yet neither are set in the nineteenth century. "As Brunsdon notes, this image of the city is a familiar one, and 'requires only a gas street lamp, a cobbled street, a horse-drawn carriage and a wisp of mist to be identified" (Louttit, p. 3). Its repetition makes it an easy space for the fantastical, since its landscape is so recognizable to an audience.

According to Hephzibah Anderson instead of "trying to change or downplay the tone or signal self-awareness about it, *Penny Dreadful* gives the audience actual dark and stormy nights, and makes them actually scary and foreboding" (Slayton, 2014). Reflective of the horror at the heart of the show, London is a space showcasing the rapid progress of change at the end of the nineteenth century, illustrated by the mix of filth, poverty, and decay, representing a past that shows the tension between perceptions of the modern and primitive. Characters, such as Sir Malcolm, Lord Gray, Lyle Ferdinand, Madam Kali, and Lord Hyde, clearly exist at the top of the social order, so that the relative opulence of their surroundings is starkly contrasted with the teeming mass of the poor scrabbling for existence in a decomposing landscape. Particularly in Season 3, when we view an underground London filled with the poor and diseased living essentially as rats in the subways of the city, Horror London is filled with the monstrous exemplified in all aspects of life. Specific details, such as the advent of electricity, advances in medical science, and new technologies like photography, foreground the action demonstrating the problematic nature of change as it separates technological advancement by social class, increasingly keeping the working classes in the literal and figurative dark. The claustrophobic decay of London consistently underscores the emotional space the characters inhabit to the point that each episode opens with a landscape intended to signpost the action. For example, Season 2's "Fresh Hell" begins on bloody murder scene, and the rest of the episode is about images of death, including the witch Evelyn Poole (Helen McCory) singing in a bath of blood (Logan, 2015).

The existence of the Demimonde, the fantasy under the world, only further reveals the ugliness at the heart of London and humanity. Magic is central to the story, but Logan clearly illustrates that magic is not the real danger, rather the realities of city life are. Indeed, when the apocalypse begins, it fills the London air with noxious smog plunging the city into twilight. Yet, the smog caused by the rise of Lucifer is no different to the smog caused by the new factories of the industrialized city, and the residents are hard pressed to notice the apocalypse has even begun. Horror London's archetypal landscape thus embodies the monstrosity at the heart of this narrative.

The creature John Clare, the most marginalized of *Penny Dreadful*'s characters, becomes the one most connected to this decaying horror-scape. Sharon Gosling argues, "As the personification of Victorian modernity, the Creature shows us what Dorian Gray's visage refuses to reveal—the damage wrought by the visionary efforts that succeeded in pulling the future ever closer to the present" (Gosling, 2015, p. 150). His attempts to become a part of the world and find some measure of acceptance are consistently viewed through an unwelcoming landscape where humans struggle to survive in streets overflowing with sewage and where evil is the only way to survive. Interestingly, the creature represents the future, saying "The future belongs to the strong, to the immortal races, to me and my kind" (Logan, 2014). Yet Clare's treatment in the city embodies the treatment of those coded as different in a space where every character is monstrous, learning about human nature through observing a primarily cruel and violent London. His short-lived occupations at the Grand Guignol Theatre and the Putney Family Waxwork museum expose this contradiction by having the creature work in spaces where monsters are the core marketing element, and yet, he is rejected and betrayed in each space because of his own monstrosity. First appearing in "Fresh Hell" (Logan, 2015), the Putney Family Waxworks specifically reflects the changing times by having its owner decry the changing needs of London's population, no longer interested in a romanticized version of the past, instead wanting more and more horror reflecting the popularity of penny dreadfuls in their day. Thus, their version of London focuses on the "Chambers of Crime," tableaus of London's most horrific murder scenes, including the murder scene at the Mariner's Inn that opens the episode. Indicative of the modern being read back into the past, Logan's London makes a very contemporary argument about city life and the tensions between the old, and the modern informed by the inclusiveness of modern technologies, once again, creating excluding class divisions, and our desires for advancement have a dramatic impact on the natural environment.

If this is a fictional world, it takes very little examination to point out the historical inaccuracies. For example, while it is true that the core characters existed in nineteenth century novels, none of their originating texts were considered penny dreadfuls, a pejorative term for short horror texts sold in weekly instalments very much like the slasher porn of today. Furthermore, Dr. Frankenstein and his creatures were born in Mary Shelley's *Modern Prometheus* in 1819, a lifetime before Bram Stoker's *Dracula* (1897) or Oscar Wilde's *Dorian Gray* (1890). The show is set specifically in 1891, strangely predating all of the 1890s origin texts except Shelley's and Wilde's. Thus, the strength of the series lies not in its verisimilitude, but in the multiple ways Logan reads the present back into the past creating a landscape that reveals more about today than the end of the nineteenth century. The "Victorian London of *Penny Dreadful* has some sort of connection to a historical reality, but at the same time is twisted and ultimately adapted to fit the mood of the show" (Louttit, 2016), placing it clearly within the broad genre of Gothic Horror while utilizing the strongest elements of an urban fantasy. For Logan, London fits with his "prime directive for the series" to "make it true. For something to be meaningful it has to be true. If you can make it true for the audience, you can make it frightening, you can make it provocative, you can make it sexy, and funny, and moving" (Logan, 2015, p. 6).

MONSTROUS INSIDERS

There is a great deal to love about *Penny Dreadful*, but a core element is the way the show pulls together those coded as Others and gives them a voice. The Monsters of the show are rightly coded as such, while their actions are often juxtaposed with the monstrous behaviors of those normally insiders in society, particularly in the forms of Sir Malcolm, surgeon Dr. Frankenstein, and the aristocratic rake Lord Gray. Class distinctions are heavily present, as are the relative horrors of living in 1890s London. Just as the show's setting reflects the popularity of penny dreadfuls, it also occurs during a period of significant transition also reflected in the horror and fantasy texts of its day. All the characters are reflective of this transition with each standing on the cusp of change. The white male characters occupy a rarefied position denied others that provides them with growth and ultimately redemption, rewarding the colonizer while damning the colonized. While the female characters are discussed later, here unpacking the male protagonists helps uncover "a different theme, reconceptualising the monster and the fear it embodies for the 21st century. Now, it is no longer solely about how to fight a monster, but how to be one" (Schäfer, 2016, p. 14).

The impetus for the narrative is the kidnapping of Sir Malcolm Murray's daughter Mina. Immediately Logan thus repositions the source, *Dracula*, simply with the addition of a father and a new best friend for Mina. Sir Malcolm is, on the surface, a typical representation of Victorian manhood and the British Aristocrat. He consistently displays an entitlement only demonstrated by a class and a culture assured of always getting what they want when they want it. With few exceptions, every person Sir Malcolm interacts with is his social inferior, and his safe space seems to be treating people that way. Reflective of the historical period, he is a man who still believes in the rightness of British Imperialism best exemplified by the 'Scramble for Africa' (1890–1914) in its early years. As Nicholas Slayton describes him, "Sir Malcolm is the renowned explorer, the Great White Hunter going after a new prey, and unleashing his ruthless style of exploration onto the streets of London" (2014). While actor Timothy Dalton adds he's "one of those men who has profited from the great advance across the globe of the British Empire" (in Gosling, 2015, p. 88). Either way, he exemplifies the British aristocrat, in an age where there were still worlds to conquer and riches to exploit.

As Logan argues that monstrosity comes from within, we slowly learn the horror at the heart of Sir Malcolm's soul, and the weaknesses in his personality. In the episode "Séance" (3:2) Vanessa, possessed by the spirit of Malcolm's son, exposes the evil/selfish deeds he thought were between him and God. In his son's voice, Vanessa accusingly reminds him of their expedition and how his father let him die of malaria,

> Father … I am … weak … Can't feel my hands. There's no water. I can't swallow. You knew I was dying … didn't you, Father? Did you name a mountain after me? (2014)

Actually, Sir Malcolm names the mountain after himself. While this act is explored further, especially in the comic series, that act of selfishness pales in comparison to her other revelation of his parenting. Now possessed by Amun-Ra, Vanessa's words take on an increasingly angry tone as the séance moves to a crescendo. "I wonder when was the moment you knew you wanted to fuck her?" She cries out.

> Vanessa heard you … heard you fucking and she was curious. She walked closer, she rounded the corner and discovered you, the two of you, you know, fucking. fucking her cunt … Vanessa saw that … fucking animal. You man. You animal. You man. You animal. Betrayer! Creature! (Logan, 2014)

Thus, Sir Malcolm's failings as a father, abandoning his dying child and sexually abusing his daughter, informs the guilt that drives his desperate need to save Mina, and therefore find some measure of redemption. In this way, it is the white male colonizer who is the monster with no supernatural excuse, just his own toxic narcissism. Even his desire to save his daughter is ultimately selfish. As he tells Dr. Frankenstein, "To save her, I would murder the world" (Logon, 2014) ignoring the reality of his years of murder as colonizer. Yet it is Malcolm who puts Mina out of her misery at the end of Season 1. Logan gives him the chance for a new sort of redemption—saving Vanessa's soul and thus preventing the coming apocalypse. More importantly, he is also given a new chosen family, and one that accepts all sides of him. Still, Malcolm ultimately fails to protect and save anyone in this chosen family during the life of the show, and in Season 4, his heart is used to resurrect Vanessa allowing Lucifer to take over her soul (*Awakening*, 2017). Malcolm is thus a failure at all the elements expected of a Victorian male, even his stiff upper lip fails him in the face of continual defeat. Repeatedly, he is presented with challenges he cannot win, despite his position at the top of the era's social order. But it is a measure of the fantastic writing that each challenge and each failure allow for his emotional growth (apparently not possible before these events) so that he begins as a selfish vain man and ends by giving his life to save others. It's true he is a monster, he asks Vanessa "Do you know how many men I've killed? In Africa we walked in blood every step" (Logan, 2015). Yet, as a white male representative of imperialism, his crimes are if not forgivable, at least without personal consequence except through loss of others. He ends the life of the show just as wealthy, just as free, and if not redeemed, then at least forgiven. For him, Ethan's words become his story arc, "There are things you can't control. There are battles you lose. At the end of the day, the only thing we have is the people we trust" (2015).

If Sir Malcolm is the leader of this tragic crew of monsters, it is Ethan Chandler (Josh Hartnett), who, like America at the end of the nineteenth century, comes out on top and is clearly the true stalwart white hero. John Logan writes that one "of the joys of the show is looking at an archetype, accepting it and then realizing there might be something more complex behind it. I think that's what it is to be a human being. You present a certain thing to the world, but behind it is a lifetime of joy, mystery, despair, shame" (in Gosling, 2017, p. 18). As our doorway into the story, Ethan begins as the archetypal American that seems to live in the British imagination where all American men are brash, trash talking cowboys. As with Sir Malcolm, Ethan is a man running away from his true self, this time a real monster within rather than a monstrous personality. Yet like Sir Malcolm, he comes from money made on the backs of colonized brown bodies and the taming of the primitive natural environment. He tells Brona, that there "are such sins at my back it would kill me to turn around" (Logan, 2016), and like a true American, his path is to keep running forward and never look back; allowing his past to feel like the monster lurking around every corner.

Ethan is a 'real' American hero both in his fictional guise as gunslinger and in his reality, providing the one true connection Vanessa is allowed through the show. Indeed, Vanessa seeks him out because she has "a need for a gentleman who's comfortable with firearms and not hesitant to engage in dangerous endeavors" (Logan, 2014). His Victorian masculinity is embedded in the notion that it is his duty to protect those in need, especially women. The two women he falls for, Vanessa Ives (Eva Green) and Brona Croft (Billie Piper), are both victims in his eyes; Brona is destroyed by poverty and dying from consumption, and Vanessa hunted by an unseen menace. In both cases, he seems unable to help them without developing feelings, reflecting the deep emotional connections he makes with those around him. Even Brona confronts his love of the dying victim with the words "You're fucking a skeleton every night. There's no future in it for either of us" (Logan, 2015). It soothes his conscience to care for those he helps (or fails to) as if somehow emotion trumps action, such as when he abandons Vanessa to go 'find' himself. Like a true Romantic hero, he wears his masculinity and empathy like a cloak that ultimately excuses his darkest actions.

His heroic nature and attraction to seeming victims hides Ethan's dual nature, that of a literal monster that takes over for him during the full moon. While it is not until Season 2 that his werewolf nature is revealed, it was still a well signaled plot point that drove the narrative and his arc in important ways from the start. In his desire to run from the destruction his monster has caused in the United States, we realize he is also running from the monstrosity of America's conquest against the native tribes belying the idea that the monster is a creature detached from his core self. As another colonizer, though this time a representative of the violent US government, Ethan is again painted as a man who sees himself with "such sins at my back it would kill me to turn around" (Logan, 2015).

The audience slowly discovers that the two-natured Ethan is actually Lupus Dei, the 'Wolf of God,' sent to protect Vanessa and prevent the return of Lucifer. However, Ethan sees his wolf form as something to suppress, helped by the fact that he has no control over his transformation and no memories afterward. What's clear about his nature, however, is that as long as he buries and ignores it, he will never be able to control it or truly access his god given power. Thus, it is not until Season 4 that Dr. Seward finally helps him 'bond' with his monster and accept it as part of himself. Once he does, he is truly able to become the Wolf of God. Still, as with Sir Malcolm, Ethan's fears and secrets essentially prevent him from saving either of the women he loves. Arguably, his failures lead to Brona being reanimated by Dr. Frankenstein, and he abandons Vanessa in her darkest hour, allowing her to fall into the arms of Dr. Sweet and willingly give herself over to Dracula. Oddly enough, this American monster is the only core character to survive the apocalypse, transformed but still alive. Thus, he becomes the transition of empires from Britain to the US. Modernity replaces the new but with the same monsters as the past.

There are multiple male characters that highlight the complexities of nineteenth century manhood as seen through contemporary eyes, but it seems they are all coded as monstrous and appropriately punished. Lauren Rocha argues of Sir Malcolm and Ethan that in "their not being self-controlled, composed men, the characters' masculinity is put into question. Unable to identify with the societal masculine paradigm, they are not shown as autonomous; instead their agency is limited, marred by their contested identities" (2016, p. 34). But these varieties still make them versions of the same toxic manhood that carries a history of conquest and marginalization of colonized bodies. Even seemingly transgressive men like Ferdinand Lyle have the protection of gender and class so that, in his case, he might be marginalized because of his sexuality, but his job as an Egyptologist trades on the stealing of antiquities from victimized populations. Perhaps then it is Dorian Gray who best exemplifies the lie at the heart of Logan's desire to make every character equally monstrous. Gray is a man who willingly sells his soul to the devil, whose debauchery is literally channeled away from him into a hidden portrait. There are no consequences for the unending horror he inflicts on those around him out of boredom, at the very worst he is cursed with a growing sense of ennui which only causes him to seek out greater pleasures (including sex with Ethan Chandler). Yes, his condition means he is alienated from everyone around him, but he is wealthy, endlessly young, and male, making his travails meaningless yet indicative of white male privilege. The white men of *Penny Dreadful* are all surely monsters, but their privilege (including being created by a white man) mean that their consequences are always born by others, whether a portrait or the destruction of a civilization. As Ethan says,

I have stood at the very edge. I have looked into the abyss. If I'd have taken one more step, I would have fallen. But no matter how far I ran away from God, he was still waiting ahead. (Logan, 2015)

Would that we all had such certainty.

THE MONSTROUS FEMININE

We are not women who crawl. We are not women who kneel ... Women who are strong, and refuse to be degraded, and choose to protect themselves, are called monsters. That is the world's crime, not ours.
– Lily (Logan, "No Beast So Fierce," 2016)

Both praise and critiques of the show tap into the ambivalent and contradictory image of 21st century womanhood. On the surface, the core female characters—Vanessa Ives and Brona Croft—reflect a liberated version of the Victorian female. Here characters like Dr. Seward (Patty Lupone) or Madam Kali (Helen McCrory) suggest a version of the late nineteenth century where women could live beyond the limited boundaries of mother/wife and where they are allowed to save themselves. Yet, as we unpack these characters and their ultimate fates, we expose the ugliness of the images as they remind us that independent womanhood must always be repressed and punished.

Vanessa Ives is arguably one of the most intriguing characters on modern television. Logan gives her the "façade of the prim and proper Victorian lady, but her dark desires underneath ... attract very evil supernatural spirits" (Slayton, 2014). Played artfully by French actress Eva Green, Vanessa becomes the tragic heart at the center of the drama, her tragedy increasingly focuses the action, and we realize that this is not really a tale about saving the damsel Mina but Vanessa's soul. What makes this character so interesting is that she is complicit in her fall from grace, surrendering by choice at core moments and ultimately choosing to give her soul over to the Dark. In this sense she is like the other white characters who are allowed an interior life, especially Ethan, infected by a monster who shares her soul that she must accept. Logan argues that "the show is about empowerment, and she controls her own destiny." Then he reveals his privileged position with the belief that "To me, whether you're male, female, gay, straight, whatever—you control your destiny. You make the choices that are right for your morality and your ethics and your heart, and that's what she does. She owns her life, and at the end of the day, she owns her death" (qtd. in Gosling, 2015).

Vanessa, like Ethan, can only be at peace once she chooses to accept all sides of herself, even those elements that challenge her role as Victorian woman. More than anything, Vanessa only looks the part of upper middle-class Lady. But right from the opening scene, the audience views the contradictions inherent in her person. Our first frame is of Miss Ives praying before a stark wall featuring a wooden cross (Logan, 2014). From the barrenness of the landscape, you might be forgiven for thinking she is a nun or some devout worshipper, such as Silas in the *Da Vinci Code* (2006) who would go on to flagellate himself. But as she prays, a spider crawls over the cross and down the wall, an image that seems accidental until that same spider appears crawling over her shoulder. As she continues to pray, more and more spiders appear, leaving us to wonder if her prayers are causing the spiders, or if she is casting a spell, or is so corrupt that her prayers result in Satan's creatures revealing themselves. However, you view this scene, it illustrates that Vanessa is a monster described by Robert Yanal as "a being in violation of the natural order" (2003). She violates this natural order from childhood with every action juxtaposed with her best friend and neighbor Mina Murray, who represents everything good and pure and seems to instinctively know how to fit into societal expectations of the upper middle-class. Her empowering character appears reflective of the ways we hope to see women displayed today in a world where *Wonder Woman* (2017) can top the movie charts. Plus, she refuses to obey the societal rules, even when the men around her keep trying to save her. She is a decision maker and one used to going her own way and seems not to care at all about the way society sees her. While not being a babe-in-spandex, she can protect herself and displays a bravery usually reserved for the male characters. We see this at multiple points, but the end of Season 1 as the team moves in to rescue Mina from the Vampires lair, Vanessa walks unafraid through the center of the action as the men fight on the peripheries. The men trust her to do her part, including recruiting sharpshooter Ethan, for Sir Malcolm recognizes her as someone not in need of saving. We might argue that Miss Ives's journey is one of acceptance, but at multiple points, she makes it clear that she recognizes her weaknesses, for as she says to Dorian Gray, "There are things within us all that can never be unleashed" (Logan, 2014). She is painted as strong enough to defeat Dracula/Lucifer, if she so chooses. As she says to the Demon in Ethan's form "If your goal is to have me surrender to you, that day will never come" (Logan, 2014).

But that day does come at multiple times in her life, and at each moment she chooses to surrender enough for the demon to take a little more of her soul, highlighting her complicity and ultimate humanity. "Vanessa's position as transgendered female within the patriarchal structures underpins her position as a monster" (Schäfer, 2016, p. 13) and a destructive one at that. Essentially abandoned by society, she must wear a cloak of masculinity or at least manhood to survive, making her independence a matter of survival not choice. As we see in "Closer than Sisters," she has been hunted by 'evil' since childhood and her complicity in Mina's kidnapping is revealed as "a direct chain of events: Sir Malcolm's tryst in the maze leading to Vanessa seducing Captain Branson in the solarium … resulting in Mina marrying Jonathan

Harker and eventually falling under the spell of her Master" (Doviak, 2014). This back-story episode, told in the form of an unsent letter, provides the audience with evidence of the horrific punishment she endures for both her resistance and surrender. Either way, her character's monstrosity appears contained in her sexuality and the demon always sends her over the edge into 'abnormal' sexuality. In "Séance," we see her copulate with a stranger in an alley (while Dorian Gray watches from the shadows), and in "Closer than Sisters," that action is further explained when we see her finally surrender to the Demon in the form of Sir Malcolm. As Rocha argues,

> The manifestation of the demon during periods of sexual expression … points to the gendered emphasis of her body. Condemned for her sexuality, the demon could also be called her sexual desire; controlled, it does not pose a threat, but when it takes over, she becomes dangerous to those around her, especially men. All the while, she continues to fight it inside her, struggling to regain control of it. (2016, p. 37)

One of the themes this character, grapples with is agency or choice. This despite Logan's claim that "whether you're male, female, gay, straight, whatever—you control your destiny" (qtd. In Gosling, 2015). Her journey seems to prove the opposite. Or as Allisonn Keele notes: "Vanessa's descent is one that begs a question of all viewers about choice. There are paths of light and darkness that we face every day, which ones do we move towards" (2014). It seems that no matter what choice she makes, those that matter most are consistently illusions, forced at the moment when she has been hounded and hunted beyond sanity or when she is at her weakest. Teenage Vanessa was unprepared for the feelings the sight of her mother and neighbor cheating with each other would evoke in her innocent mind. Yet, when she turns to her faith for help, unlike Ethan, "God didn't answer me. But another did" (Logan, 2014) even as a devout child she is unworthy of God's grace. Adult Vanessa continues to ask for help but now knows she has no choice but to fight for herself.

The demon cannot enter her body without her consent. Yet his seductive nature plays on Vanessa's isolation, promising her a chance of normality, or at least relief from the endless hunting of her soul. "Closer than Sisters" illustrates the ways she has no choice. The Demon (in Sir Malcom's form) reminds her "You sought it out and fucked it. You could have shut the door at any time. You still can. Right now" (Logan, 2015). Unlike the men in this tale, her monstrosity is really her desire to be free and is a constant punishment for her desire. Vanessa has some of the protections of her class, but unlike Sir Malcolm, that protection only comes from her ability to ignore the ways she is seen and treated and is certainly not a measure of the respect she should be allowed to garner.

Yet perhaps it is Brona/Lily who best makes this argument. Brona has been brutalized by poverty her whole life. In Northern Ireland her choice was marriage to a violent man, or a life of prostitution. Her 'choices' bring her to the Mariner's Inn in one of the poorest parts of London, where she daily witnesses those who come and go through the sailing port. Her life was one of degradation and even Ethan's attentions merely reminded her of what she was denied because she was born Irish, and a woman, and poor. But Brona is denied release once consumption takes her life. Instead she is turned into a literal creature by Dr. Frankenstein, given a new name, Lily, and a new expectation, to worship her creator. She escapes and falls into the liberating arms of Dorian Gray, a man whose only desires are pleasure and freedom from boredom. As an immortal, Lily makes female liberation her primary purpose, recruiting fellow prostitute Justine (Jessica Barden) and setting out on a path to free her sisters. This seems like a truly feminist cause, and a reflection of the enlightenment of the show. But Logan cannot help but reveal his embedded patriarchal ideas about the dangers of unfettered womanhood. In "Ebb Tide" he has Lily say:

> Please know that the day a good woman will have to undergo such indignity is almost past. We will not have to suffer our children to starve and freeze and die dishonored on cold hills. We will not be hungry forever. We will rise. (Logan, 2016)

Without context, the words seem empowering and the character an example of the burgeoning Women's Movement in both Britain and the United States. Yet her actions come after a moment of violence and in the previous episode "No Beast So Fierce" she tells Justine:

> They think as you do, the suffragettes. No, our enemies are the same but they seek equality. And we? Mastery. And they're all so awfully clamorous. All this marching around in public and waving placards. That's not it. How do you accomplish anything in this life? By craft. By stealth. By poison. By the throat quietly slit in the dead of the night. By the careful and silent accumulation of power. (Logan, 2016)

Like all women, her true desire is not equality but mastery. She has become a literal monster but one whose nature is more monstrous than the creature a man forced her to be. Once again, a woman who seeks equality is painted as insane, dangerous, murderous, and ultimately deserving of a violent end. Vanessa, Brona, Madam Kali, are all women punished for their presumptions of independence. Such women must be suffering from hysteria of a psychosexual nature that warps their minds and confuses their understanding of their place. Ultimately, regardless of his intent, Logan consistently proves that there is no true forgiveness for the woman who transgresses.

COLONIZED BODIES

What am I but an extension of you? All your sin emptied into me. I am your other half, your truest self.
> – John Clare (Logan, "And They Were Enemies," 2015)

Regardless of the genre, the colonized body remains a contested space that reflects the attitudes of white writers and their characters. The representation of ethnic identities consistently functions to make the viewing audience feel more comfortable while ignoring structural inequality and the illusory progress of race relations. Primarily because of the limited knowledge or understanding of the interior lives of peoples of color, representations of race focus and thus reinforce limited racist stereotypes. Despite John Logan's assertion that this is a show in which everyone is monstrous in their own way, as Dragos Manea writes, "no matter how diffuse or layered their image is in our memory, we nevertheless conceive a familiar figure, with certain key traits we assume to be essential" (2014, p. 40). Thus, while characters coded as non-white on the show demonstrate a veneer of diversity, as with women, their inherent lack of diversity helps reinscribe our understanding of difference and justifies racial privilege.

John Logan's casting seemed intended to reposition the ways non-whites have been presented in shows set in the Victorian Age. Thus, Dr. Henry Jekyll (Shazad Latif) is recast as the bastard son of an English Lord and his Indian wife.[3] His appearance in the final season offers a broader life for Dr. Frankenstein, finally providing him with a place to continue his work. Indeed, his character is really there to serve the white characters, and, even in the comics, he is given almost no discernible life beyond Frankenstein. While Logan does a worthy job of incorporating the ways Jekyll has had to deal with racism his entire life, as with Lily, his desire is for vengeance against the society that ostracised him. Moreover, unlike the other monsters, he makes himself and others monstrous in his desire to find a cure for violent tendencies. In this way, his actual role is to 'cure' Lily of her worrying desire for freedom, to make of her a true woman who would love Dr. Frankenstein unconditionally because he made and thus owns her. Like the colonial body he is clearly there to serve his white master, even when that master is his social and economic inferior.

Unlike the other male characters who apparently have to deal with marginalization with grace and forbearance, Jekyll is bitter and angry, carrying a rage that will ultimately help him create his alter ego Lord Hyde. In the Season 3 episode "The Day Tennyson Died," Dr. Frankenstein reminds Jekyll of their years at college:

> You remember late at night in our room, over the hookah, listing the names of all the boys who had insulted you? The recitation of your potential victims. Your nightly prayers. That anger inside you, all that rage. Have you lost it? (Logan, 2016)

The bullying he endures is simply used as more evidence of his naturally unevolved colonial behaviour, certainly not representative of his father's social class. He is a split personality with one foot in the old world and one in the new, yet unwelcome in both. With an Empire that stretched the globe, mixed ancestry was not unusual in the Victorian Age, but mixed-blood was an insurmountable stain, and Dr. Jekyll reflects not only this institutionalized racism, but the reality that English blood is not enough to dilute the savagery of Indian, African, Aboriginal or any other contaminant. While his inclusion in the narrative may appear an example of enlightenment, it is easy to note that he is yet one more example of difference coded as monstrosity. In this narrative, his need to become Lord Hyde is actually nicely justified and reflective of the problems facing the marginalized today.

> In the end, we must be that thing the world demands of us. We must take the lust and the avarice and the ambition and bury them. All the alien, ugly things! All the things we really are! The other one! The other man! We cannot allow him! (Logan, 2016)

Both Dr. Jeykll and Dr. Alexander Sweet (Christian Camargo) illustrate the fears of external forces infiltrating the British Isles bringing with them the horrors of difference and change. Both characters, one the villain and one at least not, hide their monstrous natures beneath a veneer of civility and good breeding. Unlike Sir Malcolm or Ethan Chandler, these characters are born damned by a monster they cannot hide behind their non-white skin.

In a similar vein, the one black character Sembene (Danny Sapani), provides an even more direct example of Logan's embedded ideas about difference, this time showing peoples of African descent as an intrinsically servile race, completing the show's lessons about which monsters are deserving of a life and which are not. Sembene appears as a member of the core cast of monsters from the first episode. The initial appearance of a black character in Victorian London prompted some excitement. Logan's desire to rewrite the past seemingly allowed for the appearance of a black character in an age when they have been consistently presented as invisible. For instance, in the era *Penny Dreadful* was set, there had been evidence of Africans as far back as the Roman era. During the reign of Elizabeth I, owning a 'Blackamoor' was considered the height of sophistication,[4] and by the Victorian era with the Atlantic Slave Trade at an end and as a result of centuries of discrimination, the black population stagnated at a tiny 10,000 mostly clustered into London's poorest ghettos and other port cities like Liverpool. By the 1880s, the British Empire had taken hold of much of the 'Dark Continent,' including Nigeria, South Africa, Kenya, and the Sudan, arguably keeping knowledge of Africa a core part of the ways the British saw themselves. Thus, the invisibility of ethnically diverse characters in stories about this era (think Sherlock Holmes, Victoria etc.) highlights the racism at the heart of television today.

Despite functioning in a fictional Victorian England where many of the core characters transcend or complicate archetypes, Sembene exists as a complete stereotype of Black manhood and the exotic, African. Everything about this lone black character reflects embedded white attitudes read back into the past. Sembene of the show is a Senegalese slave trader and long-time friend and confidante of Sir Malcolm. Sharon Gosling notes that "he inhabits a space at Sir Malcolm's side that seems created from mystery itself. There is no explanation of how or why he came to be in London, other than the obvious connection of Sir Malcolm's travels in Africa" (2015, p. 96). Yet this mystery is indicative of typical portrayals of Africans unimportant enough to have an interior life or experiences beyond the scope of the white characters. Even when we are provided with a small sketch of his life it is only that filtered through Sir Malcom's experiences ("The Awakening," 2017). Logan makes Sembene taciturn and mysterious even telling the actor Danny Sapani that his "mystery is his strength" (qtd in Gosling, 2015, p. 99). We know nothing about this man because there is nothing worth knowing. As Amanda Hobson writes, "The fear, pain, and privileges … of contemporary racism play out in erasure and denial of the lived experiences of individuals, who must grapple with the psychological wound that constitutes never seeing oneself represented" (2015, p. 33).

Of course, it is very clear that Sembene is Sir Malcolm's inferior and (just like the Uncle Tom archetype) wants nothing more than to give his life in service to his white boss despite the misconstrued moments where he appears to speak his mind. There are a number of clear racist elements surrounding the character that go unnoticed because they are so often used to explain blackness. For example, Sir Malcolm meets Sembene in Africa on his expedition to find the source of the Nile River. Sembene could have literally been anything—a guide, a fellow explorer, a ship captain—but instead Logan makes him a slave trader, worse still an enslaver of his own kind. Sembene says to Ethan, "I have been much feared and hated in my life. By my people, by yours. These marks mean I was a slave trader. 'Tis my sin to live with" (Logan, 2015). The manifestation of Ethan's sin is hidden in the form of his wolf, for Sembene not only must he contend with blackness, his scarification displays his sin in ways that cannot be hidden.

In this way, his monstrosity stands in shocking contrast to the transgressions of the white characters. While the sins of the other characters can all be described as poor decision making, Sembene is the only character to choose an occupation so truly immoral (even in the 1890s). This allows the audience to ignore any 'issues' this character has because they were his choices and reflective of the African nature. In Season 4 "The Awakening," when we finally get to see the tribulations that brought Sir Malcolm and Sembene together it becomes clear that Sembene saves Sir Malcolm's life twice as his search for the mouth of the Nile leads to the deaths of his son and almost every single one of Sembene's slaves. As he says to Ethan in "Possession," "I saved his [life] and now he is my responsibility" (Logan, 2014). Despite saving Sir Malcolm's life, it is Sembene who believes it is now his duty to take care of him, including cooking and cleaning, as payment. In short, a successful self-made independent businessman gives up everything to become the man servant of a visiting client. As has been typical in representations of peoples of color, Sembene would rather devote his entire life to serving others, for in the white imagination those of color are always happiest when serving their natural superiors.

While it has become such an oft-repeated archetype it is often spoken about in jest, in the white imagination, even in an enlightened production such as this, the black character must die first. Indeed, it is even more apparent in a show where no one of importance appears to stay dead.[5] His death is at the hands of Ethan in werewolf form, and so it is both worse (Sembene is a 'respected' member of this family) and better (since Ethan is not really at fault since he can't control his wolf form). In other words, Season 2 ends by destroying the inferior black body, as if it was the only main body that is disposable. To make matters worse, Sembene is essentially replaced in Season 3 by a wise medicine man from the American West, and Season 4 introduces us to more wolves coded as non-white. The black man always dies first because the black body is the least important and the one least deserving of saving. A typical trope on screen and in the real world, it is so ordinary that it garners little reflection and is always justified as self defense because of the insurmountable animalistic African nature. Placed alongside his chosen inferiority Sembene's death is entirely reflective of the embedded desire to demonize and thus marginalize blackness in ways that reverse the blame. Ultimately, it's fascinating that Logan has Sembene signpost his difference from the white cast in "What Death Can Join Together," when he says "For all the blood we share, for all the miles we have walked Malcolm, we are not the same" (Logan, 2014). Logan's non-white bodies are not the same and are therefore underserving of a happy ending, redemption, or meaningful growth.

A MONSTROUS NARRATIVE

The ultimate challenge and goal of Penny Dreadful *is really simple ... It's to say, 'We are all monsters.' Within all of us we have secrets, we have demons, we feel alienated from the world around us ... Whether those human beings are actual human beings, reanimated corpses, vampires, or any other demon you can name, they're all searching for the same thing, which is someone to look back at them with compassion.* (John Logan in Gosling, p. 14)

At its heart *Penny Dreadful* was an amazing show that brought the complexities of today's world into the dark, foggy streets of Victorian London. Logan's attempts to demonstrate that we are all monstrous and thus all searching for the same thing is a wonderful sentiment that definitely works on the surface. However, the joy of analysis is the ability to deconstruct the images provided and place them in a broader context. Thus Logan, despite coding himself as an outsider, is still a privileged white male living in a society where white men can be seen in multiple ways and have multiple dreams. His embedded attitudes about race and gender arc unrecognized by him so that the persons of color come across as tone deaf aberrations in an otherwise enlightened series. Similarly, his images of womanhood may seem liberating until you realize the end result for their behavior. In a summary of the final season finale "The Blessed Dark," Logan says,

Ethan loses a father but gains a father in Sir Malcolm. Sir Malcolm has finally lost the last remnant he has of his family, which is Vanessa, but he gains Ethan as a surrogate son. Dorian Gray is left alone, framed in a doorway as if he's in a portrait, in this wistful, poignant place. Lily is left empowered, walking out and choosing to live any sort of life rather than live the compromised life with Dorian. ("John Logan on the Series Finale," Showtime, 2017)

All of the female characters have been killed (Lily is still the reanimated Brona), the one black character is dead, and the brown characters were evil anyway so one is dead and the other forgotten about. It is true that Sir Malcolm and Ethan are now 'brutalized by loss,' but they are alive as are Lyle Ferdinand, Victor Frankenstein, and John Clare. All the white men survive this tale of horror and loss. Regardless of his words, John Logan's actions make it clear who the real monsters are.

NOTES

1   Oscar Wilde's *The Picture of Dorian Gray* (1890); Bram Stoker's *Dracula* (1897); Mary Shelley's *Frankenstein* (1818); and Robert Louis Stevenson's *Strange Case of Dr Jekyll and Mr Hyde* (1896).
2   Think for example Spike Lee's love letters to New York in movies like *Do the Right Thing* (1989) or 25th Hour (2002) or Jim Jarmusch's use of a decaying Detroit in *Only Lovers Left Alive* (2013).
3   The actor Shazad Latif is that very British mix of English, Scottish, and Pakistani.
4   "In 1601, Elizabeth I issued a proclamation expressing her 'discontentment by the numbers of blackamoors which are crept into the world" (Olugosa, 2016).
5   Broana Croft dies of consumption in Season 1 and is reanimated by Dr Frankenstein. In Season 4 Vanessa is resurrected as Lucifer using the heart of Sir Malcolm who immediately returns as a ghost.

REFERENCES

Anderson, H. (2016, May). The shocking tale of *Penny Dreadful*. *BBC Culture2*. Retrieved from http://www.bbc.com/culture/story/20160502-the-shocking-tale-of-the-penny-dreadful
Blakemont, A. J. (2015, October 8). *Urban fantasy and its illustrious origins* [Blog]. Retrieved from http://blakemont.com/urban-fantasy-origins/
Doviak, S. V. (2014, June 8). *Penny Dreadful* 'Closer than Sisters' review. *AV TV Club*. Retrieved from https://tv.avclub.com/penny-dreadful-closer-than-sisters-1798180634
Dragos, M. (2016). A wolf's wye view of London: *Dracula, Penny Dreadful*, and the logic of repetition. *Critical Survey, 28*(1), 15–29.
Gosling, S. (2015). *The art and making of* Penny Dreadful: *The official companion book to the showtime series created and written by John Logan*. London: Titan Books.
Hobson, A. (2015). Brothers under cover: Race and the paranormal romance novel. In U. M. Anyiwo (Ed.), *Race in the vampire narrative*. Rotterdam, The Netherlands: Sense Publishers.
Keene, A. (2014, June 8). *Penny Dreadful* recap: Closer than sisters. *The Collider*. Retrieved from http://collider.com/penny-dreadful-recap-season-1-episode-5/
Lawson, M. (2014, May 21). A bookish thriller for the post-literate age: Make way for the "million-dollar dreadful." *New Statesman*. Retrieved from https://www.newstatesman.com/culture/2014/05/mark-lawson-penny-dreadful-bookish-thriller-post-literate-age
Logan, J. (Creator). (2014). *Penny Dreadful: The complete first season*. Los Angeles, CA: Paramount Home Entertainment.

Logan, J. (Creator). (2015). *Penny Dreadful: The complete second season.* Los Angeles, CA: Paramount Home Entertainment.

Logan, J. (Creator). (2016). *Penny Dreadful: The final season.* Los Angeles, CA: Paramount Home Entertainment.

Louttit, C. (2016). Victorian London redux: Adapting the gothic metropolis. *Critical Survey, 28*(1), 2–14.

Rocha, L. (2016). Angel in the house, devil in the city: Explorations of gender in *Dracula* and *Penny Dreadful. Critical Survey, 28*(1), 30–39.

Schäfer, D. (2016). *Nosferatu* revisited: Monstrous female agency in *Penny Dreadful. Gender Forum: An Internet Journal for Gender Studies, 60,* 1–2.

U. Melissa Anyiwo
Department of Politics and History
Curry College

U. MELISSA ANYIWO AND AMANDA JO HOBSON

10. THE URBAN FANTASY CLASSROOM

The Urban Fantasy genre has rich applications in any classroom, easily incorporated into history surveys, women's studies, literature, communications, and a plethora of other disciplines. The following chapter provides questions and assignments directly linked to the themes covered by the authors throughout this book. Everything is suitable for any level of college study, helping you weave this text seamlessly into any course.

UNDERSTANDING URBAN FANTASY

1. Screen Gems is a movie production studio known for its urban fantasy action films, such as *Ultraviolet* (2006) and *The Mortal Instruments: City of Bones* (2013). Have students explore the worlds of Screen Gems using at least two films or movies series such as *Underworld* or *Resident Evil* and catalog the core genre themes connecting them back to urban fantasy.
    a. Compare and contrast their findings using either/and Gal's or Benefiel's chapter in this text.
    b. Have students create a movie poster of the next great Urban Fantasy action film that reflects its core themes and fits into Screen Gem's stable of products.
2. Cassandra Clare's hugely successful *Mortal Instruments Series* is equally categorized as urban fantasy and young adult. Split your class into two teams and have each team read and/or watch *Mortal Instruments: City of Bones* from one of the two genre perspectives. Have each team try to convince you that the film most accurately fits into their chosen genre.
3. Urban fantasy often deals with people (and monsters) attempting to understand the nature of goodness.
    a. Watch *Angel* "Awakening" (4:10) and "Soulless" (4:11) and have the students discuss what makes a person good or evil. Does the existence of a soul really determine a person's behavior?
    b. Watch Angel "I Will Remember You" (8:1) and Being Human UK "The Boy Who Cried Vampire" (1:4). How do other people's perceptions of monstrosity impact an individual's view of themselves?

4. Urban fantasy is often credited with its enlightened portrayal of peoples coded as different. Challenge this argument by reading Anyiwo's chapter on *Penny Dreadful* and watch the episode "And They Were Enemies" (2:10) exploring the ways Urban Fantasy reinforces images of race rather than contesting them.

5. Supernatural creatures exist across genres, but genre impacts their portrayal and characteristics. Splitting the students into small groups, have each group:
   a. Choose a supernatural creature (witch, vampire, werewolf, etc.).
   b. List the characteristics of the creature by genre (horror, romance, young adult, and urban fantasy).
   c. Create a Venn diagram or vision board that brings together the characteristics and connections to their chosen genre.

6. Transmedia storytelling reflects how urban fantasy is not only fluid across genre boundaries but also across media, moving from novels to television and film and on to graphic novels and other visual media.
   a. Have students read Guitar's chapter and define the concept of transmedia storytelling and the ways it functions in the world of *Buffy the Vampire Slayer.*
   b. As many urban fantasy narratives move from television to film then to novelizations and graphic novels (see *Penny Dreadful* and *Buffy the Vampire Slayer* as examples), have students examine pieces from different media forms and collect examples of how the method of delivery influences urban fantasy narratives.

GENDERED PERSPECTIVES

1. Urban Fantasy is often described as an empowering genre that shows strong independent women with (super)heroic powers. Challenge this concept by having your class subject *Underworld Awakening* (2012) and *Underworld: Blood Wars* (2016) to the Bechdel test.[1] Do movies present different arguments about women when directed by a man (.... *Awakening*) than by a woman (... *Blood Wars*)? What arguments does Ana G. Gal make, regarding the overall series and its claim to empowerment?

2. Now that Urban Fantasy is an accepted genre, scholars include stories that precede its origins in Laurell K. Hamilton's *Anita Blake Series*. Have students watch *Xena: Warrior Princess* "A Day in the Life" (2:15) and *Wonder Woman* "The Boy Who Knew Her Secret" (3:20 & 21) alongside

Sarah Smith's chapter on *Wonder Woman* and the Bechdel Test. Explore the ways these shows both fit and do not fit the genre.

3. Read Sarah Smith's chapter on *Wonder Woman* and the Bechdel Test and think about the ways we judge visual content.
   a. If you identify as a woman, think of a time that you had a conversation with another female. Would your conversation pass the Bechdel Test? How often would your conversations pass, or would not? Why do you think this is the case?
   b. Alternatively, if you are reading this as someone who identifies with a gender other than female, reflect on conversations you have had that would pass or would not, remembering to remove the female gender role.
   c. The Bechdel Test is rather simple in its design. Do you think it can be used as an effective tool for grading gender roles in media? How would you improve the test?

4. According to Candace Benefiel, Laurell K. Hamilton's *Anita Blake Series* attempts to deconstruct womanhood for a "new generation." Explore the ways female protagonists are presented in contemporary urban fantasy by having students read Benefiel's chapter and watch *Blood Ties* (2007–2008) "Blood Price 1" (1:1), *Lost Girl* (SyFy 2011–2015) "It's a Fae, Fae, Fae World" (1:01), and/or *Van Helsing* (Syfy, 2016–present) "Seen You" (1:2).

5. Sexual violence is central to many urban fantasy texts, used as a narrative device to create motivation for characters, as an initiator of power, or for characters to seek revenge. Choose at least two texts that rely on sexual violence as a core narrative trope from the following: Hamilton's *Danse Macabre*, Grossmen's *The Magician* or the first season of *The Magicians*, Karen Marie Moning's *Dreamfever,* and *Buffy the Vampire Slayer* "Seeing Red."
   a. Compare the context of the act of the sexual violence and the purpose it appears to serve within the narratives.
   b. Look for examples of how the characters that experience sexual violence cope with the trauma.
   c. In the fall of 2017, the #MeToo movement arose as activism addressing sexual violence. Have students posit the impact this movement might have on images of sexual violence in urban fantasy.

6. The terms 'witch' and 'wizard' are historical terms containing clear gendered expectations. Have students watch *Charmed* episodes "Witch

Trial" (2.1) and "Morality Bites" (2.2) the *Dresden Files* "Things that go bump" (1:11) and *True Blood* "Soul of Fire" (4:11) and catalog the specific ways that the magical practitioners are presented. Explore the meanings behind the images presented on screen alongside Hobson's chapter "Bewitching Bodies ...." In what ways do each of these shows add to or detract from gendered stereotypes about witchcraft?

7. Consider the specifically gendered nature of the historical witch trials and their portrayal in urban fantasy by reading Hobson's chapter. Then have students watch *Charmed* episodes "Witch Trial" (2.1) and "Morality Bites" (2.2), *Buffy the Vampire Slayer* episode "Gingerbread" (3.11), and *Penny Dreadful* episode "The Nightcomers" (2.3) and catalog the ways witch trials play a role in contemporary popular culture. In what ways are hysterias against witches specifically gendered?

8. Urban fantasy narratives often depict female protagonists as hypersexual, from Screen Gems' "Babes in Spandex" films to the cover art of novels, such as Kim Harrison's *Dead Witch Walking*. Have students examine the covers of urban fantasy novels and recreate a cover that emphasizes the female protagonists' powers instead of their sexuality.

9. *Gender Warriors* is a text that attempts to uncover and critique Urban Fantasy. Have the students examine the cover art of this text and explore the ways it replicates and/or challenges representations of women in popular culture.

ACTIVITIES

1. Sarah Smith's chapter on Wonder Woman reflects on the ways the character inspired and empowered her as a child.
   b. Have students reflect on a fictional female character and a female from their own lives that inspires them?
   c. Using a graphic organizer like a Venn diagram, have students list the traits of each person highlighting the ones that overlap.

2. Split the class into teams and have each construct their own test version of the Bechdel Test with a minimum of three requirements to assess the roles of women in media. Have them present their test using at least one example that passes and one that fails.

3. Have students watch *Buffy the Vampire Slayer* "Storyteller" (7:16) and explore the world of Buffy from Andrew's perspective. How does the nature of Buffy herself change when seen from an alternate perspective, especially that of a self-professed enemy?

4. In *Buffy the Vampire Slayer* "Hush" (4:10), everyone in town wakes up to discover they can no longer speak. Have students recreate the central premise of the episode by trying to silently communicate during class time. Have them reflect on the different ways we communicate.

5. Have students watch *Supernatural* "The Real Ghostbusters" (5:09) alongside Coker's chapter "The Problematic Fan-Girl ..." and explore the worlds of cosplay.

   a. What elements make a successful cosplay design?

   b. As Coker demonstrates, many urban fantasy creators are fans of other series. Discuss the ways fan communities and cosplay impact the creation of urban fantasy worlds.

   c. Have students design their own cosplay that reflects the various aspects of the urban fantasy genre.

6. Have students watch season 1 of the YouTube series *Carmilla* (2014–present) alongside Coker's chapter "The Problematic Fan-Girl ...." Have them create their own fan fiction from either your choice of text or their own. Visit *Archive of Our Own* for examples of fan fiction from multiple fandoms.

7. Have students read Guitar's chapter on *Buffy the Vampire Slayer* and Coker's chapter "The Problematic Fan-Girl ..." and then read or watch Cassandra Clare's "The Draco Trilogy," *Supernatural*'s "Sympathy for the Devil" (5:01), and/or season 1 of the YouTube series *Carmilla*. Discuss the ways in which fans impact the metanarratives of original source material. Is fan fiction plagiarism?

8. In order to explore issues of adaptation, read Lev Grossman's *The Magicians* and watch the first season of Syfy's *The Magicians* or read Charlaine Harris's *Midnight Crossing* and watch the first season of NBC's *Midnight, Texas*.

   a. Have students reflect on the impact of adaptations of urban fantasy from literary texts to film and television.

   b. Using another urban fantasy novel, have students create a plan for adapting the text to a television show and consider what aspects would need to be amended or removed and why. How would the adaptation be different, if creating a single film instead of a television series?

   c. Using a different urban fantasy novel, have students create a plan for adapting the television show to a graphic novel. Consider what aspects would need to be amended or removed and why. How would the adaptation be different, if no longer limited by technical considerations?

NOTE

[1] "The *Bechdel Test*, sometimes called the *Mo Movie Measure* or *Bechdel Rule* is a simple test which names the following three criteria: (1) it has to have at least two women in it, who (2) who talk to each other, about (3) something besides a man" (Bechdel Test.com).

U. Melissa Anyiwo
Department of Politics and History
Curry College

Amanda Jo Hobson
Women's Resource Center
Indiana State University

U. MELISSA ANYIWO AND AMANDA JO HOBSON

11. THE URBAN FANTASY UNIVERSE

Or What to Read or Watch Next

INTRODUCTION

With such a genre-blending universe, Urban Fantasy (UF) texts are wide ranging in their themes while all fitting clearly under the same banner. The following chapter offers a limited selection of what we believe are the best examples of the genre's core themes. Since the UF blends together so many genres, the texts listed can sit in multiple categories, thus the organization also reflects the strongest thematic elements of the text. We have also highlighted texts that have an impact on the portrayal of gender within UF, specifically narratives that engage with issues of representation of gender, characters' struggles with gender dynamics, and the reliance on sexual violence as a trope.

URBAN FANTASY WORLDS

The genre-blending of urban fantasy lends itself well to developed universes that unfold over multiple texts. The following represent the most popular worlds, often featuring a mix of monsters. These series feature ensemble casts of characters with the occasional central figure, but it is through communal efforts that the characters overcome the obstacles set forth in the narrative.

Laurell K. Hamilton, *Anita Blake, Vampire Hunter Series* (1993–present) [Book series]

> The *Anita Blake, Vampire Hunter Series* follows the adventures of necromancer Anita Blake, a kick-ass vampire hunter, whom the vampires have nicknamed the Executioner, in a world in which vampires and other supernatural creatures have announced their presence and are fighting for their rights. Beginning with the publication of *Guilty Pleasures* in 1993 through the twenty-fifth book *Crimson Death* (2016), Hamilton's work is the foundation to urban fantasy, blending horror, fantasy, romance, and detective fiction, spiralling into erotica in the middle of the series, and eventually landing in a hybrid universe unique

© KONINKLIJKE BRILL NV, LEIDEN, 2019 | DOI:10.1163/9789004394100_011

to her style, as evidenced in both the *Anita Blake Series* and her *Merry Gentry Series*, creating a complicated and intricate mythology over the course of the series. The series follows the life and relationships of Anita Blake, as she raises the dead for a living and helps solve preternatural crimes, with Anita becoming a necromancer and a living vampire—a human-succubus—making her question the line between human and monster. [Contains adult content and sexual violence]

Karen Marie Moning, *Fever Series* (2006–present) [Book series]

The *Fever Series* focuses predominantly on MacKayla "Mac" Lane. In the first novel, Mac discovers that she is a Sidhe-Seer, meaning she can see the true faces of the Fae, can sense magical items and nullify Fae powers. Through the series she meets other Sidhe-Seers, all women imbued with powers that help them fight the Fae. When the Unseelie Fae break free from their prison and invade the human world, Mac and her allies must find the way to neutralize an evil living book and stop the Fae from destroying what is left of Dublin and the rest of the world. [Contains sexual violence]

The Blade Trilogy (1998–2004) [Motion picture series]

Loosely based on the Marvel Comics character of the same name, this urban fantasy (currently at 3 films) focuses on Blade (Wesley Snipes) a hybrid vampire-human daywalker who possesses all the strengths of both species in a world where there are both 'born' and 'made' vampires. The dark and brooding trilogy functions around finding a cure for vampirism and destroying those that exist. Each movie brings to life a different cityscape reflective of both its vampiric content and the historical setting, i.e. *Blade Trinity* released after 9/11 begins in Afghanistan. The series utilizes the core themes of action horror and offers one of the few treatments of vampires of color in cinema.

Jessica Andersen, *Final Prophesy Series* (2008–2012) [Book series]

The *Final Prophesy Series*, also known as *The Nightkeepers Series*, begins as ancient Mayan demons provoke the apocalypse. The only thing that can stop the impending end of the world are the Nightkeepers, warriors able to tap into the powers of the Mayan gods. Most of the Nightkeepers have been raised by caretakers who spirited them away when their civilization collapsed, and they have no knowledge of their destiny or their heritage. Over the course of eight novels and one novella, the Nightkeepers split into pairs of "Gods-destined" mates, which allows their powers to increase exponentially. The series relies heavily on tropes from the romance genre, but it also draws on horror, fantasy, science fiction, and mystery.

Shannon K. Butcher, *Sentinel Wars Series* (2009–2015) [Book series]

The only thing that stands between murderous child-attacking creatures, the Synestryn, and the world are the Theroni, an all-male group of warriors sporting living tree tattoos with mystical powers and excellent sword fighting skills. Cursed to turn evil if their life tree loses its leaves, each Theroni warrior must find their mate thereby unlocking their access to mystical power, which can help them win the war. The series currently has nine novels and two novellas and is incomplete, but Butcher says the series will continue with a new novella.

Grace Ellis and Shae Beagle, *Moonstruck* (2017–present) [Comic book series]

Rated for all readers and targeted toward a young and new adult audience, *Moonstruck* is a comic series set in a college town of Blitheton, where supernatural beings live with humans. Barista werewolf, Julie, her maybe girlfriend werewolf Selena and her best-friend centaur Chet, embark on an adventure to solve magical mysteries. This series is queer friendly featuring trans and non-binary characters, such as Chet who uses they/them pronouns. *Moonstruck* displays a commitment to representing gender, sexuality, racial, and relationship diversity for humans and mythical beings.

Patricia Briggs, *Mercy Thompson Series* (2006–present) [Book series]

Narrator and protagonist Mercy Thompson is a mechanic and coyote shapeshifter. Unlike other urban protagonists, Mercy inherited her ability to shift from her father, who was a member of the Blackfeet Nation, making Mercy and her father "Walkers," Native American shapeshifters whose transformation is freed from the moon's cycle. Werewolves, other shapeshifters, Fae, vampires, witches, and more populate this urban fantasy series, which has ten novels and several comic book stories and adaptations to date. Indicative of the gender-blending genre, Mercy's journey reflects much of the contemporary woman in a violently male world as she navigates pack politics, relationships, marriage, step-parenthood, and trauma over the course of the series. [Contains sexual violence]

MAGIC AND WITCHCRAFT

Though every UF universe features magic or mystical creatures, not every series foregrounds witchcraft or magic wielding individuals. The following narratives center magic at the heart of the narratives, even as the types of magic users vary with necromancers, druids, magicians, witches, sorcerers, and more. The images of the witch and magic wielder within these stories rely on historical ideas about witchcraft and contemporary concepts of Wicca and neo-paganism. In these series, the characters learn that having mystical powers does not solve normal every-day problems, instead magic merely compounds those difficulties and creates a whole new set of issues. These series articulate the notion that with magic comes a great deal of responsibility, usually to save the world from the forces of darkness.

Laurell K. Hamilton, *Merry Gentry Series* (2000–2014) [Book series]

Half-human supernatural private detective Merry Gentry is in hiding and being hunted by the Seelie Fae queen, the Queen of Air and Darkness. Over the course of nine novels, Merry builds relationships with her group of consorts, as they attempt to stem the weakening of the Fae's power and usher in a newer power based in sex magic. Merry's living magic brings energy back to the fairy mound and raises power in her men and her allies. Ultimately the series quickly moves away from the urban detective to become an exploration of the uses of magic.

Jim Butcher. *The Dresden files* (2000–present) [Book Series]

Jim Butcher's series helped define Urban Fantasy, the first-person detective mystery with a heavy dose of the supernatural, from a male perspective. Harry Dresden is the classic film noir protagonist, a wizard and private investigator driven by loss to become a cynical anti-hero, who increasingly becomes the only person between humanity and the destruction of earth by supernatural forces. There are core differences in Butcher's characterization of Dresden, that highlight its male driven narrative creating a very different tone from the likes of Laurell K. Hamilton's *Anita Blake* or *Merry Gentry* series.

Sera Gamble, John McNamara, and Michael London, *The Magicians* (2015–present) [Television series]

Based on Lev Grossman's *The Magicians* novel series, the Syfy Channel's series follows six graduate students (Quentin, Alice, Elliot, Margo, Penny, and Kady) enrolled in Brakebills, a hidden magic university in New York, as well as the best friend of one of the students (Julia). For those enrolled in Brakebills, they learn to hone their magical skills through their coursework, but Julia's path to learning magic is piecemeal learning with the hedge witches. When an enemy attacks Brakebills and threatens to destroy magic in all worlds, the seven central characters must accelerate their studies to save it. The series explores sexuality, including gay and bisexual relationships, sexual pleasure, and sexual violence, and the characters also deal with issues of substance abuse, depression, and trauma. [Contains sexual violence and discussions of self-harm]

Julie Plec, *The Originals* (2013–present) [Television series]

A spinoff of the CW hit *The Vampire Diaries*, *The Originals* tells the tale of the first family of vampires, Klaus (Joseph Morgan), Elijah (Daniel Gillies), and Rebekah (Claire Holt) Mikaelson as they attempt to reclaim their place as New Orleans ruling monarchs. The show focuses on the battle between the witches of New Orleans and the vampires, pulling in much of New Orleans vodun lore. [Young Adult]

Cassandra Clare, *The Mortal Instruments Series* (2007–2014) [YA Book series 1–6]

This YA series plays with numerous urban fantasy tropes, including a secret society of magic-users alongside "the real world," wars between vampires and werewolves as well as humans and demons, and a cultural war between magic-users who want to protect normal humans and those who disdain them. 'Normal' girl Clary discovers that she is secretly a Shadowhunter, a group of humans with angelic bloodlines who fight demons and must rediscover her parents' past in order to save her mother, while caught in a love triangle between her best friend and a boy who may be her long-lost half-brother. The series also explores LGBT characters and self-acceptance, including a queer romance with an actual happy ending. (Cait Coker)

Jordan L. Hawk, *Whyborne & Griffin Series* (2012–present) [Book series]

Hawk's *Whyborne & Griffin* mixes historical fiction, fantasy, queer romance, mystery, and detective fiction set mainly in the small coastal (fictional) city of Widdershins, Massachusetts. Percival Endicott Whyborne is a scholar, working in the Ladysmith Museum translating ancient and unknown languages, when former Pinkerton turned private detective Griffin Flaherty arrives in town only to discover that the cult responsible for the death of his Pinkerton partner has been fully established in Widdershins. Whyborne learns that he has supernatural magical powers, as a sorcerer, passed down from his mother's family, which he must master in order to save Widdershins and the world. Over the course of the ten novels to date, Whyborne and Griffin travel the globe facing monsters and working to understand magic, while building a solid relationship that they must hide from the society around them due to laws against homosexuality in the Victorian era in which the novels are set.

John Logan, *Penny Dreadful* (2014–2016) [Television series]

This inventive urban fantasy from John Logan (James Bond *Spectre*, *Sweeny Todd*) takes classical figures from the nineteenth century and brings them to life in a spooky dark Victorian London. The show begins with Sir Malcolm Murray, an explorer searching for his missing daughter Mina with her former best friend the seductive clairvoyant Vanessa Ives. But it quickly becomes a complex psychological horror tale that explores the nature of monstrosity as the characters fight to save the soul of Vanessa, hunted by Dracula, here the fallen son of god. Well-known fictional characters like Dorian Gray and Dr. Frankenstein interact with new creations like the American sharpshooter and Wolf of God Ethan Chandler and a new incarnation of witches in the Nightcomers to create a fascinating version of late nineteenth century London. The show also plays with UF tropes like witchcraft, a protagonist with powers outside of their control that grow exponentially, and the overarching question about the nature of good and evil. Cancelled after only three seasons, the show continues in comic form.

Constance Burg, *Charmed* (1998–2006) [Television series]

Witches kicking the forces of evil's asses weekly, while they look beautiful and stylish and have grand and often heart-wrenching love affairs all with the support of their sisters: that is the theme for The WB's popular show about the Halliwell Sisters, otherwise known as the Charmed Ones. Wielding the "Power of Three," Prue (Shannen Doherty), Piper (Holly Marie Combs), Phoebe (Alyssa Milano) find out they descend from a line of seriously powerful witches and are the prophesized Charmed Ones, when their Grams (Jennifer Rhodes) dies unexpectedly. After Prue dies in the season three finale, Piper and Phoebe discover they have a half-sister, Paige (Rose McGowan), who had been given up for adoption, which reconstitutes the "Power of Three." The Halliwell's interact with all manner of mystical creatures over its eight-year run, including mermaids, Furies, demons, warlocks, Banshees, Wendigos, angels—including a few angels of death, Valkyries, and so much more. The sisters and their familial line do not only wield magical powers, such as premonition, empathy, telekinesis, freezing or exploding things (and people). They are also practitioners of Wicca, or "The Craft," engaging in on-screen rituals.

THE TELEVISED URBAN DETECTIVE

Television offers an excellent place to see the multiple representations of the central figure in urban fantasy, the supernatural detective. These worlds function as contemporary film noir—stylish dark urban environments featuring cynical damaged anti-heroes trying to regain their souls in a world where few people are innocent. Adding an overlay of the supernatural has created a sub-genre of its own, creating core archetypes and interchangeable premises.

Barney Cohen and James D. Parriott, *Forever Knight* (1992–1996) [Television series]

This is the earliest example of the urban vampire with a soul, creating many of the ideas that now form this archetype. The show followed the life of Nick Knight (Geraint Wyn Davies), an 800-year-old medieval knight working nights as a detective in Toronto, Ontario. As will become commonplace, Knight struggles to find redemption for his early years as a vampire when he embraced his nature, which he does by helping the helpless while searching for a cure. Along the way we meet his still hedonistic vampire 'family' Lucien LaCroix (Nigel Bennett) and Janette DuCharme (Deborah Duchêne), who serve as his constant temptation. Finally, a long drawn out tragic romance is present in the form of Natalie Lambert (Catherine Disher), a city medical examiner, who knows his secret and ultimately wins his heart. Over three seasons, the Canadian show explored many of the themes expected of the film noir police procedural, such as a weekly and season long big bad, and yet its supernatural themes allowed the show to explore darker themes in the past and the present, lending it an epic feel lacking in the non-supernatural.

Koslow Munson, *Moonlight* (2007) [Television series]

A short-lived CBS crime procedural, *Moonlight* centered on the story of Mick St. John (Alex O'Loughlin), a World War Two vet turned against his will by his bride Coraline (Shannyn Sossamon) on their wedding night. After a typical period of hedonistic pleasure, we follow private detective St. John, as he seeks to repay society for his crimes by helping those who cannot help themselves all the while searching for a cure for his condition. Here, the love interest is reporter Beth Turner (Sophia Myles), who knows what he is and tries to be more than the weekly damsel-in-distress. In this universe, vampires are wealthy, powerful, and thriving secretly in the modern world. There's even an episode where the French Revolution is presented as a vampire purge. The core hedonistic vampire Josef Kostan (Jason Dohring) provides much of the humor and moral argument about good and evil. A show before it's time, Moonlight just missed the latest vampire craze, with both the C.W.'s *Vampire Diaries* and HBO's *True Blood* beginning two years later in 2009. The show is also notable as a text that keeps the vampire away from cities defined by darkness to the shining false light of Los Angeles.

Joss Whedon and David Greenwalt, *Angel* (1999–2004) [TV Series]

A classic urban fantasy show that closely follows the themes of film noir and the anti-hero private detective. Following his departure from Sunnydale and Buffy, Angel (David Boreanaz), the vampire with a soul, heads to the City of Angels, Los Angeles, where he tries to find redemption by helping the helpless through Angel Investigations. A perfectly drawn urban fantasy that treats the City of Angels as a secondary character, Angel explores the complex nature of good and evil as he and his motley crew attempt to save the souls of those who have lost their way, losing and saving their own souls in the process. The show remained a spin off while BtVS remained on air, sharing episode arcs, and bringing over characters Cordelia Chase (Charisma Carpenter), Wesley Wyndam-Pryce (Alexis Denisof), Harmony Kendall (Mercedes McNab), Faith (Eliza Dushku), and of course Spike (James Marsters). With an expanded universe that takes the audience to other dimensions and time periods, *Angel* explored the complex nature of right and wrong, good and evil, and the nature of the soul even having Angel take over Hell's law firm Wolfram and Heart. A rich series with some standout episodes, such as "Awakening" (Whedon, 2003) and

"Not Fade Away" (Bell & Whedon, 2004) – probably the most frustrating finale of all time. Luckily the series continues in comic form.

BABES IN SPANDEX & URBAN WARRIORS

The image of the female urban warrior is surprisingly monolithic. Even when they are in novels, protagonists follow the template of Trinity visualized by the Wachowskis in the *Matrix Series* (1999–2003) and popularized by Screen Gems in the forms of Alice and Selene from the *Resident Evil* (2002–2016) and *Underworld Series* (2003–2016) respectively. Such characters are usually—shorter than average, white, heterosexual, brunette, with a serious leather/latex fetish and a passion for weaponry. These females, who appear physically strong and supernaturally enhanced, might be most easily described as fantasy images for today's males raised on video games and action films. Women who could shoot a gun, fix a car, drink a guy under the table, have awesomely dirty sex, and probably leave before you woke up. Yet the very things that appear reductive are actually the source of their empowerment suggesting a more equalitarian future for women (at least on television). Ultimately the babe-in-spandex represents two contradictory images where women are either independent action heroes or fetishized images primarily for male consumption that transmit lessons about the dangers of unfettered womanhood.

Joss Whedon, *Buffy the Vampire Slayer* (1997–2003) [Television series], (2007–present) [comic book series]

> *Buffy the Vampire Slayer* is a series that focuses on the journey of Buffy Summers (Sarah Michelle Gellar), a young high school student tasked with eradicating vampires, demons, and other forces of evil. The series follows Buffy through high school, college, and into adulthood where the forces of darkness often interrupt her desire to live a normal life. She is aided in her fight against evil with the help of watcher Giles (Anthony Stewart Head) and friends Willow (Alyson Hannigan) and Xander (Nicholas Brendan), often affectionately referred to as the Scooby gang. Buffy's romantic pursuits often become entangled with her sacred duty as slayer, since she has a penchant for falling in love with vampires, first with Angel (David Boreanaz)—a vampire with a soul—and later with Spike (James Marsters)—a vampire that eventually earns his soul back for Buffy. The show was revolutionary during its time for its feminist and queer themes. The series continues in comic book form. (Jenna Guitar) [Contains sexual violence]

Len Wiseman, *Underworld Series* (2003–2016) [Motion picture series]

This continuing series focuses on the journey of female vampire Selene (Kate Beckinsale), as she moves from slayer to a day walking hero sought as a prize in the endless war between, vampires and Lycans (werewolves). Hunted down by both species, Selene and Lycan-Vampire hybrid Michael develop a romantic bond that ultimately results in a born-hybrid daughter with psychic and superhuman healing abilities. Based on Trinity in the *Matrix Series*, Selene is the archetypal 'babe-in-spandex' dressed more for clubbing than fighting (including heeled boots) and a fighting style that blends martial arts and gun play. With each film coming in at less than ninety minutes, *Underworld* provides an easily accessible UF series that demonstrates core ideas about fighting womanhood and the working woman fighting against sexist ideals.

Paul W.S. Anderson, *Resident Evil* (2002–2016) [Movie Series 1–6]

The *Resident Evil* series is the large screen adaptation of the popular Capcom video game of the same name. Released by Sony Pictures Entertainment, there were six movies following Alice (Mila Jovovich) who discovers her purpose and reason for being while fighting the evil Umbrella Corporation that created and released a bioweapon that initiated a zombie apocalypse. Throughout the series we are introduced to characters from the video games, such as: Jill Valentine (Sienna Guillory), Carlos Olivera (Oded Fehr), Nemesis (Matthew G. Taylor), Claire Redfield (Ali Larter), etc. while dramatically changing the source content. The character Alice did not exist in the video games but was a creation by the films writer and director as a cipher for the audience. Alice becomes the archetypal urban warrior, who leads a ragtag collection of heroes to save what's left of humanity (Sarah Smith).

Jocelynn Drake, *Dark Days Series* (2008–2011) [Book Series 1–6]

The *Dark Days Series* is a classic urban fantasy with some interesting twists. Mira is a vampire with the rarest of powers, pyrokinesis. Shunned as a human, her transition to vampire only compounded her marginalization. Now feared by the very combustible vampires, she was forced to spend years as the hammer of the Vampire Ruling Council, who wiped her memory after every mission to prevent her from remembering her own strength. Over the course of six books, flame-haired Mira does begin to remember that strength and her powers grow exponentially as a result, with perfect timing as the vampire's natural enemy the Naturi are threatening to break free of their prison and destroy the world. The series explores many of the genre's typical tropes without seeming generic, with Mira's uber-masculine partner Dananus openly dealing with falling in love with a woman who is more powerful than him in every way, while they are even stronger together, discovering that joining their magic can have catastrophic results. The series also explores the gendered ways conflict is handled, and we watch Mira go from using male determined violence to defeat those coded as enemies, to working with women of all sides to come to a diplomatic solution that ultimately saves the world and ushers in a new age of inter-species cooperation.

PARA-TEXTS & THEIR OFFSHOOTS

The world-building inherent in urban fantasy lends itself to transmedia storytelling, texts that exist across multiple platforms, extending stories beyond their source material. Such artefacts include adaptations on film and television, comic series, and fan texts. All of the following choices reflect the different ways paratexts have been used to keep stories going long after an initial series ends.

Krysty Wilson-Cairns. *Penny Dreadful* (2016–present) [Comic Series]

John Logan's *Penny Dreadful* is just one more show to utilize the comic novel format to continue a story after it was cancelled, as *Buffy* and *Angel* did earlier. As a Showtime production, there are multiple marketing products featured on the show's own dedicated site such as *Clue*, the Demimonde card game, tarot cards, and an endless array of branded clothing and jewelry. However, the transmedia element comes with the comic series that began in 2015. Written by executive producers Krysty Wilson-Cairns and Andrew Hinderaker, the 5-issue prequel explored the origins of the Sir Malcolm's search for his daughter Mina and introduced us to the Dracula characters Jonathan Harker and Lucy Westerna (rewritten as a feminist gunslinger). Season 4: The Awaking, (2017–present) rejoins the narrative six months after the events of the Season 3 finale offering a post-apocalyptic landscape in which Lucifer rises from Hell to take over the world. Released from the confines of the TV screen, the story has become infinitely more epic showing a global apocalypse. The format also allows fans to experience many of the character developments skipped over in the show such as the origins of Sir Malcom and Sembene's relationship (3:2), the real nature of Dorian Gray's immortality, or the fates of Lily/Brona Croft, and Dr. Jekyll/Lord Hyde.

The Buffy Universe

It would be fair to say that it was Joss Whedon who perfected the concept of the transmedia narrative, and there remains no other paratext with such broad applications throughout culture and continuing long decades after the Buffy's cancellation in 2003. Officially referred to as the Buffy Expanded Universe, Joss Whedon has cleverly been open to multiple expansions of his initial adaption of the original camp movie. Jenna Guitar's chapter effectively details the most important aspects of the expanded universe, including a discussion of Season 8, but a few are detailed below.

Jenny Owen Youngs and Kristin Russo, *Buffering the Vampire Slayer* (2016–present) [Podcast]

> *Buffering the Vampire Slayer* is a podcast currently in its fourth season (2018) that watches and discusses each episode of *Buffy the Vampire Slayer* in chronological order and spoiler free. The co-hosts Jenny Owen Youngs and Kristin Russo read the show through a feminist and queer lens and end each episode with an original song recapping the episode. Youngs and Russo have welcomed many fellow podcasters and queer entertainers to guest on their podcast, while also interviewing original cast members from the show about their experiences on the set of BTVS. (Jenna Guitar)

Buffy Studies

The importance of Buffy to broader cultural studies is reflected in the existence of a well-defined scholarly area in ways unseen with any other paratext. Buffy Studies, like its paratext, is a truly interdisciplinary area of study that offers textual analysis in a variety of contexts beyond literature illustrating the ways that the show has become the most studied pop culture text. Whedon Studies offers the annual International Conference, *Slayage*, as well as the award-winning academic journal of the same name. Thus far the academic area has resulted in hundreds of scholarly works demonstrating that the world of Buffy and the aca-fan will be relevant for years to come.

The Dresden Files Universe

Reflective of its continuing success, there are few more expansive UF universes than Butcher's *Dresden Files*, a world that has expanded to become a complete transmedia universe across multiple formats broadening and deepening the source material. Straight adaptations include a two-volume roleplaying game (2010), and audio books read by James Marsten (2002–present). The true transmedia universe develops the core paratext by offering entirely new tales and delving more deeply into different perspectives of the first-person narrative. For example, in 2007 Canadian TV aired a production that refocused the narrative around Dresden's (Paul Blackthorne) relationship with police officer Lt. Connie Murphy (Valerie Cruz), allowing us to view the story through multiple other eyes and deepening fan understanding of the source. But the show also changed core elements such as changing the age Harry came into his powers from 16 to 33 or making the Harry's iconic mini a jeep. Butcher has prolonged this trend with a continuing graphic novel series, including the prequel *Welcome to the Jungle* (2008), multiple short stories and novellas all offering new stories.

The Wonder Woman Universe

This is a strange version of a paratext primarily because every entry significantly alters the source content. Still, this demonstrates the endless cultural relevance of an image created by a man in the 1940s.

William Moulton Marston (Charles Moulton) and artist Harry G. Peter, *Wonder Woman* (1941–present) [Comic Series]

> The red, white, and blue clad Wonder Woman character was created during World War II and the story initially depicted her fighting military forces as well as a variety of fictional supervillains for the United States. Wonder Woman has also regularly appeared in comic books featuring the Justice Society and Justice League. The island nation of Themyscira is her homeland where she is considered a demi god with the official title of Princess Diana of Themyscira, Daughter of Hippolyta. Away from the island, she adopts the name and identity of Diana Prince. She has been described in numerous comic issues as "beautiful as Aphrodite, wise as Athena, stronger than Hercules, and swifter than Hermes." Wonder Woman has no real weaknesses and is a superb combat fighter. Her story has evolved with each decade and writer/artist influence keeping her endlessly current. (Sarah Smith)

William Moulton Marston (Charles Moulton) and artist Ross, Stanley Ralph., Wonder Woman. Season 1. The New Adventures of Wonder Woman. Season 2 (1975–1979) [TV Show].

> An American television series based on the DC Comic, Wonder Woman. Lynda Carter, 1972 Miss World USA, stars as Wonder Woman/Diana

Prince. Lyle Waggoner, comedic actor and Playgirl model, stars as Steve Trevor Senior in season one and Steve Trevor Junior in seasons two and three. Season one is set in World War II during the 1940s just as the original comic and aired on ABC. Diana takes on the identity of a Navy Yeoman Petty Officer First Class. The second and third seasons are set in the 1970s with Steve Trevor being the son of the first season's character, but all other cast members (not Carter) were changed. For these two seasons, Diana assumes the identity of an agent in the Inter-Agency Defense Command (IADC), a CIA/FBI-type organization. The comic origins were kept in the series through an animated title sequence and locations within the show all illustrated with comic panels. The iconic spin was actually the suggestion of Lynda Carter when the show's producers were struggling with how to demonstrate Diana's transformation proving once again the importance of female input into characterizations of womanhood. (Sarah Smith)

Patty Jenkins, Scott Snyder, Allen Heinberg, and Jason Fuchs, *Wonder Woman* (2017) [Motion picture]

A triumphant adaptation of the initial comics, Diana (Gal Gadot), a princess of the Amazons, shares a flashback from 1918 that tells us her story. Raised on a sheltered island paradise, Diana is trained to be an unconquerable warrior. When a pilot, Steve Trevor (Chris Pine), crashes on their shores and tells of a massive conflict raging in the outside world, Diana escorts him home, heading to an early 20th Century London to stop the war she believes is influenced by the Greek God of War, Ares (David Thewlis). She enters the world of men for the first time, believing her mission is to promote peace and destroy Ares. Through her journey with Steve, Sameer (Saïd Taghmaoui), Charlie (Ewen Bremner), and The Chief (Eugene Brave Rock), she discovers her true destiny and learns the nature of humanity. The film is also important in the representation of women in films because Patty Jenkins was the first woman to direct an American studio superhero film and the film broke box office records with its release. The most modern urban warrior, Wonder Woman continues in the DC Universe. (Sarah Smith)

Marvel Cinematic Universe

Comic book adaptations have been an important aspect of popular culture since the 1960s, but when Disney purchased Marvel Studios in August 2009, the *Marvel Cinematic Universe* (MCU) began a course that would make it a cultural juggernaut. The MCU begins with the 2008 release of *Iron Man* and currently spans nineteen films, ten television shows, and new comic book arcs with more of all mediums in production already. In addition, there are a wide range of video games connected through characters, if not always through plot. The MCU is an ideal representation of a paratexual urban fantasy because engagement and thorough understanding of the MCU means spending time minimally with a large quantity of comics, television, and films. Kevin Feige, President of Marvel Studios, has been a producer on every MCU film. We are choosing to highlight a few specific examples of the MCU that offer unique engagements in the urban fantasy genre.

Ryan Coogler, *Black Panther* (2018) [Motion Picture]

> Set predominantly in the fictionalized African nation Wakanda, *Black Panther* weaves together fast-paced superhero fight sequences and special effects with political and family drama, as well as romance and fantasy. *Black Panther* follows T'Challa (Chadwick Boseman), the Black Panther, whose father was killed just days before the action of the film begins. T'Challa is surrounded by brilliant and competent women advisors that are all warriors in their own ways, including his former girlfriend Nakia (Lupita Nyong'o), his sister Shuri (Letitia Wright), Okoye (Danai Gurira) the general and leader of the Dora Milaje—the elite group of all female royal bodyguards, and Queen Mother Ramonda (Angela Bassett). The film broke box office records and demonstrated the importance of representation in films, especially superhero films. Urban landscapes play core aspects within the narrative from Compton, California, to Busan, South Korea, and the capital city of Wakanda, which is shrouded from the world by technology.

Jon Watts, *Spiderman: Homecoming* (2017) [Motion picture]

> Peter Parker, a.k.a. Spiderman, has had many incarnations on our movie and television screens. When Peter is bitten by a radioactive spider and he's given supernatural powers, the city literally becomes Peter's playground as he swings through the buildings. In the most recent incarnation, *Homecoming*, Peter (Tom Holland) actively seeks ways to help his neighbors by fighting crimes, all while trying to finish his homework and pining for a young woman in his class. He wants so badly to be useful to Tony Stark (Robert Downey Jr.) and the Avengers that he often makes the mistakes of a teenager who wants to help: he doesn't listen, he thinks he is the only one that will act, and he overreacts because he doesn't yet know how to fully use his powers or

new suit. What is most unique about *Homecoming* in the MCU is that it is deeply entrenched in young adult issues and identity development, meaning it blends many traditional urban fantasy elements. Peter must cope with saving the world just as frequently as he has to learn the difficult life lessons about growing up, responsibility, and relationships. *Homecoming* adds the influence of young adult fictions to the urban fantasy and to the MCU.

Drew Goddard, *Daredevil*, (2015–present) [Television series]

Kicking off Netflix's foray into the MCU and a partnership with Marvel Television and ABC Studios, *Daredevil* is based on a long running Marvel comic book series and was created and produced for Netflix by Drew Goddard (known for *BTVS*, *Angel*, *World War Z*, *The Cabin in the Woods*). Matt Murdock (Charlie Cox) is a lawyer by day and a vigilante crime fighter by night. Blinded as a child, Murdock develop superhuman hearing, which allows him to fight criminals by using sound waves to know their locations. His mission is to help those in need both through his law firm and his crime fighting, and he has help from his law partner Franklin "Foggy" Nelson (Elden Henson) and victim turned assistant Karen Page (Deborah Ann Woll). The first season of *Daredevil* featured well-known characters from the comic book series Wilson Fisk/Kingpin (Vincent D'Onofrio), Frank Castle/Punisher (Jon Bernthal), and Elektra Natchios (Élodie Yung) and introduced viewers to Claire Temple (Rosario Dawson), who crosses over into all of the Netflix MCU series.

Melissa Rosenberg, *Jessica Jones* (2015–present) [Television series]

Jessica Jones is the second Netflix series based in the MCU and features Jessica Jones (Krysten Ritter) as the anti-hero, who runs a private detection agency, Alias Investigations. Jones struggles with post-traumatic stress disorder (PTSD) in the aftermath of long-term sexual assault and mental abuse at the hands of Kilgrave, played brilliantly by David Tennant. Kilgrave's power is the ability to control minds and influence people's behaviors, which he used to force Jones into a sexual relationship with him including forcing her to profess love for Kilgrave. Beyond the sexual violence, Kilgrave coerces Jones to use her superhuman powers to harm others, including killing innocents, and therefore, Jones must learn to cope not only with the sexual assaults but with her guilt. The second season of *Jessica Jones* is notable because of the decision to hire only women as directors, something lauded for its impact on the representation of women behind the camera in Hollywood. [Contains sexual violence]

Cheo Hodari Coker, *Luke Cage*, (2016–present) [Television series]

Luke Cage is the third MCU television series made for Netflix in conjunction with Marvel Television and ABC Studios. The first season is heavily influenced by 1970s crime dramas, particularly Blaxploitation films, such as *Shaft* and *Foxy Brown*. Luke Cage (Mike Coulter) is an ex-con turned crime-fighter with superhuman strength and unbreakable skin, who uses his powers to protect his Harlem neighborhood from an organized crime ring headed by Cornell "Cottonmouth" Stokes (Mahershala Ali). The series highlights issues of gentrification and communities fighting for resources, while Cage seeks to rebuild relationships and create new ones, such as with Claire Temple (Rosario Dawson). Cage has virtually no physical weaknesses, only a Judas Bullet—a special exploding bullet made from alien metal—can pierce his skin, and therefore, the second season questions what Cage's weakness are, delving more into the inner emotional life of this taciturn superhero. Consistently engaging the topics of race and hypermasculinity, *Luke Cage* is an excellent example of the urban fantasy genre.

OTHER EXAMPLES

John Leekley, *Kindred the Embraced* (1996) [Television series]

Described as *Dracula* meets *The Godfather* and based on the most popular vampire RPG of all time, *Vampire the Masquerade*, *Kindred* ... gave viewers an entry into the complex world of vampires. The show focused on vampire prince Julian Lunar (Mark Frankel) and the five clans of vampires collectively called "The Kindred" who each loosely represent different emotional aspects of humanity and constantly fight amongst each other for supremacy. The short-lived show set in San Francisco was an early example of the genre where the typical love triangle contained a vampire Julian (Mark Frankel) and a human police officer, Frank Kohanek (C. Thomas Howell), fighting for the love of reporter Caitlyn Byrne (Kelly Rutherford). At only 1 season (Frankel died during their hiatus), the show offers a wonderful take on the different forms of the vampire, and turns San Francisco into a dark, menacing cityscape.

Monica Owusu-Breen, *Midnight, Texas* (2017–present) [Television series]

Based on Charlaine Harris's trilogy by the same name, *Midnight, Texas*, is a town populated with powerful but damaged preternatural beings, including a fallen angel, a vampire who does not drink blood, a half-demon, and a witch, as well as some quirky human allies, such as the freelance assassin. The story begins when psychic Manfred Bernardo (Françoise Arnaud) shows up in Midnight on the run from a client he tricked with the ghost of his grandmother in his RV. Manfred and his new friends must ward off various beings that attack the city and its inhabitants.

Neil Jordan, *Byzantium* (2012) [Motion picture]

Neil Jordan returns to the world of vampires with this Irish urban fantasy thriller set in the gloomy world of the deteriorating British seaside whose decay reflects the general decay of the vampire. Following the teenage vampire Eleanor Webb (Saoirse Ronan) and her mother Clara (Gemma Arterton), this hidden gem focuses on the position of women as both sex workers and vampires in all-male world where women are not supposed to transform. A very different use of the city, and a very different kind of vampire, this film represents one of the few non-US productions in the UF genre.

Jim Jarmusch, *Only Lovers left Alive* (2013) [Motion picture]

This melancholy and bittersweet tale about love and mortality is a very modern version of the vampire tale from the mind of auteur Jim Jarmusch. The story features the most romantic of contemporary vampires, musician Adam (Tom Hiddleston) and his bibliophile wife Eve (Tilda Swinton). Indicative of the genre, Jarmusch beautifully turns the cities of Detroit and Tangiers into dark, moody, and melancholy secondary characters, reflecting the deterioration at the heart of humanity where even human blood is contaminated. *Only Lovers Left Alive* is a contemporary work of art; a languid, rock'n'roll infused tale of joie-de-vivre lost and regained, which creates a picture of two vampires trying to survive in a decaying world.

Tim Andrew and Jeff Davis, *Teen Wolf* (2001–2014) [YA TV Series]

MTV's *Teen Wolf* centers on Scott McCall, an ordinary teenage boy whose life is changed when he is bitten by a werewolf. Now a werewolf himself, Scott becomes enmeshed in the supernatural community of the town of Beacon Hills. The series initially focuses on the war between werewolves and the Argents, a family that hunts and kills supernatural creatures. Scott becomes caught in the middle of these tensions, as a werewolf himself and as the boyfriend of Allison Argent, a fledgling hunter. Scott struggles to keep his werewolf identity a secret while also trying to uncover who is behind the string of gruesome murders committed by a fellow werewolf. An excellent example of the young adult themes typical of networks like MTV and the CW. (Lauren Rocha)

Stephen Sommers, *Odd Thomas* (2013) [Motion picture]

Short-order cook and psychic, Odd Thomas (Anton Yelchin) sees ghosts and helps stop or solve crimes. When he begins having visions of a faceless killer gunning down a swath of the town, Odd races against time to figure out who is behind the killings and why, in order to stop them from happening with help from the police chief Wyatt Porter (Willem Dafoe) and his girlfriend Stormy Llewellyn (Addison Timlin). The film is an adaptation of the first of seven novels in the *Odd Thomas Series* by Dean Koontz. In many ways, *Odd Thomas*, the film, is quintessential urban fantasy as it relies on heavily on the (sub)urban landscape as a means for Odd to figure out the clues to solving the mystery and utilizes tropes from comedy, fantasy, horror, detective fiction, romance, and thriller to draw the audience into a fun and interesting film that also has a sad and tragic side. Odd Thomas was a breakout role for Anton Yelchin, and *Odd Thomas* is a cult classic in many circles.

Bouch T. Whithouse et al., *Being Human* (Seasons 1–3, 2008–2013)

BBC's *Being Human* explores the fascinating premise of three accidental housemates trying to find their way in unforgiving times. The elegant twist is that these housemates are a vampire, a werewolf, and a ghost. Surprisingly described as a comedy, the show cleverly weaves the central urban fantasy trope of being a monster trying to fit into human society, all the while learning that humans are sometimes the real monsters to fear. The show is worth watching for the ways in which the port city of Bristol, UK functions as a microcosm of immigration by having the protagonists reflect the urban stew that is a city on the coast, including the ways it codes and marginalizes difference. Thus, Mitchell the vampire (Aidan Turner) is Irish, George the werewolf is Jewish, and Annie the Ghost (Lenora Crichlow) is an unspecified mix of cultures (though the actress is of mixed English/Trinidadian descent). As is typical of the genre, Bristol's streets reflect the moods of the show juxtaposing the bright lights of the hospital where Mitchell and George work as orderlies, with the flat greys of the working-class neighborhood where they live, and a dark underbelly filled with monsters. There are standout episodes like "The Boy Who Cried Vampire," (Brian Dooley, 2009) when Mitchell tries to be neighborly, thus more human, and makes friends with a young boy, only to find himself the victim of a witch hunt that ends in tragedy. *Being Human* ultimately explores humanity in all its beauty and ugliness, and the nature of good and evil. The show continued for two more seasons, moving first to Barry, Wales, then London, changing protagonists along the way.

REFERENCES

Andersen, J. S. (1900). *Blood spells*. New York, NY: Signet Eclipse.

Andersen, J. S. (2008). *Night keepers: A novel of the final prophecy*. New York, NY: Signet Eclipse.

Andersen, J. S. (2009). *Sky keepers: A novel of the final prophecy*. New York, NY: Signet Eclipse.

Andersen, J. S. (2010). *Demon keepers*. New York, NY: Signet Eclipse.

Andersen, J. S. (2011). *Storm kissed: A novel of the nightkeepers*. New York, NY: Signet Eclipse.

Andersen, J. S. (2012). *Magic unchained: A novel of the nightkeepers*. New York, NY: Signet Eclipse.

Andersen, J. S. (2012). *Spellfire: A novel of the nightkeepers*. New York, NY: Signet Eclipse.

Anderson, P. (Director). (2004). *Resident evil* [Motion Picture]. New York, NY: Screen Gems.

Anderson, P. (Director). (2008). *Resident evil: Extinction* [Motion Picture]. Culver City, CA: Sony Pictures Home Entertainment.

Anderson, P. (Director). (2010). *Resident evil: Afterlife* [Motion Picture]. Culver City, CA: Sony Pictures Home Entertainment.

Anderson, P. (Director). (2012). *Resident evil: Retribution* [Motion Picture]. Culver City, CA: Sony Pictures Home Entertainment.

Anderson, P. (Director). (2017). *Resident evil: The final chapter* [Motion Picture]. Culver City, CA: Sony Pictures Home Entertainment.

Briggs, P. (2006). *Moon called*. New York, NY: Ace Books.

Briggs, P. (2007). *Blood bound*. New York, NY: Ace Books.

Briggs, P. (2010). *Bone crossed*. New York, NY: Ace Books.

Briggs, P. (2011). *River marked*. New York, NY: Ace Books.

Briggs, P. (2011). *Silver borne*. New York, NY: Ace Books.

Briggs, P. (2012). *Iron kissed*. New York, NY: Ace Books.

Briggs, P. (2013). *Frost burned*. New York, NY: Ace Books.

Briggs, P. (2014). *Night broken*. New York, NY: Ace Books.

Briggs, P. (2016). *Fire touched*. New York, NY: Ace Books.

Briggs, P. (2017). *Silence fallen* (Midwest Best Sellers).

Burge, C. M. (Creator). (2014). *Charmed: The complete series* [Television series]. Hollywood, CA: Paramount Pictures.

Butcher, J. (2010). *The Dresden files collection: 1–6*. New York, NY: ROC.

Butcher, J. (Writer), Butcher, J., & Marsters, J. (Narrator). (2018). *Brief cases: More stories from the Dresden files* [Audio book]. New York, NY: Penguin Audio.

Butcher, J., & Powers, M. (Writers). (2015). *Jim Butcher's the Dresden files omnibus: Volume one*. Runnemede, NJ: Dynamite Comics.

Butcher, J., Powers, M., & Butcher, J. (2015). *Jim Butcher's the Dresden Files omnibus, volume 1: Welcome to the jungle; Storm front; Fool moon; Restoration of faith.*

Butcher, S. K. (2009). *Burning alive*. New York, NY: Onyx.

Butcher, S. K. (2009). *Finding the lost*. New York, NY: Onyx.

Butcher, S. K. (2010). *Living nightmare*. New York, NY: Signet Eclipse.

Butcher, S. K. (2010). *Running scared*. New York, NY: Onyx.

Butcher, S. K. (2012). *Dying wish*. New York, NY: Signet Eclipse.

Butcher, S. K. (2013). *Falling blind*. New York, NY: New American Library.

Butcher, S. K. (2014). *Willing sacrifice*. New York, NY: Penguin Group.

Butcher, S. K. (2015). *Binding ties*. New York, NY: Penguin Group.

Clare, C. (2007). *City of bones*. New York, NY: M.K. McElderry Books.

Clare, C. (2008). *City of ashes*. New York, NY: M.K. McElderry Books.

Clare, C. (2009). *City of glass*. New York, NY: M.K. McElderry Books.

Clare, C. (2011). *City of fallen angels*. New York, NY: M.K. McElderry Books.

Clare, C. (2012). *City of lost souls*. New York, NY: M.K. McElderry Books.

Clare, C. (2014). *City of heavenly fire*. New York, NY: M.K. McElderry Books.

Cohen, B., & Parriott, J. D. (Creators). (2003). *Forever knight* [Television series]. Culver City, CA: Columbia Tristar Home Entertainment.

Coker, C. H. (Creator). (2017). *Luke cage: The complete first season* [Television series]. Los Angeles, CA: Netflix.

Coogler, R. (Director). (2018). *Black Panther* [Motion picture]. Burbank, CA: Marvel Studios.

Davis, J., & Reed, C. (Producers). (2012). *Teen wolf: The complete season one*. Beverly Hills, CA: Twentieth Century Fox Home Entertainment.

Drake, J. (2008). *Nightwalker: The first dark days novel*. New York, NY: HarperCollins.

Drake, J. (2009). *Dawnbreaker*. New York, NY: EOS.

Drake, J. (2009). *Dayhunter*. New York, NY: EOS/Harper Collins Publishers.

Drake, J. (2010). *Pray for dawn: The fourth dark days novel*. New York, NY: EOS.

Drake, J. (2010). *Wait for dusk: The fifth dark days novel*. New York, NY: EOS.

Drake, J. (2011). *Burn the night: The final dark days novel*. New York, NY: Harper Voyager.

Ellis, G. (Writer), & Beagle, S. (Illustrator). (2018). *Moonstruck: Volume 1* [Graphic novel]. Portland, OR: Image Comics.

Ellis, G. (Writer), & Beagle, S. (Illustrator). (2018). *Moonstruck: Volume 2* [Graphic novel]. Portland, OR: Image Comics.

Foerster, A. (Director). (2016). *Underworld: Blood wars* [Motion picture]. Culver City, CA: Columbia.

Frankfurt, P., Snipes, W., Engelman, B., & Arad, A. (Producers). (1998). *Blade collection*. Burbank, CA: Warner Bros. Home Entertainment.

Gamble, S., McNamara, J., & London, M. (Creators). (2016). *The magicians: Season one*. New York, NY: Syfy.

Gamble, S., McNamara, J., & London, M. (Creators). (2017). *The magicians: Season two*. New York, NY: Syfy.

Gamble, S., McNamara, J., & London, M. (Creators). (2018). *The magicians: Season three*. New York, NY: Syfy.

Goddard, D. (Creator/Producer). (2015). *Daredevil*. Los Angeles, CA: Netflix.

Hamilton, L. K. (1993). *Guilty pleasures*. New York, NY: Ace Books.

Hamilton, L. K. (1994). *The laughing corpse*. New York, NY: Ace Books.
Hamilton, L. K. (1995). *Circus of the damned*. New York, NY: Ace Books.
Hamilton, L. K. (1996). *Bloody bones*. New York, NY: Ace Books.
Hamilton, L. K. (1996). *The lunatic café*. New York, NY: Ace Books.
Hamilton, L. K. (1997). *The killing dance*. New York, NY: Ace Books.
Hamilton, L. K. (1998). *Blue moon*. New York, NY: Ace Books.
Hamilton, L. K. (1998). *Burnt offerings*. New York, NY: Ace Books.
Hamilton, L. K. (2000). *A kiss of shadows*. New York, NY: Ballantine Books.
Hamilton, L. K. (2000). *Obsidian butterfly*. New York, NY: Ace Books.
Hamilton, L. K. (2001). *Narcissus in chains*. New York, NY: Ace Books.
Hamilton, L. K. (2002). *A caress of twilight*. New York, NY: Ballantine Books.
Hamilton, L. K. (2003). *Cerulean sins*. New York, NY: Berkley Books.
Hamilton, L. K. (2004). *Incubus dreams*. New York, NY: Berkley Books.
Hamilton, L. K. (2004). *Seduced by moonlight*. New York, NY: Ballantine Books.
Hamilton, L. K. (2005). *A stroke of midnight: A novel*. New York, NY: Ballantine Books.
Hamilton, L. K. (2006). *Danse macabre*. New York, NY: Berkley Books.
Hamilton, L. K. (2006). *Micah*. New York, NY: Jove.
Hamilton, L. K. (2006). *Mistral's kiss: A novel*. New York, NY: Ballantine Books.
Hamilton, L. K. (2007). *A lick of frost: A novel*. New York, NY: Ballantine Books.
Hamilton, L. K. (2007). *The harlequin*. New York, NY: Berkley Books.
Hamilton, L. K. (2008). *Blood noir*. New York, NY: Berkley Books.
Hamilton, L. K. (2008). *Swallowing darkness: A novel*. New York, NY: Ballantine Books.
Hamilton, L. K. (2009). *Divine misdemeanors: A novel*. New York, NY: Ballantine Books.
Hamilton, L. K. (2009). *Skin trade*. New York, NY: Berkley Books.
Hamilton, L. K. (2010). *Bullet*. New York, NY: Berkley Books.
Hamilton, L. K. (2010). *Flirt*. New York, NY: Berkley Books.
Hamilton, L. K. (2011). *Hit list*. New York, NY: Berkley Books.
Hamilton, L. K. (2012). *Beauty*. New York, NY: Penguin.
Hamilton, L. K. (2012). *Kiss of death*. New York, NY: Penguin.
Hamilton, L. K. (2013). *Affliction*. New York, NY: Penguin.
Hamilton, L. K. (2013). *Dancing*. New York, NY: Penguin.
Hamilton, L. K. (2014). *A shiver of light*. New York, NY: Del Ray Books.
Hamilton, L. K. (2014). *Jason*. New York, NY: Penguin.
Hamilton, L. K. (2015). *Dead ice*. New York, NY: Penguin.
Hamilton, L. K. (2016). *Crimson death*. New York, NY: Penguin.
Hamilton, L. K., Green, J., & Alves, W. (2008). *Anita Blake, vampire hunter*. New York, NY: Marvel.
Hamilton, L. K., Ritchie, S., Ruffner-Booth, J., & Booth, B. (2007). *Anita Blake, vampire hunter: Volume 1*. New York, NY: Marvel.
Hawk, J. L. (2014). *Whyborne & Griffin: Books 1–3*.
Hawk, J. L. (2015). *Whyborne & Griffin: Books 4–6*.
Jarmusch, J. (Director). (2014). *Only lovers left alive* [Motion picture]. Culver City, CA: Sony Pictures Home Entertainment.
Jenkins, P. (Director). (2017). *Wonder woman* [Motion picture]. Burbank, CA: Warner Bros. Home Entertainment.
Jordan, N. (Director). (2012). *Byzantium* [Motion picture]. New York, NY: IFC Films.
King, C. (Author), Logan, J. (Creator), & Hervás, J. (Illustrator). (2017). *The awaking* [Graphic novel]. London: Titan Comics.

Leekley, J. (Creator). (2013). *Kindred, the embraced: The original vampire saga* [Television series]. New York, NY: Spelling Entertainment and Paramount Pictures.

Logan, J. (Creator). (2014). *Penny Dreadful: The complete first season*. Los Angeles, CA: Paramount Home Entertainment.

Logan, J. (Creator). (2015). *Penny Dreadful: The complete second season*. Los Angeles, CA: Paramount Home Entertainment.

Logan, J. (Creator). (2016). *Penny Dreadful: The final season*. Los Angeles, CA: Paramount Home Entertainment.

Mårlind, M., & Stein, B. (Directors). (2012). *Underworld: Awakening*. Culver City, CA: Sony Pictures Home Entertainment.

Marston, W. M., & Ross, S. R. (Creator/Developer). (2005). *The new adventures of Wonder Woman*. Burbank, CA: Warner Home Video.

Moning, K. M. (2006). *Darkfever*. New York, NY: Delacorte Press.

Moning, K. M. (2007). *Bloodfever*. New York, NY: Delacorte Press.

Moning, K. M. (2008). *Faefever*. New York, NY: Delacorte Press.

Moning, K. M. (2009). *Dreamfever: A novel*. New York, NY: Delacorte Press.

Moning, K. M. (2011). *Shadowfever*. New York, NY: Delacorte Press.

Moning, K. M. (2012). *Iced: A novel*. New York, NY: Delacorte Press.

Moning, K. M. (2015). *Burned: A fever novel*. New York, NY: Delacorte Press.

Moning, K. M. (2016). *Feverborn: A fever novel*. New York, NY: Delacorte Press.

Moning, K. M. (2017). *Feversong: A fever novel*. New York, NY: Delacorte Press.

Moning, K. M. (2018). *High voltage*. New York, NY: Delacorte Press.

Munson, T. O., Koslow, R., O'Loughlin, A., Myles, S., Sossamon, S., & Dohring, J. (2009). *Moonlight: The complete series*. Neutral Bay: Warner Brothers Entertainment.

Owusu-Breen, M. (Writer/Producer). (2017). *Midnight, Texas* [Television series]. New York, NY: NBC.

Plec, J. (Creator). (2014). *The originals: The complete first season*. Burbank, CA: Warner Brothers Entertainment.

Plec, J. (Creator). (2015). *The originals: The complete second season*. Burbank, CA: Warner Brothers Entertainment.

Plec, J. (Creator). (2017). *The originals: The complete fourth season*. Burbank, CA: Warner Brothers Entertainment.

Rosenberg, M. (Creator). (2017). *Jessica Jones: The complete first season*. Los Angeles, CA: Netflix.

Sommers, S. (2013). *Odd Thomas*. Los Angeles, CA: Image Entertainment.

Watts, J. (Director). (2017). *Spiderman: Homecoming*. Culver City, CA: Sony Pictures.

Whedon, J. (Creator). (2001). *Tales of the slayers* [Graphic novel]. Milwaukie, OR: Dark Horse Comics.

Whedon, J. (Creator). (2003). *Angel* [Television series]. Beverly Hills, CA: Twentieth Century Fox Home Entertainment.

Whedon, J. (Creator). (2005). *Buffy the vampire slayer: The chosen collection* [Television series]. Beverly Hills, CA: Twentieth Century Fox Home Entertainment.

Whedon, J. (2007). *Buffy the vampire slayer omnibus* [Graphic novel]. Milwaukie, OR: Dark Horse Books.

Whendon, J. (Creator). (2016). *Buffy, the high school years: Freaks & geeks* [Television series]. Beverly Hills, CA: Twentieth Century Fox Home Entertainment.

Whedon, J., & Greenwalt, D. (Creators). (2006). *Angel: The complete first season* [Television series]. Beverly Hills, CA: Twentieth Century Fox Home Entertainment.

Whedon, J., & Greenwalt, D. (2011). *Angel omnibus* [Graphic novel]. Milwaukie, OR: Dark Horse Books.

Whedon, J., Jeanty, G., Owens, A., & Chen, J. (2007). *Buffy the vampire slayer: Season eight* [Graphic novel]. Milwaukie, OR: Dark Horse Books.

Whedon, J., Jeanty, G., Owens, A., & Chen, J. (2012). *Buffy the vampire slayer: Season nine* [Graphic Novel]. Milwaukie, OR: Dark Horse Books.

Whithouse, T. (Creator). (2013). *Being human: The complete series* [Television series]. London: BBC.

Wilson-Cairns, K., Hinderaker, A., & King, C. (Writers). (2017). *Penny Dreadful: Volume 1* [Graphic novel]. London: Titan Comics.

Wiseman, L. (Director). (2003). *Underworld.* Beverly Hills, CA: Twentieth Century Fox Home Entertainment.

Wiseman, L. (Director). (2006). *Underworld: Evolution.* Culver City, CA: Sony Pictures Home Entertainment.

Witt, A. (Director). (2004). *Resident evil: Apocalypse.* Culver City, CA: Columbia TriStar Home Entertainment.

U. Melissa Anyiwo
Department of Politics and History
Curry College

Amanda Jo Hobson
Women's Resource Center
Indiana State University

NOTES ON CONTRIBUTORS

EDITORS

U. Melissa Anyiwo is a Professor of Politics & History and Coordinator of African American Studies at Curry College in Massachusetts with a relentless obsession for all things dark and monstrous. A transplanted Nigerian-British citizen whose dissertation focused on stereotypical images of African American women— "Mammy" and "Jezebel"—from the sixteenth century to the present, she regularly writes and presents on racial and gender archetypes including *From the Kitchen to the White House: Michelle Obama & the Redemption of Black Womanhood*, and "That's Not What I Signed Up For": Teaching Millennial's about Difference through First-Year Learning Communities" in *Outside/In in Teaching Race & Anti-Racism in Contemporary America: Adding Subtext to Colorblindness* (2013).

Anyiwo's passion for the vampire as racial stereotype has yielded multiple presentations including "Bad Girls? The Female Vampire on Film & Television," and "Selene and the Redeeming of the Female Vampire in the Underworld Series," "Not Cinderella but Prince Charming" The Destruction of Masculinity in Laurell K Hamilton's Anita Blake series, and "The True Monstrosity of Monsters: the Hidden Solution to Otherness in True Blood and Blade Trinity." Her published work includes "Using Vampires to Explore Diversity and Alienation in a College Classroom" (2014) and the edited collections *Buffy Conquers the Academy* (2013), *Race in the Vampire Narrative* (2015), and *Gender in the Vampire Narrative* (2016).

Finally, leaving no doubt that she's a vampirologist, Anyiwo was featured in the Warner Brothers documentary "Lestat, Louis, and the Vampire Phenomenon" for the *Interview with the Vampire 20th Anniversary Edition* (2014) and is the current cochair of the Vampire Studies Area at the National Popular Cultures and American Cultures Association.

Amanda Jo Hobson is the Assistant Dean of Students and Director at the Women's Resource Centre at Indiana State University. In her role as a student affairs administrator, her work focuses on issues of social justice and equity in higher education, and she regularly presents about a wide-range of diversity issues, including gender justice, bystander intervention, and sexual violence. Her doctoral work at Ohio University's School of Interdisciplinary Arts centers on issues of intersectionality of identity in feminist genre film with a specific emphasis on horror films and pornography. Amanda presents on the construction and portrayal of gender, sexuality, and race within contemporary popular culture and art, such as "Gender Blending and Genre Bending in the *Anita Blake, Vampire Hunter Series*," "Apocalyptic Vampires," and Vampiric Icons: Visions of Vampires from Dirty to Debonair in Less than 200 Years. Additionally, she regularly uses popular culture to educate about social justice, including presentations on "Horror Films as Social

Commentary," "Feminist Horror Films," and "Monstrosity in Popular Culture." She has been invited to deliver lectures on the topic of vampires in popular culture, including a talk at BalletMet of Columbus, Ohio, for their production of *Dracula*.

Her published work includes "'We Don't Do History': Constructing Masculinity in a World of Blood" in *Race, Gender, and Sexuality in Post-Apocalyptic TV and Film* (Palgrave Macmillan, 2015) and "Brothers Under Covers: Race and the Paranormal Romance Novel" in *Race in the Vampire Narrative* (Sense Publishers, 2015). She is the co-editor with U. Melissa Anyiwo of *Gender in the Vampire Narrative* (Sense Publishers, 2016). Amanda can be found most days reading endless novels, watching horror movies, and hanging out with her adorable fifteen-year old furry kid, Beaker.

CONTRIBUTORS

Candace Benefiel was an associate professor and humanities librarian at Texas A&M University for many years. She had a Master of Library Science from the University of Texas at Austin and a Master of English from West Texas State University and was also a doctoral candidate at Texas A&M with a dissertation in progress on the vampire in literature at the time of her death in August 2017. Candace was a well-known scholar on the popular vampire and a mainstay in the Vampire Studies Area for the Popular Culture Association's national conference. Her scholarship included a plethora of articles in the *Journal of Popular Culture, College and Research Libraries*, and many others. Her book, *Reading Laurell K. Hamilton* (ABC-Clio, 2011) is a valuable resource in the fields of vampire and urban fantasy studies.

Cait Coker is a doctoral candidate at Texas A&M University. Her background is in genre history, fandom and fan studies, and the history of women's writing and publishing. Her articles have appeared in *TXT Magazine, Transformative Works and Cultures, Journal of Fandom Studies*, and *Foundation: The International Review of Science Fiction*

Ana G. Gal, Ph.D., is an English instructor at the University of Memphis. Her research focuses on the Gothic tradition, with particular emphasis on how Western representations of monstrous bodies have evolved in literature, film, television, and graphic novels since the nineteenth century. Her most recent published work includes "Good Bad Boys and the Women who Love Them: Romantic Triangulation and the Ideal of Conformist Assimilation in The Vampire Diaries and True Blood" in Hero or Villain?: *Essays on Dark Protagonists of Television* (McFarland, 2017) and "Performative Femininity and Female Invalidism in John Keats's 'La belle dame sans merci' and S.T. Coleridge's Christabel" in *Gender in the Vampire Narrative* (Sense Publishers, 2016). She is currently researching how contemporary vampire television shows, under the guise of feminism and progressivism, work toward legitimizing the commodification of female bodies and sexual violence against women.

Jenna Guitar is a PhD candidate at the University of Rhode Island in the English department where she also teaches courses in Gender and Women's Studies. Her research interests include Gothic literature, fandom studies, popular culture, and Queer theory. She has previously published the chapter "Glee Goes Gaga: Queering Concepts of High School Identity Formation" in the edited collection, *Glee and New Directions for Social Change* (Sense, 2015).

Lauren Rocha is the First-Year Writing Coordinator and a professor in the English Department at Merrimack College. She is fascinated by beauty culture, monsters, and the Gothic. Her recent publication "That Geek Look: Beauty and the Female Geek Body" in *Age of the Geek: Depictions of Nerds and Geeks in Popular Media* (Palgrave Macmillan, 2018) explores beauty culture and the female body in the popular television series *The Big Bang Theory*, *Criminal Minds*, and *Doctor Who*. Her other publications include "Angel in the House, Devil in the City: Explorations of Gender in *Dracula* and *Penny Dreadful*," "Beneath the Surface: The Masculine Self and Body in Sheridan Le Fanu's 'Green Tea'," and "Wife, Mother, Vampire: The Female Role in the *Twilight* Series."

Sarah A. Smith, M.S., M.B.A., is an Online Learning Manager for Partner in Publishing (PIP). With over 14 years of experience in developing and implementing a wide array of instructional technology training and professional development opportunities at all levels of expertise, focused on facilitating student learning and integrating technology with curriculum. Inspired by her love of the visual image, Sarah earned a BA in Graphic/Information Design from and a Master's in Education Technology at Central Connecticut State University and a Master's in Business Administration from Curry College. Finding a quiet retreat in Quincy, Massachusetts, Sarah challenged her superhero persona by purchasing a fixer upper. Now, she works on the landscape while her puppy Frankie chases squirrels. Sarah is a console gamer and enjoys co-op games on her Xbox, and of course, all things Wonder Woman.

Printed in the United States
By Bookmasters